History of Taxation in India

Ancient India to Modern Times

The gardener plucks fruits and flowers, but does not harm the trees; the bee sucks the honey but does not damage the flowers. In the same way the king should collect his taxes but should not cause any suffering to his subjects. One who kills the goat at best gets one meal; one who feeds it well can get milk for several years.

—Chanakya in *Arthashastra*

Just as the sun extracts water from the reservoirs and gives it back in the form of showers, so does the ruler extract tax from his subjects and gives it back to them in the form of prosperity.

—Mahakavi Kalidasa in *Raghuvansham*

History of Taxation in India

Ancient India to Modern Times

By

M.M. Sury

New Century Publications
New Delhi, India

NEW CENTURY PUBLICATIONS
4852 / 24, 1st Floor,
Ansari Road, Daryaganj,
New Delhi – 110 002 (India)

Tel.: 011-4101 7798; 4358 7398; 98117 88655
E-mail: info@newcenturypublications.com
www.newcenturypublications.com

Editorial office:
4800 / 24, Bharat Ram Road,
Ansari Road, Daryaganj,
New Delhi – 110 002

First Published: **2022**

ISBN: **978-81-7708-539-6**

Published by New Century Publications and printed at Milan Enterprises, New Delhi

Designs: Patch Creative Unit, New Delhi

PRINTED IN INDIA

About the Book

Taxes are imposed so that a government may perform its traditional functions (defence, and maintenance of law and order), undertake welfare and developmental activities, and make provision for public goods to satisfy collective needs of the people. It has also to pay for its own administration.

References to taxes in ancient India are found in *Manu Smriti,* Kautilya's *Arthashastra* and other sources. Similarly, vivid accounts of tax system in medieval India are found in contemporary court chronicles, particularly *Ain-i-Akbari* compiled by Abul Fazl, one of Akbar's courtiers. Travel accounts of visitors, especially those who came from the West, also throw light on the Mughal system of revenue administration.

The tax system of British India reflected characteristics of a traditional agricultural economy. Revenues of the central government were dominated by customs duties as domestic requirements for manufactured goods were met mostly by imports, chiefly from Britain. Import duties were levied on almost all items of imports whereas major items subject to export duties were jute and tea in which India enjoyed near-monopoly in the world market.

After Independence in 1947, the Indian tax system has undergone major structural changes. It has become comprehensive and complicated over the years. It has successfully mobilised resources to finance developmental, welfare and administrative activities of the public authorities.

Restructuring of the tax system constituted a major component of fiscal reforms initiated in 1991. The main focus of the tax reforms was on simplification and rationalisation of both direct and indirect taxes with the objective of augmenting revenues and removing anomalies in the tax structure. Tax reforms in recent years have brought the tax system much closer to best international tax practices.

A historic tax reform in the form of goods and services tax (GST) was introduced in India from July 1, 2017.

This book provides an exhaustive and critical account of various aspects of the Indian tax system in historical settings. It places current developments in the field of taxation in perspective.

The book contains 22 chapters which have been organized into 3 parts.

Part I (chapters 1 and 2) is titled Taxes in Ancient and Medieval India. The detailed analysis given in *Manu Smriti* and *Arthashastra* on the subject shows the existence of a well-planned taxation system, even in ancient times. Taxes were paid in the form of gold coins, cattle, grains, raw materials and also by rendering personal services. Similarly, there were various types of taxes during the Sultanate period and the Mughal rule. Land revenue by far was the most important source of income for the Mughal rulers. The land revenue system adopted by Akbar has been greatly admired by historians.

Part II (chapters 3 to 8) is titled Taxes during British Rule. It explains and examines the financial administration of the British rulers and the introduction of income tax, excise duties and sales tax by them. Rationalization of customs duties, and the working of federal-provincial financial relations are also discussed in this part.

Part III (chapters 9 to 22) is titled Post-Independence History of Taxation. This part is further sub-divided into Part III (A) and Part III (B).

Part III (A) (chapters 9 to 14) is titled Multiple and Punitive Taxation during Pre-reforms Period (1947 to 1990). It explains the policy of integrated direct tax system introduced soon after Independence in 1947. It also describes the structure of income tax, excise duties, customs duties and sales tax.

Part III (B) (chapters 15 to 22) is titled Moderate and Rationalized Tax System in the Post-reforms Period (Since 1991). It deals with approach to tax reforms, rationalization and simplification of income tax, excise duties and customs tariff, introduction of service tax, and states' switch over from sales tax to value added tax (VAT). It also discusses the main features of goods and services tax (GST) introduced from July 1, 2017.

The book also contains an appendix which lays out current constitutional provisions pertaining to distribution of taxation powers between the Centre and the States.

About the Author

M.M. Sury received his B.A. (Hons.), M.A., and Ph.D. degrees in economics from the University of Delhi. He taught economics in the same University for 42 years. Specialising in fiscal economics, he has published extensively on the Indian fiscal system in recognised national and international journals, including *Small Industry Bulletin for Asia and the Pacific* (United Nations, Bangkok), *Bulletin for International Fiscal Documentation* (International Fiscal Association, Amsterdam), *Asian-Pacific Tax and Investment Bulletin* (Singapore), *Journal of the Indian School of Political Economy* (Pune), *Indian Economic Journal* (Bombay), and *Margin* (New Delhi). He was a Visiting Fellow at the International Bureau of Fiscal Documentation, Amsterdam (May 1989), a Fellow at the Indian Institute of Advanced Study, Shimla (1991-92) and a Visiting Fellow in the Department of Law and Management, University of Mauritius, Mauritius (September-October, 2000). He was Economic Adviser of First Delhi State Finance Commission (1996-97).

Contents

Part III (B): Moderate and Rationalized Tax System in the Post-reforms Period (Since 1991)

Preface

Taxes are as old as civilizations. Taxes are imposed so that a government may perform its traditional functions (defence, and maintenance of law and order), undertake welfare and developmental activities, and make provision for public goods to satisfy collective needs of the people. It has also to pay for its own administration. It needs financial resources for these purposes and taxation is one method of transferring money from private to public hands. Taxation is necessary because what the government gives it must first take away.

References to taxes in ancient India are found in *Manu Smriti,* Kautilya's *Arthashastra* and other sources. *Arthashastra* embodies values, norms, and beliefs pertaining to public administration, economics, ethics and diplomacy. Taxes in ancient India were levied both in cash and in kind and were collected by local officers. Major sources of revenue for the king included land tax, octroi, taxes on liquor shops, gambling houses and on professionals like dancing girls.

Similarly, vivid accounts of tax system in medieval India are found in contemporary court chronicles, particularly *Ain-i-Akbari* compiled by Abul Fazl, one of Akbar's courtiers. Travel accounts of visitors, especially those who came from the West, also throw light on the Mughal system of revenue administration. *Ain-i-Akbari* describes, *inter alia,* matters pertaining to taxes, other revenues, expenditure, salaries of public officers etc. Travel accounts of visitors, especially those who came from the West, also throw light on the Mughal system of revenue administration.

The tax system of British India reflected characteristics of a traditional agricultural economy. Revenues of the Central Government were dominated by customs duties as domestic requirements for manufactured goods were met mostly by imports, chiefly from Britain and other Commonwealth countries. Import duties were levied on almost all items of imports whereas major items subject to export duties were jute and tea in which India enjoyed near-monopoly in the world market.

Another important source of tax revenue for the Central Government was excise duty levied on a few commodities. Excise taxation in its modern form dates back to 1894 when for the first time a duty at the rate of 5 per cent *ad valorem* was imposed on cotton yarn of more than twenty counts. Excise at the rate of 6 *annas* per Imperial Gallon was imposed on motor spirit in 1917 and on kerosene at the rate of one *anna* per Imperial Gallon in 1922. Another landmark in the history of excise taxation was the year 1934 when excise duties were imposed on sugar, matches, and steel ingots. Duties were imposed on tyres in 1941 and on vegetable products, and tobacco in 1943, mainly to meet the exigencies of war finances. The year 1944 saw excise duties being imposed on coffee, tea and betel nut. Cigarettes came within the excise net in 1948 and mill-made cotton cloth in 1949.

Among the direct taxes, the only important source of revenue was the income tax introduced in India by the British in 1860 to overcome the financial difficulties created by the events of 1857.

As for the British Indian Provinces, the chief source of income was land revenue followed by provincial excises, mainly on liquor. Although under the Government of India Act, 1935, Provincial Governments had been authorised to levy sales tax, it formed a very low component of their revenue till Independence in 1947.

The Princely States did not form part of the structure of public finance of British India. They had separate budgets and separate sources of revenue. The maritime States imposed their own customs duties.

After Independence in 1947, the Indian tax system has undergone major structural changes. It has been successfully used to mobilise resources to finance administrative and developmental activities of public authorities.

The Constitution of India adopted on November 26, 1949, became operative on January 26, 1950. It provides for two layers of Government, one at the Central level, and the other at the level of the States. A federal polity of this kind requires division of powers and responsibilities between the Centre and the States. The Constitution describes in detail the legislative powers and functions of the two tiers of Government.

Restructuring of the tax system constituted a major component of fiscal reforms initiated in 1991. The main focus of the tax reforms was on simplification and rationalization of both direct and indirect taxes with the aim of augmenting revenues and removing anomalies in the tax structure. Tax reforms were necessary in the sense that in the absence of these reforms the Indian economy would have been isolated in the world market.

The post-1991 period has witnessed a sharp decline in the rates of income tax, excise duty and customs tariff. The theory that high rates of duty lead to higher revenue collection has been discarded in favour of lower rates with fewer exemptions and concessions. In short, tax reforms are geared to build a structure which is simple, relies on moderate tax rates but with a wider base and better enforcement.

A historic tax reform in the form of goods and services tax (GST) was introduced in India from July 1, 2017. GST is a tax on goods and services with comprehensive and continuous chain of set-off benefits up to the retailer level. It is essentially a tax only on value addition at each stage, and a supplier at each stage is permitted to set-off, through a tax credit mechanism, the GST paid on the purchase of goods and services. The power to levy GST is derived from Article 246A of the Constitution which confers concurrent powers to both Parliament and State Legislatures to make laws with respect to GST.

This book provides an exhaustive and critical account of various aspects of the Indian tax system in historical settings. It places current developments in the field of taxation in perspective.

Delhi
July 6, 2022

M.M. Sury

Abbreviations/Acronyms

BCD	Basic Customs Duty
CBEC	Central Board of Excise and Customs
CBIC	Central Board of Indirect Taxes and Customs
CCCN	Customs Co-operation Council Nomenclature
CENVAT	Central Value Added Tax
CGST	Central Goods and Services Tax
CST	Central Sales Tax
CVD	Countervailing Duty
DTEC	Direct Taxes Enquiry Committee
EC	Empowered Committee
E-filing	Electronic filing
FPS	Faceless Penalty Scheme
FRBM Act	Fiscal Responsibility and Budget Management Act
GATT	General Agreement on Tariffs and Trade
GDP	Gross Domestic Product
GST	Goods and Services Tax
GST Council	Goods and Services Tax Council
GSTN	Goods and Services Tax Network
HSN	Harmonized System Nomenclature
IGST	Integrated Goods and Services Tax
IT	Information Technology
ITC	Input Tax Credit
ITEC	Indirect Taxation Enquiry Committee
ITR	Income Tax Return
LTFP	Long-Term Fiscal Policy
MANVAT	Value Added Tax at the Manufacturing Stage
MODVAT	Modified Value Added Tax
MoF	Ministry of Finance
NDC	National Development Council
NFAC	National Faceless Assessment Centre
NFApC	National Faceless Appeal Centre
NRIs	Non-resident Indians
PAN	Permanent Account Number
PAYE	Pay-As-You-Earn
RBI	Reserve Bank of India
RFAC	Regional Faceless Appeal Centre
SACD	Special Additional Customs Duty
SAD	Special Additional Duty
SEZs	Special Economic Zones
SGST	State Goods and Services Tax

SITC	Standard International Trade Classification
SPV	Special Purpose Vehicle
SRP	Self-Removal Procedure
TEC	Taxation Enquiry Commission
TRC	Tax Reforms Committee
UT	Union Territory
UT-GST	Union Territory Goods and Services Tax
VAT	Value Added Tax
WTO	World Trade Organization

Unit and Currency Conversion Table

Unit Conversion

1 lakh	= 0.1 million
10 lakh	= 1.0 million
1 crore	= 10.0 million
100 crore	= 1.0 billion

Currency Conversion

The unit of currency in India is Indian Rupee, symbolized as ₹. As per reference rate of Reserve Bank of India (RBI) for July 11, 2022,

US$ 1	= 79.40
UK£ 1	= 95.04
Euro (€) 1	= 80.49
Japanese Yen (¥) 100	= 57.98

Fiscal Year

Fiscal year in India runs from April 1 to March 31 of the following year

Pre- and Post-metric Systems of Currency and Measures in India

Metric system of currency in India was introduced from April l, 1957

In the Pre-metric system, one Rupee was = 16 annas and one anna was = 4 paise

In the Post-metric system,

One Rupee = 100 paise

One mile = 1.6 kilometres

One yard = 0.9144 metre

One acre = 0.4046 hectare

Part I
Taxes in Ancient and Medieval India

1

Taxes in Ancient India

Taxes are as old as civilizations. Taxes are imposed so that a government may perform its traditional functions (defence, and maintenance of law and order), undertake welfare and developmental activities, and make provision for public goods to satisfy collective needs of the people. It has also to pay for its own administration. It needs financial resources for these purposes and taxation is one method of transferring money from private to public hands. Taxation is necessary because what the government gives it must first take away.

1.1 *Manu Smriti* on Taxation

In India, the system of direct taxation as it is known today has been in force in one form or another even from ancient times. There are references in *Manu Smriti* to a variety of tax measures. Manu, the ancient sage and law-giver stated that the king could levy taxes, according to *Shastras*. He advised that taxes should be related to the income and expenditure of the subject. He, however, cautioned the king against excessive taxation and stated that both extremes should be avoided namely either complete absence of taxes or exorbitant taxation. According to him, the king should arrange the collection of taxes in such a manner that the subjects did not feel the pinch of paying taxes. He laid down that traders and artisans should pay one-fifth of their profits in silver and gold, while the agriculturists were to pay one-sixth, one-eighth and one-tenth of their produce depending upon their circumstances. The detailed analysis given by Manu on the subject clearly shows the existence of a well-planned taxation system, even in ancient times. Not only this, taxes were also levied on various classes of people like actors, dancers, singers and even dancing girls. Taxes were paid in the shape of gold coins, cattle, grains, raw materials and also by rendering personal services.

1.2 Mahakavi Kalidasa on Taxation

In his work *Raghuvansham*, Mahakavi Kalidasa, the greatest Sanskrit scholar of ancient India, observed, "Just as the sun extracts water from the reservoirs and gives it back in the form of showers, so does the ruler extract tax from his subjects and gives it back to them in the form of prosperity". This is similar to what modern economists call tax incidence, expenditure incidence and budget incidence. Incidence in economics refers to the distributional effects of a fiscal measure. Thus, tax incidence means 'who bears the burden of taxes?' While expenditure incidence means 'who benefits from public expenditure?' Similarly, budget incidence relates to the combined effects of an equal increase in tax and public expenditure on the distribution of income. It is also called net incidence and is obtained by summing, algebraically, both the tax incidence (negative) and expenditure incidence (positive) for each of the sub-groups.

1.3 Kautilya's *Arthashastra* on Taxation

References to taxes in ancient India are found in *Arthashastra* the famous work of Kautilya (also known as Chanakya or Vishnugupta). He wrote, "The gardener plucks fruits and flowers, but does not harm the trees, the bee sucks the honey but does not damage the flowers. In the same way the king should collect his taxes but should not cause any suffering to his subjects. One who kills the goat at best gets one meal; one who feeds it well can get milk for several years". This is what Adam Smith called the canon of convenience in his famous work *Wealth of Nations* published in 1776. All canons of taxation propounded by Adam Smith were recorded much earlier by Indian scholars in ancient times.

Arthashastra embodies values, norms, and beliefs pertaining to public administration, economics, ethics and diplomacy. Taxes in ancient India were levied both in cash and in kind and were collected by local officers. Major sources of revenue for the king included land tax, octroi, taxes on liquor shops, gambling houses and on professionals like dancing girls. Kautilya's *Arthashastra* deals with the system of taxation in an elaborate and planned manner. This well-known treatise on statecraft—written sometime in 300 B.C., when the Mauryan Empire was at its glorious upwards move—is truly amazing for its deep study of the civilisation of that time and the suggestions which should guide a king in running the State. A major portion of *Arthashastra* is devoted by Kautilya to financial matters including financial administration. The Mauryan system, so far as it applied to agriculture, was a sort of state landlordism and the collection of land revenue formed an important source of revenue to the State. The State not only collected a part of the agricultural produce which was normally one-sixth but also levied water rates, octroi duties, tolls and customs duties. Taxes were also collected on forest produce as well as from mining of metals. Salt tax was an important source of revenue and it was collected at the place of its extraction.

Kautilya describes in detail the trade and commerce carried on with foreign countries and the active interest of the Mauryan Empire to promote such trade. Goods were imported from China, Ceylon and other countries and a levy known as *vartanam* was collected on all foreign commodities imported into the country. There was another levy called *dvarodaya* which was paid by the concerned businessman for the import of foreign goods. In addition, ferry fees of all kinds were levied to augment the tax collection.

Collection of income tax was well-organised and it constituted a major part of the revenue of the state. A big portion was collected in the form of income tax from dancers, musicians, actors and dancing girls. This taxation was not progressive but proportional to the fluctuating income. An excess profits tax was also collected. General sales tax was also levied on sales. Even gambling operations were centralised and tax was collected on these operations. A tax called *yatravetana* was levied on pilgrims. Though revenues were collected from all possible sources, the underlying philosophy was not to exploit or over-tax the people. The revenues collected in this manner were spent on social services such as laying of roads, setting up of educational institutions, setting up of new villages and such other activities beneficial to the community.

The reason why Kautilya gave so much importance to public finance and the taxation system in the *Arthashastra,* is not far to seek. According to him, the power of the government depends upon the strength of its treasury. However, he regarded revenue and taxes as the earning of the sovereign for the services which were to be rendered by him to the people and to afford them protection and to maintain law and order. Kautilya emphasised that the King was only a trustee of the land and his duty was to protect it and to make it more and more productive so that land revenue could be collected as a principal source of income for the state. According to him, tax was not a compulsory contribution to be made by the subject to the state but the relationship was based on Dharma and it was the King's sacred duty to protect its citizens in view of the tax collected and if the King failed in his duty, the subject had a right to stop paying taxes, and even to demand refund of the taxes paid.

Kautilya has also described in great detail the system of tax administration in the Mauryan Empire. It is remarkable that the present day tax system is in many ways similar to the system of taxation in vogue about 2,300 years ago. According to the *Arthashastra*, each tax was specific and there was no scope for arbitrariness. Precision determined the schedule of each payment, and its time, manner and quantity being all pre-determined. The land revenue was fixed at one-sixth share of the produce and import and export duties were determined on *ad valorem* basis. The import duties on foreign goods were roughly 20 percent of their value. Similarly, tolls, road cess, ferry charges and other levies were all fixed. Kautilya's concept of taxation is more or less akin to the modern system of taxation. His overall emphasis was on equity and justice in taxation. The affluent had to pay higher taxes as compared to the not so fortunate. People who suffered from diseases were exempted from tax or given suitable remissions. The revenue collectors maintained up-to-date records of collection and exemptions. The total revenue of the state was collected from a large number of sources as enumerated above.

Kautilya also laid down that during war or emergencies like famine or floods, etc. the taxation system should be made more stringent and the king could also raise war loans. The land revenue could be raised from one-sixth to one-fourth during the emergencies. The people engaged in commerce were to pay big donations to war efforts.

In short, Kautilya's *Arthashastra* was the first authoritative text on public finance, administration and the fiscal laws in India. His concept of tax revenue was a unique contribution in the field of tax administration.

2

Taxes in Medieval India

The term medieval India generally refers to the period beginning with the Muslim domination of India. This period can be sub-divided into: (a) Delhi Sultanate (1206 to 1526), and (b) Mughal rule (1526 to 1857).

The Delhi Sultanate was an Islamic empire based in Delhi which stretched over large parts of Indian subcontinent for about 320 years (1206 to 1526). Five dynasties ruled over the Delhi Sultanate sequentially: Mamluk dynasty (1206 to 1290), Khilji dynasty (1290 to 1320), Tughlaq dynasty (1320 to 1414), Sayyid dynasty (1414 to 1451) and Lodi dynasty (1451 to 1526).

2.1 Sultanate Period

There were various types of taxes during the Sultanate period, the following being the prominent ones.

2.1.1 *Khums*: *Khums* means one-fifth (or 20 percent). In Islamic law, *khums* was a 20 percent tax which was paid to the state of Islam on all items regarded as *ghanima* (booty seized in war). In the early and middle history of Islam, *ghanima* was property and wealth which was looted by the Muslim army after attacking the non-believers. *Fai* was that property and wealth which was gained from confiscation without fight. After paying the *khums* (20 percent), the rest 80 percent was distributed among the army commanders and soldiers who attacked the non-believers.

2.1.2 *Khiraj*: The expression *khiraj* literally means the revenue derived from a piece of land. It is a type of individual Islamic tax on agricultural land and its produce. It was levied by Muslim rulers on their non-Muslim subjects, collectively called *dhimmi*. Muslim landowners paid *ushr*, which carried a much lower rate of taxation. In India, *khiraj* was introduced by Firoz Shah Tughlaq (reigned 1351 to 1388). It was levied on cultivation, amounting to about 50 percent of the peasant's produce.

2.1.3 Other Taxes: Allauddin Khilji (reigned 1296 to 1316) made several sweeping reforms in the field of revenue system. He was the first Sultan who paid attention to measurement (*pamaish*) of the cultivable land. He made the harshest possible increase in tax demand. He fixed state demand to be half of the produce per *biswa* yield. Not only this, he also imposed house tax (called *ghari*) and pasture tax (called *charai*) on grasslands used for grazing of animals. There was another tax known as *sharab* which was one-tenth of crop production levied on farmers to develop and maintain water supply facilities. However, these harsh measures proved to be unsustainable. As soon as he died, the system was lost into oblivion.

2.2 Mughal Rule

In 1526, Zahir-ud-Din Babur from Ferghana in Central Asia defeated the Delhi Sultan Ibrahim Lodhi at the first battle of Panipat. Babur (reigned 1526-1530) was so much engrossed in various wars during his short rule that he could hardly find any time for revenue administration. Babur, founder of the Mughal rule in India, had no tax policy as such. To quote, "In October 1528, he had to levy a tax on his *amirs* of 30 percent of their salaries, since he had given away everything in India and did not have enough funds at his disposal for war equipment, gunpowder and the operation of cannons". [1]

His successor Hamayun (reigned 1530 to 1540 and 1555 to 1556) was a weak ruler who found himself in trouble soon after his accession to the throne. He had to spend most of his time in exile. Hence, he also did not get any chance to improve the revenues of the state. Resultantly, the revenue administration under Babur and Hamayun continued to function as it was under the Sultans of Delhi.

Akbar (reigned 1556-1605) was a minor at the time of his accession. He first paid attention to the security and consolidation of the empire. Having entrenched himself on the throne, he did make efforts to strengthen the revenue system. Vivid accounts of tax system during Mughal rule are found in contemporary court chronicles, particularly *Ain-i-Akbari* [2] compiled by Abul Fazl, one of Akbar's courtiers. The work describes, *inter alia*, matters pertaining to taxes, other revenues, expenditure, salaries of public officers etc.

Many of the European travellers (French physician Francois Bernier, Italian merchant Niccolao Manucci and French trader in luxury goods Jean-Baptiste Tavernier) who visited Mughal India left behind enthralling accounts of their experiences, including Mughal system of revenue administration. Moreover, some of the Mughal rulers themselves documented the events of their rule through autobiographical accounts (e.g. Babur's *Baburnama* and Jahangir's *Tuzuk-i-Jahangiri*).

2.2.1 Land Revenue: Land revenue (known as *khiraj*) by far was the most important source of income for the Mughal rulers. It was commonly charged from the peasants at one-fifth of the net produce, though the rate varied for different rulers.

Abul Fazl writes that no moral limits could be set for the demands of the ruler from his subjects. The subject ought to be thankful even if he were made to part with all his possessions by the protector of his life and honour. He justifies the imposition of taxes by the ruler saying that these are the remuneration of sovereign, paid in return for protection. Mughals had a notion that the ruler was the owner of all land under him.

The land revenue system adopted by Akbar has been greatly admired by historians. It was based on sound principles and the state issued instructions to the officers periodically to keep it up-to-date. The demand of the state being fixed, the scope for extracting more from the peasants than due was little. Revenue officials were generally honest. Any extraction/extortion, if brought to notice, was punished. In the case of drought or floods, the land revenue was often remitted.

To tone up the land revenue, Akbar, first of all, collected complete information about land and reorganized the whole land revenue system. Raja Todar Mal was Akbar's finance Minister. He introduced *zabti* system. He undertook an extensive survey of crop yields and prices for a period of 10 years (1570-1580). Each province was divided into revenue circles with its own rates of revenue for each crop and this revenue system was known as *zabt*. It was prevalent in areas where Mughals could survey the land and keep regular accounts.

The levy of land revenue was based on survey settlements calculated after a detailed measurement and classification of the cultivated areas. The nature of the crops grown and the average prevailing market prices were also taken into account in arriving at the final assessment. This assessment system, evolved after many experiments, became the basis for the survey settlement of the British rulers

The land revenue system introduced by Akbar continued throughout the Mughal period without any significant change.

2.2.2 Import and Export Duties: Both Akbar and Jahangir (reigned 1605-1627) interested themselves in the foreign seaborne trade. The Mughals welcomed the foreign traders and provided ample protection and security for their transactions. Akbar encouraged trade by linking together various parts of the country through an efficient system of roads and abolishing many inland tolls and taxes. A very low rate of customs duty of 2.5 percent *ad valorem* was levied. That the tax policy of some Mughal rulers was guided by religious considerations also is clear from the following account, "In the large market cities, in the sea harbours and at the borders of the Empire, import and export duties of 2.5 percent *ad valorem* were levied; later on Aurangzeb doubled this percentage for Hindus who had to make use of Muslim friends to evade this taxation. There were monopolies on some goods, for instance on salt and saltpetre. The monopoly on indigo yielded a few million rupees to the Treasury". [3]

Exports from India included handicrafts, cotton cloth, indigo, spices, opium, sugar, and drugs of various kinds. Imports consisted of bullion, horses, precious stones, velvet, brocade, perfumes, wines and other luxury goods for the upper classes.

2.2.3 *Jizya* (or *Jizyah*): *Jizya* was an Islamic yearly tax levied on non-Muslims (mostly Hindus). It was first levied in India by Qutb-ud-din Aibak (reigned 1206-1210), the founder of the Mamluk dynasty. *Jizya* rate was usually a fixed annual amount depending on the financial capability of the payer. *Jizya*, abolished by Akbar, was reintroduced by Aurangzeb in 1679.

2.2.4 Other Sources: Though the land revenue was the chief source of state revenue, there were certain other taxes to supplement the income of the state. These included toll tax, mints, fines levied on criminals, indemnity from vanquished or defeated rulers, and tributes and gifts received from subordinate rulers. The indemnity was paid either lump sum or regularly as a token of subordination to the emperor.

It is thus concluded that the revenue administration during medieval period underwent many improvements and income of the state continued to grow. Land revenue was the most important source of income and it remained so during the British rule.

However, Aurangzeb (reigned 1658-1707), who inherited an overflowing treasury from his father Shahjahan (reigned 1627-1658) squandered huge amounts in his 25 years long futile Deccan wars against Marathas. The *Deccan Ulcer* ultimately resulted in an almost empty treasury for his successors. Moreover, his religious orthodoxy and his hostile policy towards Hindus seriously damaged the stability of the Mughal Empire.

Endnotes

1. Ferdinand H.M. Grapperhaus, *Tax Tales from the Second Millennium* (International Bureau of Fiscal Documentation (Amsterdam), 1998, pp. 113-114.
2. *Akbarnama* is the official chronicle of the reign of Akbar written by his court historian Abul Fazl. It is in three volumes. The third volume, called *Ain-i-Akbari*, describes, *inter alia*, the administrative system of the Empire including revenues. It is famous for its rich statistical details about things as diverse as crop yields, wages, prices and sources of revenue.
3. Ferdinand H.M. Grapperhaus, *Tax Tales from the Second Millennium*, op. cit., p. 143.

Part II
Taxes during British Rule

3

Financial Administration of the British

Prior to 1947, India was a dependency of the United Kingdom and encompassed the entire area which now forms the three countries of India, Pakistan, and Bangladesh. It consisted of the British Indian Provinces, and the Indian Princely States. The political and economic scene changed greatly after 1947 when India emerged as an independent country merging with itself the former Princely States (called Part B States), but excluding areas of the other two countries mentioned above.

3.1 System of Financial Control

Till 1857, when India was under the rule of the East India Company, there was hardly any centralized or systematic financial administration in the country. After the events of 1857, the administration of India was taken over directly by the British Government in 1858. It established a highly centralized system of financial and administrative control with the purpose of consolidating its hold on the vast territory of India. The system of centralized financial control was exercised through the establishment of Finance Department which functioned rather well till the late 1930s. A Comptroller and Auditor-General was appointed in 1860 by amalgamating audit and accounts functions. However, in the absence of a Government responsible to the legislature, he submitted his Annual Reports to the secretary of State for India in Britain.

In matters of rules, regulations, procedures, compilation of annual budgets, audit and accounts etc., the Indian system of financial administration was based on the pattern of treasury control prevalent in Britain. All revenues were required to be credited to a Public Account. Similarly, annual budgets included demands for grants and appropriation accounts as also taxation proposals. They were, however, passed with the Governor-General's approval instead of that of the legislature as was the practice in Britain.

The Government of India was also responsible for the financial administration of Provincial Governments till the introduction of Provincial Autonomy in 1937 when popularly elected Provincial governments responsible to legislatures were established. From 1921 onwards, the Central Legislative Assembly, with a non-official majority, was for the first time given the right to discuss and pass the Annual Budget of the Government of India in respect of *non-reserved* subjects, as also to pass the Finance Bill containing taxation proposals. A committee on Public Accounts, with 8 non-official members of the Central Legislative Assembly and 4 official members (including the Finance Member as chairman) was also constituted to receive and examine Annual Reports of the Auditor-General.

The system of financial control in accordance with the rules and orders in force prior to Independence was continued after August 15, 1947, pending the framing of the new constitution of India. When the new constitution was promulgated on January 26, 1950, the then prevailing system of financial control was permitted to continue, with necessary changes.

3.2 Structure of Government Tax Revenue

The tax system of British India reflected characteristics of a traditional agricultural economy. Revenues of the Central Government were dominated by customs duties as domestic requirements for manufactured goods were met mostly by imports, chiefly from Britain and other Commonwealth countries. Import duties were levied on almost all items of imports whereas major items subject to export duties were jute and tea in which India enjoyed near-monopoly in the world market.

The Princely States did not form part of the structure of public finance of British India. They had separate budgets and separate sources of revenue. The maritime States imposed their own customs duties.

Out of a Central tax revenue of ₹ 73.90 crore in 1938-39, customs accounted for ₹ 40.51 crore, Central excises ₹ 8.66 crore, and income tax ₹ 13.74 crore (Table 3.1).

Table 3.1: Structure of Central and Provincial Tax Revenues: 1938-39

(₹ crore)

Central Tax Revenue		**Provincial Tax Revenue***	
Total taxes	73.90	Total taxes	56.07
of which		*of which*	
Customs	40.51	Land revenue	25.40
Taxes on income	13.74	State excises	13.08
Corporation tax	2.04	Stamps	9.53
Central excise duties	8.66	Registration	1.09
Salt duty	8.12	Devolution of taxes from the Centre	3.98

Note: Figures relate to undivided India.

* Data refer to nine Provinces including Sind and N.W.F.P. (now in Pakistan).

Source: Government of India, Ministry of Finance, *Report of the Taxation Enquiry Commission* (Chairman: John Matthai), 1953-54, Volume I, Tables 4 (p. 20), 5 (p. 23), and 7 (p. 25).

As for the British Indian Provinces, the chief source of income was land revenue followed by provincial excises, mainly on liquor (Table 3.1). Although under the Government of India Act, 1935, Provincial Governments had been authorised to levy sales tax, it formed a very low component of their revenue till Independence. The Province of Bombay levied a tax on the sale of tobacco in 1938. A retail sales tax on motor spirit and lubricants was imposed by Central Provinces (now Madhya Pradesh) in the same year. A multi-point general sales tax was levied in Madras Province at the rate of half percent in 1939 under the Madras General Sales Tax Act.

3.3 Commercial Banks

India has a long and chequered history of financial intermediation, particularly commercial banking. At the beginning of the 20th century, India had insurance companies (both life and general) and a functional stock exchange. Even before the setting up of the Reserve Bank of India in 1935, the country had market for money, Government securities and foreign exchange. The financial system was, however, characterised by paucity of funds and instruments, limited number of players and lack of depth and openness. It was primarily a bank-based system.

Commercial banking in India during the pre-Independence period was largely characterised by the existence of private banks organised as joint stock companies. Most banks were small and had private shareholding of the closely-held variety. They were largely localised and many of them failed. They came under the purview of the RBI that was established as a central bank for the country in 1935. But the process of regulation and supervision was limited by the provisions of the RBI Act, 1934 and the Companies Act, 1913. The indigenous bankers and moneylenders had remained mainly isolated from the institutional part of the system. The usurious network was still rampant and exploitative. Co-operative credit was the only hope for credit in rural areas but the movement was successful only in a few regions.

3.3.1 Presidency Banks: In 1806, the Bank of Calcutta was established as a joint stock bank with limited liability, which was brought under the Royal Charter in 1809 and renamed as Bank of Bengal. Subsequently, the Bank of Bombay and the Bank of Madras were established by the East India Company in 1840 and 1843 respectively. The business of these Presidency banks was initially confined to discounting of bills or other negotiable private securities, keeping cash accounts, receiving deposits, and issuing and circulating cash notes. The major innovations in banking method and organisation came with the establishment of Bank of Bengal. These included the following:

1. Use of joint stock system for raising capital.
2. Conferring of limited liability on shareholders by means of a charter.
3. Provision for the note issue which could be accepted for public revenue payments.
4. General provision for acceptance of deposits from the general public.
5. Imposition of explicit limit on credit and the kind of securities it could accept.
6. Provision for regulatory changes in the board of directors.

The Royal Charter governed the three Presidency banks, which was revised from time to time. There were no legally recognised commercial banks with special right within India other than the Presidency banks. The East India Company's government reserved the right to regulate the monetary and credit system to itself.

3.3.2 Paper Currency Act, 1861: With the passing of the Paper Currency Act, 1861, the right to issue currency notes by the Presidency banks was abolished and the same function was entrusted to the Government. With the collapse of the Bank of Bombay, the New Bank of Bombay was established in January 1868. In 1876, the Presidency Bank Act came into existence, which brought the three Presidency banks under the common statute and restriction on business. In terms of Act XI of 1876, the

Government of India decided on strict enforcement of the charter and the periodic inspection of the books of these banks. In 1921, the three Presidency banks and their branches were merged to form the Imperial Bank of India, which acquired the triple role of a commercial bank, a banker's bank and a banker to the government.

3.3.3 Banking Crisis, 1913: A banking crisis that occurred during 1913 revealed weaknesses of the banking system such as the maintenance of an unduly low proportion of cash and other liquid assets, the grant of large unsecured advances to the directors of banks and to the companies in which the directors were interested. Some of the banks seem to have resorted to certain undesirable activities and practices. After hectic and uncontrolled expansion, there followed the inevitable crash. In West Bengal, the position was especially grave. Four scheduled banks and a large number of non-scheduled banks failed. The amount of money lost, mostly the savings of the middle class, was over ₹ 26 crore. The issue of failures of banks was investigated in detail by the Indian Central Banking Enquiry Committee (1929-1931), the terms of reference of which included "the regulation of banking with a view to protecting the interest of the public". The Report of the Indian Central Banking Enquiry Committee emphasised the need for enacting a special Bank Act, covering the organisation, management, audit and liquidation of banks. The authoritative recommendations of the Committee have been an important landmark in the history of banking reforms in India.

3.3.4 Indian Companies (Amendment) Act, 1936: The first attempt at banking legislation in India was the passing of the Indian Companies (Amendment) Act, 1936, incorporating a separate chapter on provisions relating to banking companies. There were two important features of the new legislation, which embodied some of the recommendations of the Indian Central Banking Enquiry Committee. For the first time, a determined effort was made to evolve a working definition of *banking* and to segregate banking from other commercial operations. The special status of scheduled banks was recognised though certain provisions of the amended Act, such as building up of reserves, were made applicable only to non-scheduled banks, on the ground that the scheduled banks could be left to the general supervision and control of the RBI. These provisions, however, touched only the fringe of the problem of banking regulation.

3.3.5 Bank Failures and Remedial Measures: The failure of the Travancore National and Quilon Bank (TNQ Bank) in the middle of 1938 created a public scare. The role of the Reserve Bank of India (RBI) in this episode came under public and media gaze. The banking crisis of 1938 was largely a localised affair confined to South India. However, it was observed that majority of the non-scheduled banks continued to be without any control as they were not willing to submit their operations to the RBI's regulation. Between 1939 and 1949, as many as 588 banks failed in various States.

The RBI submitted to the Central Board, in October 1939, a Report on the non-scheduled banks, with special reference to the distribution of their assets and liabilities. The Report mentioned that several of these banks had poor cash reserves, low investment ratio, over extension of the advances portfolio and a large proportion of bad and doubtful debts. There had been a mushroom growth of banks whose financial position was suspect and all this information was given only on the basis of dressed-up balance sheets, which did not disclose many of the more unsatisfactory features. The RBI's proposal for a Bank Act was sent to the Government of India in November 1939, and circulated by the Government in January 1940 among banks, banking and commercial associations, prominent members of the public and the press, with the request that the replies be sent to the RBI within a period of six months. The replies received indicated that generally the business community and their associations welcomed the draft Bill. However, based on the comments received from various local Boards of the Bank, the RBI wrote to the Government that the opinion in the country was not ripe for undertaking elaborate bank legislation at that point of time.

The efforts were revived again in September-October 1943 for a more comprehensive Bank Act. On April 6, 1945, the Finance Member moved in the Legislative Assembly a motion for reference of the Bill to a Select Committee. The motion was adopted by the House in April 1946, but the Committee could not meet until November 1946. The amendments and suggestions made by the Committee formed the basis for the Banking Companies Act, 1949. The regulatory measures taken on an *interim* basis included the Banking Companies (Inspection) Ordinance, 1946 and the Banking Companies (Restriction of Branches) Act, 1946. The Bill as amended by the Select Committee was introduced in the Legislative Assembly on February 8, 1949 and was passed on February 17, 1949 as the Banking Regulation Act.

Thus, the banking regulation and supervision function of RBI is governed by the provisions of the Act, which comprehensively deals with several aspects of the banks ranging from setting up of a bank to amalgamation besides several operational issues. The Department of Banking Operations, which was entrusted with the administration of the Act, was originally organised in August 1945 to provide the requisite administrative machinery to discharge the several duties and responsibilities, which were expected to devolve upon the RBI after the passing of the Banking Companies Bill.

3.3.6 Regulation and Supervision: During the initial phase of commercial banking developments in India, banks were regulated and governed by the East India Company's Government, the Royal Charter and the Government of India. Before the enactment of the Banking Regulation Act, 1949, the provisions of law relating to banking companies were contained in the Indian Companies Act, 1850 which was based on the English Companies Act, 1844. In 1857, an Act for the incorporation and regulation of joint stock companies and other associations either with or without limited liability of the members thereof was passed. But under this Act, the privilege of limited liability was not extended to a company formed for the purpose of banking or insurance. This disability was removed by the Act of 1860, based on the English Companies Act, 1857. The law relating to companies was re-enacted in a comprehensive form in the Companies Act, 1913, which was made applicable to banking companies as well.

The decades of 1930s and 1940s had witnessed proliferation of banks, which were not regulated and supervised statutorily in a comprehensive manner. As a sequel, several banks failed.

The supervisory powers conferred initially in 1940 vested the RBI with the right to inspect banking companies on a restricted scale in consultation with the Government of India. The purpose of these inspections was limited to satisfy the RBI regarding the eligibility for a license, opening of branches, amalgamation, and compliance with the directives issued by it. With the prior consent of banking companies concerned, the RBI undertook to inspect their books and accounts with a view to determining the real or exchangeable value of their paid-up capital and reserves for the purpose of considering their eligibility for inclusion in the Second Schedule to the Reserve Bank of India Act. Specific powers to inspect banking companies were granted to the RBI by the Banking Companies (Inspection) Ordinance, 1946. The Ordinance made the prior consent of a banking company unnecessary for its inspection and also widened the objective of the inspection.

In order to protect the interests of the depositors and develop the banking system on sound lines, the regulation and supervision of the banking system was entrusted to the RBI by enacting the Banking Regulation Act, 1949. The Banking Regulation Act is modified from time-to-time in response to financial developments.

3.4 Money Market

Money market prior to Independence was characterised by paucity of instruments, lack of depth and dichotomy in the market structure. The inter-bank call money market was the core of the Indian money market. Before the establishment of the RBI in 1935, the money market consisted of two fairly distinct sectors, *viz.* the organised and unorganised sectors. While the organised sector consisted of the Imperial Bank of India—a quasi-central bank till 1935, the Indian joint-stock banks and the exchange banks, the indigenous bankers such as the shroffs, money lenders, chit funds etc. formed the unorganised part. Co-operative credit institutions occupied an intermediate position between the two sectors.

The Imperial Bank, the foremost commercial bank of the country and a few of the leading Indian joint-stock banks discounted *hundis* (internal bills of exchange). This was the main credit instrument of the unorganised sector which provided the only link between the two sectors. Owing to the absence of a proper central bank, the money market was characterised by sharp imbalances between the supply and demand for funds, wide fluctuations in interest rates during the busy and slack seasons and marked regional variations in interest rates. The Imperial Bank could not, however, lend stability to the money market as it had to borrow from the Government at high rates of interest. Nevertheless, the bank rendered assistance to the money market by using the large Government balances at its disposal, which constituted its major investible resources.

The Bank Rate was the prime lending rate at which the Imperial Bank generally advanced money against Government securities. This rate was determined by the Committee of the Central Board of the Imperial Bank and depended on the demand for money which in turn was determined almost entirely by the requirements of trade, particularly foreign trade, in staple commodities such as foodgrains, raw cotton, raw jute and jute manufactures. The rates of interest on loans, including the Bank Rate, fluctuated according to the ebb and flow of this trade. The Imperial Bank would usually not reduce the Bank Rate when its cash to liabilities ratio (an indication of liquidity) was found to be low. Apart from the Bank Rate, the Imperial Bank also periodically announced a *hundi* rate, which was generally equal to or slightly higher than the Bank Rate. Through the rates which the Imperial Bank charged on its advances and the discount of *hundis,* and by its willingness or refusal to extend financial assistance, it could profoundly influence the provision of credit as well as money market rates.

After the formation of the RBI in 1935, the organised market comprised the RBI, the Imperial Bank, foreign banks and the Indian joint stock banks. *Quasi*-Government bodies and large-sized joint stock companies also participated in the money market as lenders, the money lent by them being usually termed as *house money*. Financial intermediaries such as call loan brokers, general finance and stock brokers also functioned in the market. Although the magnitude of funds dealt within the call market was not large in relation to the deposit resources of banks, it was the most sensitive segment of the money market. The Imperial Bank did not participate in the call money market, but other banks obtained loans and advances from it. Subsequently, however, banks increasingly shifted their demand for accommodation to the RBI. Besides the call money market, there was no other significant segment in the market.

With the establishment of the RBI in April 1935, the task of determining the Bank Rate was taken over by it from the Imperial Bank. It was on July 4, 1935, i.e. the day before the scheduled banks were to lodge their statutory deposits with the RBI, that the Bank Rate of 3.5 percent was officially announced for the first time by the RBI. It was the standard rate at which the RBI was prepared to buy or re-discount bills of exchange or other eligible commercial papers. Subsequently, the official rate of the Imperial Bank was re-designated as the Imperial Bank advance rate (as distinct from the Imperial Bank *hundi* rate), which was to be the rate for advances against Government securities and the benchmark for the calculation of interest on other advances on which a fluctuating rate of interest was charged.

At the time of Independence in 1947, money market structure in India was loose though not entirely uncoordinated. The indigenous bankers enjoyed rediscount facilities from the Imperial Bank and other commercial banks which, in turn, had access to the RBI. Recourse on the part of the indigenous money market to the resources of the organised market took place usually during the busy season when the crops were being harvested and moved from the producer to the wholesaler.

3.5 Payment Systems

The Paper Currency Act of 1861 conferred upon the Government of India the monopoly of note issue bringing to an end note issues of private and Presidency Banks.

In 1881, the Negotiable Instruments Act (NI Act) was enacted, formalising the usage and characteristics of instruments like the cheque, the bill of exchange and promissory note. The NI Act provided a legal framework for non-cash paper payment instruments in India.

With the steady growth in volumes of trade and commerce and the growing confidence of the public in the usage of cheques etc., transactions through the use of these payment instruments grew at a rapid pace. With the development of the banking system and higher turnover in the volume of cheques, the need for an organised cheque clearing process emerged amongst the banks. Clearing associations were formed by the banks in the Presidency towns and the final settlement between member banks was effected by means of cheques drawn upon the Presidency Banks. With the setting up of the Imperial Bank in 1921, settlement was done through cheques drawn on that bank.

The Calcutta Clearing Banks' Association, which was the largest bankers' association at that time, adopted clearing house rules in 1938. The association had twenty-five large banks as its members and eight sub-members. There were two ordinary clearings on each business day, except on Saturday when there was one clearing. However, the association did not cover many banks functioning in Calcutta. The cheques, drafts etc. of such non-clearing banks were collected by the clearing banks only on payment of charges. This affected their business prospects adversely, as the public was not likely to maintain accounts with banks whose cheques suffered a serious handicap of market acceptability.

To overcome this problem, these banks formed themselves into a group called the Metropolitan Banking Association with fifty members, which conducted the Metropolitan Clearing House, in 1939. This association arrived at an understanding with the Calcutta Clearing House in 1940. In addition, two other clearings were conducted in Calcutta: Pioneer clearing and the Walks Clearing.

The Bombay Clearing House was the only association to conduct clearings in Bombay. It had no parallel systems and institutions comparable to the Metropolitan Clearing House of Calcutta. The uniform procedures and charges for collection of non-clearing banks' cheques, drafts, dividend warrants etc. were adopted by the Bombay Clearing House in 1941-1942.

After the setting up of Reserve Bank of India under the RBI Act 1935, the clearing houses in the Presidency towns were taken over by the Reserve Bank of India.

3.6 Reserve Bank of India (RBI)

There is only one central bank in a country whose main function is to control the operations of the rest of the banking system. [1] Reserve Bank of India (RBI), the central bank of India, is the apex institution responsible for managing and supervising the monetary and financial system of the economy.

The Imperial Bank of India (nationalized in 1955 and renamed as State Bank of India), which emerged as a consequence of the amalgamation of 3 Presidency Banks of Bengal, Bombay and Madras in 1921, assumed certain central banking functions except currency management. The control of currency management continued to be with the Government of India in order to ensure that the central banking entity did not appropriate powers greater than those mandated by the political authority. The Reserve Bank of India Act was placed on the statute book on March 6, 1934. The RBI commenced operations on April 1, 1935 and was nationalised on January 1, 1949. The head office of the Bank is in Mumbai and its executive head is called the Governor.

The objective of establishing the RBI, as stated in the preamble to the RBI Act 1934, was to "regulate the issue of bank notes and the keeping of the reserves with a view to securing monetary stability in India and generally to operate the currency and credit system of the country to its advantage". The Bank's functions as laid down in the statutes were: (a) issue of currency (b) banker to Government; and (c) banker to other banks. Except in the sphere of agriculture, the Bank was not entrusted with any great promotional role and that too on a limited scale.

When the Reserve Bank of India Act, 1934 came into effect, an important function of the RBI was to hold the custody of the cash reserves of banks, granting them accommodation in a discretionary way and regulating their operations in accordance with the needs of the economy through instruments of credit control. With regard to the banking system of the country, the primary role of the RBI was conceived as that of the lender-of-last-resort for the purpose of ensuring the liquidity of the short-term assets of banks.

During most of the pre-Independence period, RBI was a private bank, though formed under a statute and overseen by the then colonial government. The functions of the RBI during this phase were confined essentially to traditional central banking, *i.e.* note issue authority and banker to the Government. During the war and post-war years, its major preoccupation was facilitation of war finance, repatriation of sterling debt and planning and administration of exchange control.

The initial phase of RBI was marked by several war and post-War developments including the separation of Burma (modern Myanmar) in 1937, partition of the country in 1947 and nationalisation of the RBI, which altered the area of operations of the RBI. After the separation of Burma, the RBI acted as currency authority of that country till 1942 and as banker to the Burmese Government till March 1947. Upon the partition of the country in 1947, the RBI rendered central banking services to the Dominion of Pakistan until June 1948. In terms of the Pakistan Monetary System and Reserve Bank (Amendment) Order, 1948, the RBI ceased to function as central bank for Pakistan from July 1, 1948.

3.7 Drain of Indian Wealth

Drain of wealth theory pertains to the economic critique of colonial rule in India that was advocated by the early nationalists. They described the continuous one way flow of wealth from India to Britain for which India received no returns. One of the earliest propagators of the drain of wealth theory was Dadabhai Naoroji. [2] In 1867, he put forward the idea that the colonial rule was draining and bleeding India of its wealth. He lamented that the perversion of economic laws in India by the British rule was draining India of its prosperity and destroying the nation. In his book *Poverty and Un-British Rule in India*, Dadabhai Naoroji brought attention to the draining of India's wealth into Britain. Naoroji described the following six factors which resulted in the external drain.

1. India was governed by a foreign government.
2. India did not attract immigrants which could have brought labour and capital for economic growth.

3. India paid for Britain's civil administration and occupation army.
4. India bore the burden of empire building in and out of its borders.
5. Opening the country to free trade was actually a way to exploit India by offering highly paid jobs to foreign personnel.
6. The principal income-earners in India bought outside of India or left with the money as they were mostly foreign personnel.

Another form of movement of wealth away from India was the financial capital. It included the money paid to banks, insurance companies, shipping companies etc. in Britain for the services they rendered in India.

Yet another mode of drain was the remittances which the Company made to Britain. This included: (a) salaries and pensions paid to the employees of the Company back in Britain, (b) interest amount on loans raised by the Company in Britain, (c) dividends paid to the shareholders of the Company, (d) salaries and pensions paid to the British civilian and military personnel posted in India which, in turn, were remitted by them to Britain and (e) store purchases made in Britain by the Secretary of State on behalf of Government of India for the civilian and military departmental needs.

Such remittances by the Company later came to be known as the *home charges* when the British Parliament took over administrative control of India. Though the amount remitted varied every year, it was estimated to be in the range of 1 to 3 crore rupees per annum.

To quote, "Government remittance abroad was a politically sensitive item of the balance of payments. Every year, the government paid to Britain a sum of money in sterling, which was called the 'home charges' in the nineteenth century. About half of the home charges in the pre-war years consisted of debt service. The second most important item was payment for maintenance of an army and marine force. A third major component was pension payments for officials who had served India and retired to Britain. India Office expenses and stores purchased were the other items of expenditure. These payments, Indian nationalists argued, reduced the capacity of the domestic economy to generate savings and investment, an argument that became known as the drain". [3]

Naoroji estimated a 200-300 million pounds loss of India's revenue to Britain that was not returned. Naoroji described this as vampirism, with money being a metaphor for blood, which humanised India and attempted to show Britain's actions as monstrous.

Another well-known argument supporting the drain of wealth was given by R.C. Dutt. In his work *Economic History of India,* Dutt had equated the drain of wealth to moisture being sucked out of Indian soil to fertilize the lands in England. He commented that the economic drain out of India was so severe that it had impoverished one of the most prosperous countries on earth. He lamented that India was reduced to a land of famines which were frequent, widespread and fatal as a result of this drain.

Endnotes

1. Central banks occupy a pivotal position in the institutional fabric of an economy. The functions of a modern central bank are vastly different from what was expected from the early central

banks founded in Europe in the 17th century. The evolution of central banking in the Indian context has its own specificity. The RBI, while discharging its statutory responsibilities, has played a crucial role in the nation building process, particularly in the development of the financial sector. In fact, institution building constitutes a distinguishing feature of central banking in India.

2. Sir Dadabhai Naoroji Dordi (September 4, 1825 to June 30, 1917) also known as the *Grand Old Man of India* was an Indian Parsi scholar, trader and politician who was a Liberal Party member of Parliament in the United Kingdom House of Commons between 1892 and 1895, and the first Indian to be a British MP. Naoroji was one of the founding members of the Indian National Congress.
3. Tirthankar Roy, *The Economic History of India* (Third Edition, 2011), Oxford University Press, New Delhi, p. 97.

4

Income Tax

Consequent upon the financial difficulties created by the events of 1857, income tax was introduced in India for the first time by the British in the year 1860. [1] However, the imposition of income tax remained irregular till the year 1886 when a systematic legislation was enacted for its operation on a permanent basis. Since then the form of income tax has undergone a series of changes to meet the changing requirements of Government finances and economic policy.

4.1 Income Tax Act, 1860

The Act of 1860 was passed only for five years and therefore it lapsed in 1865. It was replaced in 1867 by a licence tax on professions and trades and the latter was converted into a certificate tax in the following year. The certificate tax was replaced in 1869 by a general income tax which after remaining in force for four years was abolished in 1873. In 1876, the Government imposed a licence tax on traders to create a famine fund to deal with the famine of 1876-78. This licence tax on traders remained in operation till 1886 when it was merged in the Income Tax Act of that year. Noting the haphazard nature of enactments, the Indian Taxation Enquiry Committee, 1924-25, remarked, "...the whole period (1860-1886) was one of continuous trial and error with different schemes of direct taxation, no less than 24 Acts being passed in 26 years". [2]

4.2 Income Tax Act, 1886

The Act of 1886 levied a tax on the income of residents as well as non-residents in India. The Act defined agricultural income and exempted it from tax liability in view of the already existing land revenue, a kind of direct tax (in the 1860 legislation, agricultural income was also subject to taxation). The absolute exclusion of agricultural income from the purview of income tax law continued till the Government of India Act, 1935 made it a provincial (State) subject. This provision was retained in the Constitution of independent India.

The Act of 1886 exempted life insurance premiums paid by an assessee on policies on his own life or on that of his wife, a provision that has continued till now. Under another provision of the Act, a Hindu undivided family was treated as a distinct taxable entity, a position maintained by all subsequent Income Tax Acts.

The assessment and collection procedures of income tax in the early days of its operation were simple and somewhat arbitrary. As the Taxation Enquiry Commission, 1953-54 noted, "The Income Tax Act of 1886 laid an obligation only on companies to file every year statements of their net income and it was entirely within the discretion of the Collector to devise means for finding out other persons likely to have taxable income and to adopt the appropriate method of determining their income...the procedure for assessment was summary, and the Collector could intimate the amount of income and tax determined by him to the assessee either through a list published in his office or through an individual notice". [3] In 1886-87, the total income assessed was ₹ 33 crore and the net collection from income tax was ₹ 1.37 crore. The Act of 1886 remained in force for 32 years, i.e. until 1918 and during this period a number of amendments were made in it including the introduction of the principle of graduation in income tax in 1916 and of super tax in 1917.

4.3 Income Tax Act, 1918

The Act of 1918 brought under charge also receipts of casual or non-recurring nature pertaining to business or profession. This was contrary to the generally accepted meaning of income that it should, *inter alia*, be received with some degree of regularity. The Act granted exemption to contributions to provident funds governed by the Provident Funds Act.

Although income tax in India has been a charge on net income since inception, it was in the Act of 1918 that specific provisions were inserted for the first time pertaining to business deductions for the purpose of computing net income. Prior to that, deductions were granted on the basis of executive orders. For example, there was no specific provision for depreciation allowance in the Act of 1886 but the Act of 1918 inserted in the statute itself the provision for depreciation allowance on the straight-line method.

The Act of 1918 remained in force for a short period and was replaced by a new Act (Act XI of 1922) in view of the reforms introduced by the Government of India Act, 1919.

4.4 Income Tax Act, 1922

The Act of 1922 provided for the first time the set off of loss from one source against income from other sources in the same year. An amendment of the Act in 1939 permitted carry forward of unabsorbed business losses for a period of six years with the restriction that carried forward loss could be set off only against the profits of the same business. Pursuant to a recommendation of the Income Tax Investigation Commission (1948), the income tax law was appropriately amended in 1953 to provide for the set off of speculative losses, even during the same year, only against speculative gains.

Under the Act of 1886, the paying officers had the obligation to deduct tax at source from the salaries of Government servants and employees of local bodies. However, the Act of 1922 extended to all employers the responsibility to deduct tax at source on salaries. Prior to 1922, there was no separate department for income tax administration. The assessment and collection of income tax was done by the land revenue officers as a subsidiary duty. It was only in 1922 that a separate Central Department was created to deal with income tax administration.

4.5 Recommendations of the Indian Taxation Enquiry Committee, 1924-25

Government of India appointed this Committee (Chairman: Sir Charles Todhunter) to examine in detail the entire field of taxation in India. Its terms of reference were as follows: (a) to examine the manner in which the burden of taxation is distributed at present between the different classes of the population, (b) to consider whether the whole scheme of taxation—central, provincial and local—is equitable and in accordance with economic principles, and, if not, in what respects it is defective and (c) to report on the suitability of alternative sources of taxation.

Chapter IX of its report contained recommendations pertaining to income tax.

A major recommendation of the Committee pertained to the distribution of income tax revenue between the Centre and the Provinces. Prior to 1919, income tax was a 'divided head' of revenue. However, the Montague-Chelmsford Reforms resulted in a complete separation of Central and Provincial finances, and income tax became a part of the Central revenues. The Todhunter Committee opined that in the event of any division of taxes between the Centre and the Provinces, the choice of income tax as the main balancing factor was inevitable. The Government of India Act, 1935, did assign to the Provinces a part of the net proceeds of income tax levied by the Centre.

The Committee examined, for the first time, the desirability of differentiation between earned and unearned incomes for the purpose of income tax. The Committee, however, rejected the idea, maintaining that it was premature in the context of the Indian conditions. It was in 1945 that a distinction between earned and unearned incomes was introduced when assessees were allowed to exclude from their earned incomes a fixed proportion subject to a maximum limit.

4.6 Recommendations of the Income Tax Enquiry Committee, 1935

This Committee was appointed by the Government of India "to make an investigation of the Indian income tax system in all its aspects and to report upon both the incidence of the tax and the efficiency of its administration". Many amendments based on its recommendations became law in 1939. According to one such amendment, the then prevailing *step* rates system of income tax was changed to a *slab* rates system in 1939. Under the step system of rates, all persons in a particular income bracket bear the same effective rate on every rupee of their income. Under a slab system of rates, tax on each slab of income is calculated separately and then added up. Under another amendment, closely-held companies were required to distribute 60 percent of their net of tax profits as dividend. The Income Tax (Amendment) Act, 1939, provided also for the taxation of profits of the business of mutual life insurance which had remained exempt from tax prior to 1939.

In 1939, as a result of the recommendations of the Committee, the entire income of a resident, whether accruing in (British) India or outside, became chargeable to tax. The remittance basis, therefore, faded into the background except for its applicability to persons 'resident but not ordinarily resident' and to a small portion of the foreign income of 'resident and ordinarily resident' persons in some instances. The liability of non-residents to tax on income deemed to accrue or arise in India through business connection was amplified to cover income arising through certain other activities also. At the same time, resident, non-resident and not ordinarily resident persons were, for the first time, defined in the law.

The entire income of local authorities was being treated as exempt even from 1886, and the Income Tax Acts of 1918 and 1922 placed the exemption on a statutory footing. Pursuant to a recommendation of this Committee, the scope of the exemption was restricted by the Income Tax (Amendment) Act of 1939. The income arising to a local authority from business became liable to tax, except where the business consisted of the supply of a service or commodity within its own jurisdictional area.

4.7 Excess Profit Tax

Another notable development in the evolution of income tax was the imposition of excess profit tax in 1940. It was levied on profits earned by businesses and professions between September 1, 1939 and March 31, 1946. A 'standard profit' was calculated for each accounting year falling within the above years. Standard profit was approximately equated with the profits earned in normal times, i.e. in the pre-War years. Companies started before 1936 had the following five options to choose from for determining standard profit: profits during 1935-36 or 1936-37 or average of the profits during 1935-36 and 1936-37 or 1936-37 and 1937-38 or 1937-38 and 1938-39. In the case of companies started after 1936, the 'capital standard' was used. Thus, a statutory 8 percent of the capital invested was considered the standard rate of profit. Excess profit tax was levied at the rate of 50 percent on the excess over the standard profits earned between September 1, 1939 and March 31, 1941. For the period between April 1, 1941 and March 31, 1946, the rate of excess profit tax was 66.66 percent.

4.8 Income Tax Investigation Commission, 1947

Shortly after Independence, the Government appointed the Income Tax Investigation Commission (Chairman: Srinivas Varadachariar) 1947 to: (a) investigate and report on all matters relating to taxation of income, with particular reference to preventing evasion and avoidance, and (b) to investigate specific cases referred to the Commission by the Government. The Commission submitted its report in 1948 and recommended several changes in the law to plug loopholes in the income tax system. For example, it recommended that the law should be amended so as to allow speculative losses to be set off only against speculative gains. A number of Commission's recommendations were incorporated in the law by the Income Tax (Amendment) Act, 1953.

During British rule, revenue-raising was the main purpose of income tax system. There were hardly any concessions/exemptions for savings, investments, industrial growth, and other desirable socio-economic objectives. Incentives for such activities started building up in the system soon after Independence. Thus, a provision introduced in 1949 exempted from tax new industrial undertakings for the first five years of their manufacturing operations.

4.9 Rate Structure

Prior to 1916, income tax was levied at a flat rate of 5 *pies* in a rupee on all incomes above ₹ 2,000. With a rupee containing 192 *pies*, the rate of tax worked out to 2.6 percent approximately. It was in 1916 that the income tax came to be levied at graduated scale and this principle has been followed since then. In 1945-46, the maximum rate of income tax was 57 pies in a rupee (29.7 percent). In 1946-47, there was a steep rise in the maximum rate of income tax to 15.5 *annas* [4] in a rupee (96.9 percent). The Taxation Enquiry Commission, 1953-54, recommended 92 percent rate of tax (including surcharge) on the highest slab of income.

See also chapters 10 and 16 of this book.

Endnotes

1. For historical details of income tax in India, see: (a) Government of India, *Report of the Indian Taxation Enquiry Committee* (President: Sir Charles Todhunter), 1924-25, chapter 9, pp. 189-191; (b) Government of India, *Income Tax Investigation Commission* (Chairman: Sir Srinivasa Varadachariar), 1947, pp. 1-4; (c) Government of India, Ministry of Finance, *Report of the Taxation Enquiry Commission* (Chairman: John Matthai), 1953-54, Volume II, chapter 1.
2. *Report of the Indian Taxation Enquiry Committee*, 1924-25, *op. cit.*, Volume 1, para 259.
3. *Report of the Taxation Enquiry Commission,* 1953-54, *op. cit.*, Volume II, chapter 1, p. 16.
4. Metric system of currency in India was introduced from April 1, 1957. In the pre-metric system, one Rupee was = 16 *annas* and one *anna* was = 4 *paise* and one *paisa* was = 3 *pies*. In the post-metric system, one Rupee = 100 *paise*.

5

Excise Duties

In India, the history of excise taxation in its modern form can be traced back to the year 1894 when excise duty at the rate of 5 percent was imposed on yarn above twenty counts. Since then, the Indian excise system has undergone various changes. Excise at the rate of 6 *annas* [1] per Imperial Gallon was imposed on motor spirit in 1917 and on kerosene at the rate of one *anna* per Imperial Gallon in 1922. Another landmark in the history of excise taxation was the year 1934 when excise duties were imposed on sugar, matches, and steel ingots. Duties were imposed on tyres in 1941 and on vegetable products and tobacco in 1943, mainly to meet the exigencies of war finances. The year 1944 saw excise duties being imposed on coffee, tea and betel nut. Cigarettes came within the excise net in 1948 and mill-made cotton cloth in 1949. Before 1944, excise duties were levied under separate enactments for different goods, e.g. tobacco levies were imposed under the Tobacco (Excise Duty) Act, 1943. About 16 such separate laws were in force till 1944. However, in that year the various enactments were consolidated into the Central Excises and Salt Act and the Central Excise Rules, 1944.

Prior to Independence in 1947, excise taxation in India was selective in terms of commodity coverage and modest from revenue angle. Excise duties were not important as a source of revenue due to the narrow production base of the Indian economy.

The relative share of Central excises in total tax revenue of the government was 4.7 percent and 4.4 percent in 1920-21 and 1925-26 respectively. The policy of *discriminating protection* [2] followed from the mid-1920s did give some impetus to domestic industry and the share of excise revenue increased to 8.8 percent in 1931-32. At the start of the Second World War, the contribution of excise revenue was 10.7 percent (Table 5.1).

Table 5.1: Pre-Independence Trends in the Relative Share of Excise Duties in Total Tax Revenue of the Central Government: Selected Years

(₹ crore)

Year	Total Tax Revenue	Central Excise Revenue	Col. 3 as percent of Col. 2
1	2	3	4
1920-21	60.85	2.85	4.7
1925-26	72.86	3.21	4.4
1931-32	75.62	6.19	8.2
1938-39	81.37	8.72	10.7

Source: Government of India, Ministry of Finance, *Report of the Taxation Enquiry Commission* 1953-54, Volume II, p. 258, Table 3 (excerpted).

The selected commodities on which excise duties were imposed included cotton textiles, salt, motor spirit, and kerosene. A commodity-wise history of excise taxation is as follows.

5.1 Cotton Textiles

Cotton textile mills were first built in India in the 1850s. By 1896 their number had risen to 167 and by 1923 to 323. Following pressure from Britain, an excise duty of 5 percent, corresponding to the duty imposed on imported goods, was imposed in 1894 on Indian yarn above twenty counts. It was in the nature of a countervailing duty on domestic yarn and hence on cloth which competed with imported goods from Lancashire. In 1896, excise duty on yarn was changed to duty on cloth at a reduced rate of 3.5 percent. Simultaneously, import duty was reduced to the same level as the excise duty. The policy of equal duties on imported and domestically produced goods continued till 1917. It was from this year that the period of differential duties started with the raising of the import duty on cloth to 7.5 percent. It was further raised to 11 percent in 1921. The domestic producers thus enjoyed protection to the extent of 7.5 percent on cloth. The Indian Fiscal Commission 1921-22, examined in detail the question of protection to domestic industries and recommended that the Tariff Board should consider the rate of import duty necessary for the protection of the domestic industry. When duty is imposed on local production, the import duty should be enhanced by a like amount. Following its recommendations, the Government adopted what came to be called the policy of 'discriminating protection' under which tariff protection was granted to selected industries against foreign competition. The industries which benefited from the policy of discriminating protection included, *inter alia*, iron and steel, cement, textiles, sugar, paper, matches, and jute.

5.2 Salt

Excise on salt was another important source of revenue for the Government during pre-Independence days. The commodity was preferred for taxation because of its inelastic demand and also because it is used in small quantity by all strata of society. Even a low rate of duty on this essential commodity yields some revenue for the exchequer without anybody feeling the pinch. However, the duty was opposed on the ground that it falls on an absolute necessity of life. Since salt is necessary for human existence, duty on it is in the nature of a poll tax. Even the poorest of the poor are made to contribute to state exchequer.

The Indian Taxation Enquiry Committee, 1924-25, examined in detail the pros and cons of salt duty. It opined, "It may be concluded that, if it is desirable to impose any tax on the mass of the community at all, there is much to be said for the continuance of the salt tax. The present rate of duty is appropriate and causes no serious hardship". [3] Excise duty on salt remained a major source of revenue till Independence. Abolition of salt duty was chosen by Mahatma Gandhi to spearhead his non-co-operation movement against the British rulers. The duty on salt was abolished with the achievement of Independence in 1947.

5.3 Petroleum Products

Excise duty at the rate of 6 *annas* (₹ 0.37) per Imperial Gallon (4.55 litres) was imposed on motor spirit in 1917. The purpose of this levy was to restrict consumption of petrol to conserve supplies for war needs. Kerosene was another petroleum item placed on the tariff list in 1922. The rate of duty was one *anna* (₹ 0.06) per Imperial Gallon. The duty on motor spirit was mainly a tax on transport while the burden of kerosene duty fell chiefly on almost all classes of the population. For the next 34 years (i.e. until 1956) there was no addition to the list of petroleum products subject to excise tariff. It may be mentioned here that before Independence, the Indian oil industry was characterised by small-scale, localised operations under foreign firms. The Assam Oil Company (a subsidiary of Burmah Oil Company) produced about half a million tonnes of crude oil in Assam. A small refinery of the company at Digboi processed this crude. With the Digboi refinery producing about 7 percent of the total consumption of petroleum products in India, the remainder was imported and marketed by various foreign oil companies operating in India, the chief among them being Burmah Oil, and Stanvac.

5.4 Tobacco

Taxation of tobacco and tobacco products in India was suggested, for the first time, by the Indian Taxation Enquiry Committee, 1924-25. It observed, "The absence of any internal taxation on tobacco is a feature which distinguishes the fiscal system of India from that of almost every other civilised country in the world. The considerations which have led in other countries to the selection of tobacco as one of the principal subjects for consumption taxation apply with equal force to India. It is a typical instance of a conventional luxury whose use goes down to the poorest classes, and it is an article the consumption of which can be varied greatly both in quality and quantity according to the means of the consumer". [4] Following the recommendations of the Committee, the taxation of tobacco was examined on various occasions, but the administrative difficulties involved in implementing such a levy prevented its imposition. Moreover, taxation of tobacco was a State subject before the enactment of the Government of India Act, 1935. After this enactment, the power to impose tobacco excise was vested in the Central Government.

Excise on unmanufactured tobacco was levied for the first time with effect from April 1, 1943 with a view to mobilising additional resources to meet the requirements of the Second World War. The levy was imposed under the Tobacco (Excise Duty) Act, 1943 which was subsequently merged with the consolidated Central Excises and Salt Act, 1944. The revenue realised from tobacco in the first year of the excise, viz. 1943-44 was ₹ 9.65 crore.

The rates of duty levied on unmanufactured tobacco in 1943 were designed on a progressive scale depending upon the intended use of the commodity. In addition to this, a graduated duty on the basis of value slabs was imposed on the higher grades of the manufactured cigars and cheroots. The tobacco tariff was extended in 1948 when an excise duty was imposed on cigarettes on the same pattern as the tariff for cigars and cheroots, namely value slabs for fixation of rates. Duty on unmanufactured tobacco brought the excise machinery into contact with a large number of growers and licensees and thus led to tariff complexities and administrative difficulties.

5.5 Other Products

Excise duty on silver was imposed in 1930. To quote, "It was in 1934 that the first step in the rationalisation of excise levies was made and their coverage extended. Excise duties were imposed mainly as a revenue measure on sugar, matches, steel ingots and mechanical lighters. Sugar and matches production had made rapid strides under heavy protection in the years following the First World War and the stage had been reached when they could be taxed". [5] Duties were imposed on tyres in 1941 and on vegetable products and tobacco in 1943, mainly to meet the exigencies of war finances. The year 1944 saw excise duties being imposed on coffee, tea, and betel nut. Cigarettes came within the excise net in 1948. Prior to 1944, excise duties were levied under separate enactments for different goods. For example, tobacco levies were imposed under the Tobacco (Excise Duty) Act, 1943. About 16 such separate laws were in force till 1944. However, in that year the various enactments were consolidated into the Central Excises and Salt Act and the Central Excise Rules, 1944.

According to Lakdawala and Nambiar, "In the early stages of its evolution, the Indian excise system has had a basic purpose and philosophy behind its development. The main objective was either to restrict internal consumption of such commodities whose supply was scarce or to make good the loss of revenue resulting from the shrinkage of revenue from protective customs duties on imports of parallel commodities. The initial imposition of duties on items such as motor spirit and kerosene belonged to the first category while the subsequent levies on items such as tyres, textiles and cigarettes belonged to the second category". [6]

5.6 Rules of Excise Taxation

The Indian Fiscal Commission, 1921-22 enunciated the following five golden rules of excise taxation which, with necessary modifications, seem to be relevant to this day.

1. "Excise duties should ordinarily be confined to industries which are concentrated in large factories or small areas.
2. They may properly be imposed for the purpose of checking the consumption of injurious articles and especially on luxuries coming under this category.
3. Otherwise they should be imposed for revenue purpose only.
4. While permissible on commodities of general consumption, they should not press too heavily on poorer classes.
5. When an industry requires protection, any further necessary taxation on its products may, if the other conditions are fulfilled, take the form of excise duty *plus* an additional import duty. The latter should fully countervail the former and may be pitched at a higher price". [7]

See also chapters 12 and 17 of this book.

Endnotes

1. One *anna* was equal to 1/16th of a rupee before the introduction of the metric system of currency from April l, 1957.
2. In 1921, the Indian Fiscal Commission was appointed to examine the tariff policy of the Government of India. It submitted its report in 1922. The recommendations of the Fiscal Commission were debated in the Legislative Assembly in February 1923 and a resolution was passed accepting in principle the need to tailor India's tariff policy for encouraging Indian industries. As suggested by the Fiscal Commission, a Tariff Board was set up which investigated the claims of a number of industries for protective duties. Following the recommendations of the Tariff Board, the Government adopted what came to be called the policy of *discriminatory protection* under which tariff protection was granted to select industries against foreign competition. The industries which benefited from the policy of discriminating protection included, *inter alia,* iron and steel, cement, textiles, sugar, paper, matches, and jute.
3. Government of India, *Report of the Indian Taxation Enquiry Committee* (President: Sir Charles Todhunter), 1924-25, Volume I, para 168.
4. Ibid., para 155.
5. Government of India, Ministry of Finance, *Report of the Central Excise Reorganisation Committee* (Chairman: A.K. Chanda), 1963, p. 4.
6. D.T. Lakdawala and K.V. Nambiar, *Commodity Taxation in India* (Ahmedabad: Sardar Patel Institute of Economic and Social Research), 1972, p. 41.
7. Government of India, *Report of the Indian Fiscal Commission* (Chairman: Ibrahim Rahimatoola), 1921-22, p. 87.

6

Customs Duties

Prior to 1857, the regulation of customs duties in India was haphazard and lacked all-India uniformity due to unstable political and economic conditions. Rates of import duty, though not uniform, were relatively low, ranging from 3 to 5 percent *ad valorem* on raw materials and manufactured articles. These rates were doubled in the case of goods imported from countries other than Britain.

Having consolidated political power after the disturbances of 1857, the British Indian Government introduced in 1859 a uniform all-India customs tariff which replaced separate provincial rates of duty. Various customs and tariff enactments were passed from time to time but the following two were the main: (a) The Sea Customs Act, 1878, and (b) The Tariff Act, 1934.

After Independence, the Sea Customs Act and other allied enactments were repealed by a consolidating and amending legislation entitled the Customs Act, 1962. Similarly, the Tariff Act of 1934 was repealed by the Customs Tariff Act, 1975. Customs tariff has been subjected to a series of changes to act as a policy instrument to generate revenue, protect the domestic industry, conserve and ration foreign exchange and frame general international trade policy.

6.1 Period 1859 to 1894

Under the uniform all-India tariff, introduced by the British in 1859, almost everything imported into India was assessed at 10 percent of its value for purposes of customs duty. Some important articles, viz. tobacco, beer, wines, and spirits were taxed at 20 percent. Likewise, nearly all exports from India paid 3 percent rate of duty. High rates of customs duty soon proved counter-productive and by mid-1860s a process of lowering import tariff had started. Moreover, the country was also showing signs of recovery from the trauma of 1857. Import duties were reduced to 7.5 percent in 1864 and further down to 5 percent in 1875. Import duties were abolished in 1882, except those on arms and liquors. For all practical purposes, the import of goods into India was free until 1894. According to K.T. Shah, "...from 1875 to 1900, the Indian customs policy became the subject of a violent controversy between doctrinaire free traders and passionate protectionists; and in consequence there were frequent changes. The ruling caste, taking their cue from the prominent British statesmen, adopted an attitude of uncompromising freedom in trade, irrespective of India's economic or financial interests. The Indian public opinion of the day, such as it was, was gradually driven by the sheer intolerance of the rulers in their second-hand exposition of the free trade principles, to an attitude of equally unyielding protectionism". [1]

Broadly speaking, from mid-1870s the Government of India was well on the path of establishing freedom of trade. Even in the case of exports, exemptions from duty were granted freely and in 1875 the only commodities which were still subject to export duties were rice, indigo, and lac.

6.2 Period 1894 to 1919

The euphoria for free trade which dominated Government's policy between 1875 and 1890 gave way to economic realism with the beginning of 1890s. The loss of revenue from the abolition of import duties was felt to be adversely affecting Central finances. Hence, in a reversal of tariff policy, a general import duty of 5 percent was re-imposed in 1894. A notable exception to this rate was the duty free import of railway materials and machinery. Similarly, a low duty of 1 percent was imposed on iron and steel. There were a few commodities, viz. arms, liquors, and tobacco which were subject to a comparatively high rate of duty. This arrangement continued till the outbreak of the First World War.

The outbreak of the War led to an urgent need for additional revenues and customs duties came in handy for the Government. The general rate of import duty was raised from 5 percent to 7.5 percent in 1916. In the same year, an export duty was imposed on jute. A duty on raw hides and skins at 5 percent *ad valorem* was imposed in 1919.

Export duties formed an important part of the customs tariff soon after the events of 1857. They were gradually abolished and between 1880 and 1916, rice was the only item subject to export duty. The financial difficulties created by the First World War led to their revival. Jute and tea were brought under the export duty net in 1916, and hides and skins in 1919. Justifying the export duty on rice, the Indian Taxation Enquiry Committee, 1924-25, observed, "Though rice is not a monopoly of India, the export duty has been in operation for many years without any bad effects. Its justification lies in special circumstances. The only countries which export appreciable quantities of rice are India, Siam (now Thailand), and Indo-China. The Indian share of the trade varies between one-third and one-half. As each of these countries levies an export duty, the Indian duty does not handicap the producer and its remission would in fact put an equivalent amount of money into the hands of the producers and the middlemen". [2] Export duty on tea was justified on similar grounds because India's principal competitor Ceylon (now Sri Lanka) also imposed export duty on tea.

6.3 Inter-War Period

The general rate of import duty was raised from 7.5 percent to 11 percent in 1921, and further up to 15 percent in 1922. A new category of *luxury goods* (such as motor cars, silk goods, and watches) was introduced in 1921 for which a 20 percent rate was prescribed and the same was increased to 30 percent in the following year. Although, the successive upward revisions in import tariff were made for additional revenue, they did provide the much-needed protection to the domestic industry.

In 1921, the Indian Fiscal Commission was appointed to examine the tariff policy of the Government of India. It submitted its report in 1922 with the following main recommendations:

1. That the Government of India should adopt a policy of protection to be applied with discrimination along the lines indicated in this report.
2. That discrimination be exercised in the selection of industries for protection, and in the degree of protection afforded, so as to make the inevitable burden on the community as light as is consistent with the due development of industries.
3. That the Tariff Board in dealing with claims for protection should satisfy itself: (a) that the industry possesses natural advantages, (b) that without the help of protection it is not likely to develop at all, or not so rapidly as is desirable, and (c) that it will eventually be able to face world competition without protection.
4. That raw materials and machinery be ordinarily admitted free of duty and that semi-manufactured goods used in Indian industries be taxed as lightly as possible.
5. That industries essential for purposes of national defence and for the development of which conditions in India are not unfavourable be adequately protected, if necessary.
6. That no export duties be ordinarily imposed except for purely revenue purposes and then only at very low rates; but that when it is considered necessary to restrict the export of foodgrains, the restriction be effected by temporary export duties and not by prohibition. [3]

The recommendations of the Fiscal Commission were debated in the Legislative Assembly in February 1923 and a resolution was passed accepting in principle the need to tailor India's tariff policy for encouraging Indian industries. As suggested by the Fiscal Commission, a Tariff Board was set up which investigated the claims of a number of industries for protective duties. Following the recommendations of the Tariff Board, the Government adopted what came to be called the policy of *discriminatory protection* under which tariff protection was granted to select industries against foreign competition. The industries which benefited from the policy of discriminating protection included, *inter alia,* iron and steel, cement, textiles, sugar, paper, matches, and jute.

An adverse consequence of the high rates of customs duty during and after the First World War was the encouragement to smuggling. The Indian Taxation Enquiry Committee, 1924-25, examined the smuggling problem at length and observed, "...while the present high tariff offers great temptations to the smuggler, there is a lack of cohesion in the preventive arrangements, which certainly offer many facilities for his operations. It is not desirable to recite instances of the way in which advantage has been taken of these facilities, but it may be said that, though there is no evidence that any considerable percentage of the customs revenue is lost through smuggling, it is clear that there is a loss amounting at least to several lakhs a year". [4]

The economic depression of early 1930s resulted in heavy deficits in the finances of the Central Government. The general rate of import tariff was raised to 25 percent as a part of additional taxation efforts introduced under the Indian Finance Act, 1931.

During the inter-War period, customs duties remained the single largest source of Central revenues. In 1921-22, they accounted for 39.5 percent or two-fifths of the Central revenues. By 1938-39, their share had gone up to almost one-half, 48.9 percent to be exact. At the end of the Second World War, i.e. in 1944-45, their contribution was as low as 11.9 percent: ₹ 39.77 crore out of total revenue of ₹ 334.40 crore (Table 6.1).

Table 6.1: Pre-Independence Trends in the Relative Share of Customs Duties in Total Revenues of the Central Government

(₹ crore)

Year	Total Central Revenues	Customs	Col. 3 as percent of Col. 2
1	2	3	4
1921-22	80.00	31.61	39.5
1936-37	81.45	38.11	46.8
1938-39	82.90	40.51	48.9
1944-45	334.40	39.77	11.9

Figures for 1921-22 and 1936-37 are inclusive of those for Burma. Figures for 1938-38 and 1944-45 relate to undivided India.

Source: Government of India, Ministry of Finance, *Report of the Taxation Enquiry Commission,* 1953-54, Volume I, p. 23, Table 5 (excerpted).

6.4 Second World War

In the Finance Act of 1942, an overall surcharge of one-fifth on all duties was imposed. It continued from year to year till 1951 when it was increased to one-fourth in the wake of Korean boom. In 1944, the rate of surcharge on certain items, viz. potable spirits, cigars, cigarettes, and tobacco was increased from one-fifth to one-half. During the War, an export duty at 3 percent was imposed on cotton cloth and yarn but the same was converted into an export cess in 1945.

Another important wartime development was the introduction of import control (quotas) to ensure that available foreign exchange and shipping space were utilised for essential imports. The policy of import control continued during the post-War period to meet conditions created by the partition of the country, particularly the import of massive quantities of foodgrains.

It is pertinent to note that during the pre-Independence period, maritime Princely States enjoyed the right to levy and retain sea customs duties at their own ports. However, the States were not allowed, through conventions with the British Indian Government, to levy such duties at rates lower than those charged at entry into British Indian ports. This arrangement ensured that there was no undue diversion of trade from British Indian ports to ports developed and maintained by the States. The maritime Princely States of British India with their major ports mentioned in parentheses were the following: Travancore State (Trivandrum, Quilon, Alleppey), Cochin State (Cochin), Bhavnagar State (Bhavnagar), Junagadh State (Verawal, Mangrol), Porbandar State (Porbandar), Baroda State (Okha), Nawanagar State (Bedi, Rozi), Morvi State (Navlakhi), and Cutch State (Mandvi, Kandla).

The authority of the Princely States in terms of sea customs and ports was well-recorded in the Report of the Indian States Enquiry Committee (Financial), 1932. It observed, "...the revenue they (Princely States) derive from these customs duties is substantial, elastic, and an important part of their total revenues, from which their State expenditure (including that on nation building activities) has to be met; that the appointment of staff by which they collect, and the manner in which they disburse, the revenue so realised from customs duties are entirely matters for their own decision; and, in particular, that they cannot be debarred from utilising that revenue in the maintenance and development of the ports at which the customs duties are levied". [5]

See also chapters 13 and 19 of this book.

Endnotes

1. K.T. Shah, *Sixty Years of Indian Finance* (London: P.S. King and Son Ltd., 1927), pp. 282-283.
2. Government of India, *Report of the Indian Taxation Enquiry Committee* (President: Sir Charles Todhunter), 1924-25, Volume I, para 157.
3. Government of India, *Report of the Indian Fiscal Commission* (Chairman: Ibrahim Rahimatoola), 1921-22 pp. XV and XVI.
4. *Report of the Indian Taxation Enquiry Committee,* 1924-25, op. cit., para 152.
5. Government of India, *Report of the Indian States Enquiry Committee* (Financial), 1932 (Chairman: J.C.C. Davidson), para 240.

7

Sales Tax

Entry 48 of List II in the Seventh Schedule of the Government of India Act, 1935, vested in the Provinces the power to levy 'taxes on the sale of goods and on advertisements'. The government of the Central Provinces (now Madhya Pradesh) was the first to take advantage of this provision when it levied a retail sales tax on motor spirit and lubricants in 1938. This so-called *petrol tax* was a selective sales tax imposed through the Central Provinces and Berar Sales of Motor Spirit and Lubrication Taxation Act, 1938. In 1939, Madras levied a general multi-point sales tax through the Madras General Sales Tax Act, 1939. The tax levied at the rate of half percent was ostensibly meant to compensate the loss of revenue resulting from the policy of prohibition.

7.1 Initial Legal Hurdles

Since its very inception, sales tax has been a controversial levy embroiled in legal wrangling. Thus, soon after its enactment, the Central Provinces Act referred above was challenged by the Central Government as unconstitutional. It may be recalled that Entry 45 of List II in Seventh Schedule of the Government of India Act, 1935 had given the Central Government the power to levy excise on tobacco and other goods manufactured or produced in India. Hence, the Central Government maintained that sales tax on motor spirit and lubricants by Central Provinces was *ultra vires* because the power to levy excise on such products belonged to it (Central Government). Deciding in favour of the Provincial Government, the Federal Court observed that such taxes were in no way connected with the production or manufacture of goods, but were imposed on their sale.

In another legal battle, the Central Government contested the Madras General Sales Tax Act, 1939 referred to above. Being a multi-point sales tax, it covered sales by manufacturers also which was challenged by the Central Government. Once again, the Federal Court decided in favour of the Provincial Government and held that it had the power to tax sales of every kind, including sales by a manufacturer or producer.

The above two judicial pronouncements made it clear that the Provinces were competent to tax sales of any commodity and at any stage. In other words, a clear-cut distinction was drawn between the two, excise to be a tax on the act of production or manufacture, and the sales tax to be a levy on the act of sale.

Initial legal squabbling over, sales tax gained rapid popularity among the Provinces with the beginning of 1940s. Bengal adopted a single-point general sales tax levied at retail level in 1941. In the same year, Punjab introduced a general sales tax broadly based on the multi-point model of Madras. A general sales tax on the lines of single-point system of Bengal was introduced by Bihar in 1944 and by Bombay in 1946. Other Provinces followed suit and by 1948, all of them were operating sales tax in one form or the other with the notable exception of Jammu and Kashmir. This State was the last to introduce sales tax in 1962.

7.2 Beggar-my-neighbour Policies

There was no provision in the Government of India Act, 1935, to restrict or prohibit the Provinces from levying sales tax on inter-State transactions. In other words, the Act did not require the Provinces to levy sales tax only on those transactions which exclusively took place in their respective territories.

Taking advantage of this loophole in the Act, almost all the Provincial legislatures enacted sales tax laws which enabled them to tax goods exported from one State to another. These practices led to multiple taxation of the same transaction by different Provinces. As one scholar remarked, "Perhaps, the most important problem relating to sales taxation in the pre-Constitution period was the taxation of inter-State sales. All the Provinces, with the exception of West Bengal, were collecting sales tax on goods being sent to other Provinces and were, in effect, indulging in *beggar-my-neighbour policies*". [1]

In order to sort out these problems and to ensure all-India co-ordination, the Government of India convened a conference of the Finance Ministers of States in October, 1948. At this conference, attempts were made to achieve some degree of uniformity in the taxation of inter-State sales. However, these attempts failed in view of the widespread disagreement among the States. In particular, States which produced important raw materials/manufactured goods were opposed to changes that would result in the exclusion of inter-State trade from the purview of their sales tax laws. In short, the system of sales tax during the pre-Constitution period was arbitrary and bereft of national considerations.

See also chapters 14 and 20 of this book.

Endnote

1 Walter Mahler, *Sales and Excise Taxation in India* (New Delhi: Orient Longman Ltd., 1970), p. 151.

8

Federal-Provincial Financial Relations

This chapter traces the course of fiscal federalism in India from 1870 through 1947, the year of Independence. The pre-1947 arrangements for intergovernmental financial transfers had a strong bearing on the framing of Indian constitution, operative since January 26, 1950.

The present fiscal structure of India is the result of a gradual evolution over the last 150 years. Although it is desirable to look back at the historical developments of a subject to understand its current features, the situation is different in the present case. The political and economic scene in India is greatly different today from what existed during British rule. Before 1947, India was a dependency of the United Kingdom and consisted of British India, and the Princely States. It encompassed the entire area which now forms the four countries of India, Pakistan, Burma, and Bangladesh. The Princely States enjoyed internal financial autonomy and therefore did not form part of the public finances. They had separate budgets and separate sources of revenue. Neither there was any plan of economic development nor was there any attempt to build a welfare society.

Presently, India is an independent country and it includes the former Princely States but excludes the other three countries mentioned above. Due to changed circumstances there is lack of continuity and comparability of information and data. Still, a look back at the pre-1947 intergovernmental financial relations is necessary because they had a bearing on the framing of the Constitution of independent India.

8.1 Mayo Scheme, 1870

After the events of 1857, the British Crown assumed sovereignty over India from East India Company in 1858. The British had realised that governance of so vast and diverse a country of sub-continental size through centralisation of all power was difficult and some degree of decentralisation of authority to Provinces (or States) was necessary. [1] Prior to 1871, the administration of the country was rigidly centralised, characterised by absolute imperial control over Provincial revenues and expenditures. Provinces were entirely dependent on annual cash assignments from the Centre for the maintenance of their administration.

The first beginning towards decentralisation of finances was made when the resolution of Lord Mayo was issued on December 14, 1870. The Mayo resolution explained the scheme by which the Government of India envisaged enlargement of the powers and responsibilities of the Provinces. Thus, services like jails, police, education, medical, roads and civil works were transferred to the administrative control of the Provinces and to meet their costs, the departmental receipts under these heads were also assigned to them. This was done to encourage their interest in collections as well as to induce economy in expenditure. This arrangement came to be known as *Provincial Financial Settlements*. However, due to the inadequacy of these new heads of revenue, the existing system of fixed grants from Central revenues also continued. To quote, "The system of decentralisation was welcomed by the Provinces, because friction with the Central Government was thereby obviated and much useless correspondence avoided. But it did not give adequate resources to the Provinces nor provide conditions for the progressive administration of the services transferred to them. The only consideration which really weighed with the Government of India was that of administrative convenience". [2]

Satisfied with the Mayo scheme, the Government decided to carry it further and the next step towards decentralisation was taken in 1877 when subjects like land revenue, and general administration were transferred to the Provinces. The Mayo settlements were subject to revision annually but from 1882, they were made on quinquennial basis. Over the period 1882 to 1904, these settlements gave rise to the system of *divided heads of revenue.* Under the system, the Centre retained the entire profits of the commercial departments and the proceeds of revenue whose locale was no guide to its true incidence, such as the net receipts from customs, salt and opium. As the income derived from these sources was not sufficient to cover the central expenditure, other sources of revenue including income-tax were divided between the Central and Provincial Governments. The Central Government retained a proportion—fixed in the case of each Province, but not uniform as between the Provinces—of the proceeds of the main heads of revenue collected in the Provinces, based on an assessment of the respective needs of the Provinces. In practice, since no definite standards of needs had been evolved, allocations to the Provinces were largely a result of history. The revenue from *divided heads*, being insufficient to meet the needs of the Provincial Governments, was supplemented by means of fixed cash assignments, recurring as well as non-recurring, which continued to remain an important feature of the system.

In 1904, the settlements were made quasi-permanent and in 1911 began the period of permanent settlements. As the Indian Taxation Enquiry Committee (1924-25) observed, "The intention of the Government in adopting this change was on the one hand to give more elasticity to the settlements and more freedom to Local Governments in working them, and, on the other hand, to protect the general taxpayer of India against possible mismanagement in any particular province, and to put an end to the frequent and undesirable controversies over the adequacy of the existing settlements". [3]

8.2 Government of India Act, 1919

The next landmark in the history of Centre-State financial relations was the Montague-Chelmsford Report on Constitutional Reforms which led to the passing of the Government of India Act, 1919. The Act sought to secure for the Provinces a greater degree of financial independence by abolishing the *divided heads* and effecting a complete separation between the Central and Provincial heads of revenue. Thus, revenue heads like income tax, non-alcoholic excises including salt, customs, currency and mint, and contributions from railways, and post and telegraph came to the share of Central Government while relatively inelastic sources of revenue like land revenue, alcoholic excises, irrigation charges, judicial stamps, forest receipts, and registration fee were assigned to the Provinces. These arrangements enabled the Provinces to run their administration with the help of revenue raised by themselves. The Provincial budgets were separated from that of the Government of India and each Province presented its own budget and levied taxes assigned to it. With revenue heads distributed on these lines, it was estimated in the Report that there would remain a large deficit in the Government of India budget. It was, therefore, proposed in the Report that the Provinces should make contributions to the Central budget.

8.2.1 Meston Settlement, 1920: The Financial Relations Committee presided over by Lord Meston was appointed to advise on the amounts of provincial contributions, and also on the claims of Bombay to a share of the proceeds of income tax. The Meston Committee reported in March 1920.

While recognising that it would not be possible permanently to exclude Provincial Governments from some form of direct taxation upon the industrial and commercial earnings of their people, the Committee advised against the division of income tax with the Provinces. They recommended that general stamps be made provincial for financial and administrative reasons.

The Committee proposed a scheme of initial contributions and of standard contributions to be attained over a period of 7 years. The standard contributions, which were based on the relative taxable capacity of the Provinces and other economic factors, never came into operation. The initial contributions were computed on the increased spending power of each Province resulting from the new scheme of distribution, i.e. the additional income which each Province would acquire on the separation of the sources of revenue. The scheme of contributions was subjected to criticism from various quarters. Some Provinces disliked the initial contributions, others the standard contributions, and industrial Provinces like Bombay were opposed to the whole basis of the revised scheme.

The Joint Select Committee of Parliament on Draft Rules made under the Government of India Act, 1919, suggested a gradual reduction of the aggregate contribution of all Provinces and underlined the idea that contributions should cease at the earliest possible moment.

The Committee was opposed to provincialising income tax but recommended that some share in the growth of revenue from taxation of income should be granted to all Provinces in so far as that growth was attributable to an increase in the amount of incomes assessed in each Province. The scheme of financial arrangements contained in the Report on Indian Constitutional Reforms, as modified on the recommendations of the Joint Select Committee on Draft Rules, was incorporated in the Devolution Rules under the Government of India Act, 1919, which were promulgated in December 1920.

The recommendations of the Joint Select Committee relating to income tax provided that a Province should receive 3 pies in each rupee of the amount by which the assessed income of any year exceeded that of the year 1920-21. Inasmuch as collection might not accurately reflect the income tax revenue due to the economic activity of a Province, some ad hoc adjustments were made on account of industrial units located in a Province different from the Province in which they were assessed to income tax. The operation of the rule gave unequal results as between Provinces. It did not lead, on the whole, to any significant accretion to provincial revenues and, in particular, virtually failed to secure for the larger industrial Provinces a share in the yield of income tax. The rule, however, represented a slight departure in principle from the scheme of complete division of sources originally proposed, and thus marked the beginning of the use of income tax as a balancing factor.

From the very beginning, the scheme of *provincial contributions* came in for sharp criticism from various quarters, particularly from the Provinces themselves. The trends in the Central and Provincial budgets in the early 1920s vindicated the stand of critics and the demand for abolition of contributions grew still more persistent with the result that contributions were abolished from 1928-1929. Provincial contributions under the Meston Settlement during the 1920s provide, perhaps, the only example of transfer of funds from the Provinces to the Centre in the long history of fiscal federalism in India.

There were some important lessons to be learnt from the Reforms of 1919. According to the Fourth Finance Commission, "The failure of the system of a rigid division between the Central and Provincial heads of revenue introduced by the Government of India Act of 1919 could not be prevented by the Meston award and the ultimate result was unsatisfactory both to the Centre and to the units. The experience of the nineteen-twenties led, however, to the emergence of the idea that the authority most suited for discharging a particular governmental function need not necessarily be the authority most suited to raise the financial resources required to discharge the function. The taxes on income had already been recognized before 1919 as a balancing factor and it continued to be recognized as such after 1935. But it also came to be recognized that other taxes could appropriately be levied and collected by the Central Government and distributed, wholly or partly, to the Provinces or States. The Government of India Act of 1935 recognised this principle and the Constitution adopted in 1950 made clear provision for: (i) the assignment of the taxes raised by the Union Government under article 269 wholly to the States, (ii) for the obligatory division of the income-tax proceeds between the Union and the States, and (iii) for the division, with the approval of Parliament, of the proceeds of the Union excise duties". [4]

However, the framework of fiscal federalism set up in 1919 remained unaltered, by and large, till the Government of India Act, 1935 came into operation. The period covered by the Government of India Act, 1919, was marked by frequent discussions on the structure of financial relations between the Centre and the units. A principal objective of these discussions was to equip the Provincial Governments with greater financial resources. The inadequacy of the existing resources, both of the Centre and the units, and a search for fresh avenues of taxation, also represented a thread running through the discussions.

8.3 Indian Taxation Enquiry Committee, 1924-25

In the meantime, the Indian Taxation Enquiry Committee (President: Sir Charles Todhunter), 1924-25 examined, *inter alia*, the division of sources of revenue between the Centre and the Provinces. It recommended that the excise duty on country-made foreign liquor, excise on opium, and general stamps should be transferred to the Centre. The recommendation regarding said excises on liquor and opium was rejected by the Government in view of administrative difficulties involved. Similarly, owing to stiff opposition from the Provinces, the proposal to centralise general stamps was dropped and only duties on documents of commercial nature were transferred to the Central Government. The proposal of the Committee to give the provinces a small share of the receipts of the corporation tax was also rejected by the Government.

A major recommendation of the Committee pertained to the distribution of income tax revenue between the Centre and the Provinces. Prior to 1919, income tax was a *divided head* of revenue. However, the Montague-Chelmsford Reforms resulted in a complete separation of Central and Provincial finances, and income tax became a part of the Central revenues.

The Todhunter Committee expressed itself against giving the Provinces power to levy and administer an income tax as well as against the imposition by the Centre of surcharges for the benefit of the Provinces. It suggested that the most appropriate solution for this problem was the assignment to the Provinces of a share of the tax. In regard to its distribution, the Committee proposed that this should be based primarily on the principle of domicile. It proposed to give the Province the proceeds of a basic rate on personal incomes, graduated proportionally to the general rate. Under its scheme, collection on incomes not pertaining to residents in particular Provinces (such as the tax on undistributed dividends of companies or on incomes of persons resident outside the Province or the country) and the whole of super tax would be retained by the Centre. In addition to the allotment made on the basis of personal incomes, the allocation of which would be based entirely on domicile, the Committee also recommended a partial recognition of the principle of origin by assigning to each Province a small portion of the receipts of the corporation profits tax. It contemplated that this might be distributed on the basis of the collections of each Province.

In short, the Todhunter Committee opined that in the event of any division of taxes between the Centre and the Provinces, the choice of income tax as the main balancing factor was inevitable. The Government of India Act, 1935, did assign to the Provinces a part of the net proceeds of income tax levied by the Centre.

8.4 Indian Statutory Commission, 1930

In its report submitted in 1930, this Commission accepted the general principles of the scheme drawn up by its Financial Assessor, Sir Walter Layton, for the divisions of resources between the Central and Provincial Governments. Layton envisaged the use of income tax as the main balancing factor in the reallocation of revenues between the Centre and the Provinces. He suggested that in order to meet the claims of the industrial

Provinces a substantial part of the revenue from income tax should be assigned to the Provinces. He endorsed the general method of division proposed by Todhunter Committee and recommended that one-half of the income tax paid by residents of a Province (including tax on dividends received by them from companies carrying on operations outside the Province) be assigned to the Province concerned. Super tax would remain entirely Central, subject to reconsideration after 10 years. The Provincial Governments were also to have the option of levying a surcharge on tax collected on the incomes of residents in the Province limited to half the tax transferred to them, i.e. one-fourth of the total tax. Significantly, the Commission also suggested that the exemption of agricultural incomes from income tax should be abolished by definite stages and the whole of the proceeds of the taxation of these incomes should be assigned to the Province of origin.

Sir Layton further recommended that a Provincial Fund be formed out of the proceeds of certain new excises on such commodities as cigarettes and matches and, when the centre budgetary position permitted, the duty on salt, for distribution among the Provinces on a per capita basis. The Commission endorsed this proposal.

8.5 Peel Committee I, 1931

The Federal Structure Committee of the Second and Third Round Table Conferences appointed two sub-committees to consider the problem of allocation of resources between the Centre and the Provinces. Both the sub-committees were presided over by Viscount Peel. The first sub-committee (Peel Committee I) submitted its report in 1931. Report of the second sub-committee (Peel Committee II) came in 1932. In between these two reports was submitted in 1932 the report of an Expert Committee presided over by Lord Percy.

Peel Committee I suggested that all income tax proceeds should be transferred to the Provinces with collection and administration being in federal hands. It suggested, though obliquely, that federal tax revenues should be mostly derived from indirect taxation. Any resultant federal deficit could be met from provincial contributions which would be gradually terminated over a 10 to 15 year period. Later, if any permanent federal surplus were to materialise, the federal government should be free to allocate the surplus to the Provinces as an alternative preferable to reduction of taxation. The Committee suggested that it was desirable that the Constitution itself should lay down the proportions in which funds thus available should be divided among the Provinces, whether according to respective revenues or to population or to some other criteria. It recommended that an expert committee should advise on this aspect as also on the criteria by which the proceeds of income tax should be allocated among the Provinces. Accordingly, the Percy Committee was appointed to examine the issues raised by Peel Committee I.

8.5.1 Percy Committee, 1932: The basis of distribution of income tax among the Provinces was considered in detail by Percy Committee. It held that a proper basis of distribution of income tax receipts should satisfy the following three tests:

1. It should be simple, easily understood and administratively workable.

2. It should give results likely to be accepted as fair between Province and Province.
3. It should be compatible with the idea of a federation of autonomous units.

It opined that an allocation on the basis of collections would lead to gross injustice as between Province and Province and ruled it out. While distribution by population had equally no scientific basis it could be adopted with advantage for the distribution of taxes on certain forms of income not easily assignable to any locality. Theoretically, the basis of origin had much to commend it, but it would be administratively unworkable unless the allocations were made on arbitrary lines. Hence, the Committee did not recommend the adoption of this basis. Finally, it expressed itself in favour of the basis of residence in one of two forms, either the basis of personal income assessed or assessable in each Province or the amount of income tax attributable to each Province.

As regards the question of distribution of income tax between the Centre and the Provinces, the Percy Committee expressed the view that if the entire proceeds of income tax were transferred, the Centre would be faced with a substantial deficit. It, therefore, proposed the following scheme:

1. Corporation tax (super tax on companies), tax paid by residents in federally administered areas and tax paid on salaries of federal officers should be retained by the Centre.
2. Of the remainder of the net proceeds, a Province should receive the amount of personal super tax on the basis of collections from residents, an estimated amount of personal income tax creditable to it, and a share on the basis of population of the tax on non-residents and undistributed profits of companies, both to be taken as an estimated percentage of the total collections.

In order to ensure stability of provincial budgets, it suggested that the share of income tax due to the Provinces should not be altered from year to year even if the data for this were readily available on the basis suggested by it. Instead, it should be fixed for a term of years, subject to revision every 5 years in the light of data of personal income tax for the previous quinquennium. The federal government would have the power to impose a surcharge, for its own purposes, on any tax levied by it for the benefit of the Provinces. Federal grants, if and when they became feasible, should be made on population basis as the Committee believed that the surplus would arise mostly from taxes on consumption.

8.6 Peel Committee II, 1932

It proposed a two-fold division of the proceeds of taxes on income: (a) share which would be assigned as a permanent constitutional arrangement to the federal government and (b) share which would be assigned as a permanent constitutional arrangement to the Provinces. The federal government would be entitled to a share based on the proceeds of heads of tax which were not derived solely from the residents in British India, such as corporation tax, tax on federal officers, tax in federal areas, tax on Government of India securities and taxes on the incomes of persons not resident in British India. The whole of the remaining proceeds from income tax were to be assigned to the Provinces. However, the federal government should retain a block amount out of the provincial share of income tax until sufficient time had elapsed for the development of new sources of revenue. The Committee was in favour of the federal government having the power to levy for its own purposes a surcharge on the heads of income tax permanently assigned to the Provinces. Most of the members of the Committee were also agreed that the Provinces should have a right to levy a surcharge on the personal tax levied on its residents under the heads permanently allocated to the Provinces, subject to a maximum of 12.5 percent. The Committee also proposed subventions from the Centre to deficit Provinces in approved cases and on certain conditions, to enable them to balance their budgets on the basis of providing for bare necessities.

8.7 White Paper on Indian Constitutional Reforms, 1931

The White Paper issued by Government in December 1931 contemplated that a prescribed percentage, not being less than 50 percent nor more than 75 percent, of the net revenue derived from taxes on income, other than agricultural income, except taxes on the income of companies should be assigned to the Provinces on a prescribed basis. It also proposed that the federation should retain for the first 3 years a prescribed sum out of the provincial share which would continue to be retained for a further period of 7 years with a reduction of one-eighth of the original sum in each successive year. Both the federation and the Provinces were to have power to levy surcharges on income tax for their own purposes.

Proposals contained in the White Paper introduced two new features into the plan for the division of sources of revenue. Firstly, the federal legislature was to be empowered by a law to assign to the units the whole or part of the yield of salt duties, excise duties, other than those specifically assigned to the units, and export duties. Secondly, it also suggested that in respect of certain taxes, including terminal taxes and death duties, while the power to levy the tax would be vested solely in the federation, the proceeds would be distributed to the Provinces. However, the federation would have the right to impose a surcharge for federal purposes.

8.8 Joint Parliamentary Committee on Indian Constitutional Reforms, 1934

This Committee was, by and large, in agreement with the proposals contained in the White Paper. It left the provincial share of income tax to be prescribed by an Order-in-Council, but could not visualise any prospect of the Provinces' share of income tax exceeding half of the net revenue from the source. The Committee did not favour the proposal to empower the Provinces also to impose surcharges on personal income tax. The modified proposals relating to income tax and other matters were incorporated in the Government of India Act, 1935.

It is noteworthy that the idea of devolving the whole of income tax to the Provinces leaving the Centre to cover the consequent deficit by provincial contributions was abandoned, and a measure of elasticity in the distribution of income tax was introduced by limiting the provincial share to a part of the net proceeds and giving the Centre power to retain, for a transitional period, a fixed amount out of the provincial share to give it time to adjust its finances.

8.9 Government of India Act, 1935

The Government of India Act, 1935 was a watershed in the evolution of Centre-State financial relation. To quote, "While under all the previous Government of India Acts, the Government of India was unitary, the Act of 1935 prescribed a federation, taking the Provinces and the Indian States (i.e. Princely States) as Units. But it was optional for the Indian States to join the federation; and since the Rulers of the Indian States never gave their consent, the Federation envisaged by the Act of 1935 never came into being". [5] Nevertheless, the Act was a step towards consolidation and enhancement of Provincial autonomy in matters of resources and functions. It laid the foundations for the structure of Centre-State relations as incorporated in the present Constitution of India. The Act divided taxation heads into the following three broad categories.

1. Taxes levied by and meant exclusively for the Central Government.
2. Taxes levied by and meant exclusively for Provincial Governments.
3. Taxes levied by the Centre but shared with the Provinces or completely assigned to them.

The Act also provided for grants-in-aid from the Centre to the Provinces in need of assistance.

The main provisions of the Act of 1935 relating to the subject under study were as follows.

1. Agricultural income tax was included in the list of Provincial subjects.
2. Provision was made under Section 138 of the Act for the assignment to Provinces of a percentage of the net proceeds of taxes on income other than agricultural income.
3. Section 140 of the Act provided that duties on salt, Central duties of excise, and export duties, while levied and collected by the Centre would, if an Act of Central legislature so provided, be assigned wholly or in part to the Provinces.
4. Under Section 142 provision was made for the payment of grants-in-aid of the revenues of such Provinces as might be in need of assistance.
5. The Act also provided for the levy by Central legislation of duties in respect of succession to property other than agricultural land, stamp duties, terminal taxes on goods and passengers carried by railway or air and taxes on railway fares and freights, and for the distribution of net proceeds to the Provinces.

8.9.1 Indian Financial Enquiry Report, 1936: Fiscal arrangements of the Act of 1935 left several questions to be decided and Sir Otto Niemeyer was appointed to make recommendations on matters which under Sections 138(1) and (2), 140(2) and 142 of the Act had to be prescribed or determined by Order-in-Council and on certain other ancillary matters. The scope of the enquiry was made comprehensive by a supplementary reference which enabled it to be extended to cover a review of the existing liabilities of the Provincial Governments to the Centre.

In respect of income tax, having regard to the dual considerations of the necessity of safeguarding the financial stability of the Centre and the obvious future needs of the Provinces, Sir Otto Niemeyer felt it was desirable that the maximum practicable distribution should be achieved. He recommended that 50 percent of the net proceeds of income tax should be assigned to the Provinces.

As regards the distribution of the provincial share, he expressed the view that the mere accident of place of collection was an unsuitable guide and that the residence of the individual though it might be a convenient practical dividing line for the avoidance of double taxation between separate political units, was not in itself a very scientific criterion, particularly in a federation. Even supposing it were practicable to ascertain to what part of the country particular fractions of income and the incidence of the taxation burden properly adhered, it was, he pointed out, still arguable that in a federation other considerations also were involved, particularly if the benefits and incidence of other forms of common taxation were unequally divided as between the various partners.

After a consideration of the various elements of the problem, he came to the conclusion that substantial justice would be done by fixing the scale of distribution partly on residence and partly on population. He recommended distribution among the Provinces according to the fixed percentages given in Table 8.1.

Table 8.1: Distribution of Provinces' Share in Income Tax among the Provinces Recommended by Sir Otto Niemeyer

Province	**Percent**
Madras	15
Bombay	20
Bengal	20
United Provinces	15
Punjab	8
Bihar	10
Central Provinces	5
Assam	2
North-West Frontier Province	1
Orissa	2
Sind	2
Total	**100**

Source: *Report of the Finance Commission,* 1952, p. 20.

Sir Otto Niemeyer also recommended that the Centre should retain for the first 5 years out of the provincial money a sum equivalent to the amount by which the central share plus the contribution from Railways fell short of ₹ 13 crore a year and that the amount retained from the provincial share should be surrendered to the Provinces over a further period of 5 years. As part of the assistance he contemplated for the jute-growing

Provinces, Sir Otto Niemeyer recommended that the provinces' share of the jute export duty be raised by 12.5 percent to 62.5 percent of the net proceeds of the duty.

In short, his main recommendations as contained in the Indian Financial Enquiry Report 1936 were the following.

1. That 50 percent of the net proceeds of income tax should be assigned to the Provinces.
2. That the share of jute-growing Provinces in the jute export duty be raised by 12.5 percent to 62.5 percent of the net proceeds of the duty.
3. The outstanding debts (to the Centre) of Bengal, Bihar, Assam, North-West Frontier Province, and Orissa, contracted prior to April 1, 1936 be cancelled, and the outstanding debt of the Central Provinces be reduced.
4. Annual grants of varying amounts were also recommended for United Provinces, Assam, North-West Frontier Province, Orissa, and Sind (Table 8.2).

The aforesaid recommendations were accepted by the authorities and embodied in the Government of India (Distribution of Revenues) Order, 1936. This Order, subject to a change made in 1940, continued to regulate the allocation of resources between the Centre and the units until the partition of the country in August 1947.

Table 8.2: Annual Grants to the Provinces Recommended by Sir Otto Niemeyer

(₹ lakh)

United Provinces	25 for a fixed period of 5 years
Assam	30
North-West Frontier Province	100 subject to consideration at the end of 5 years.
Orissa	40 with ₹ 7 lakh additional in the first and ₹ 3 lakh additional in each of the next 4 years.
Sind	105 for 10 years, with ₹ 5 lakh additional in the first year, and thereafter falling until the grant ceased in about 45 years time

Source: *Report of the Finance Commission,* 1952, p. 21.

Following the outbreak of Second World War, and the increasing expenditure it entailed on the Centre, steps had to be taken to strengthen Central finances. It was decided that for the duration of the war, the Centre should be permitted to retain a fixed sum of ₹ 4.5 crore out of the provincial share of income tax. The Order-in-Council was amended accordingly to secure this and the modified provision regulated the distribution of the tax from 1940-41 to 1945-46. In each of the next 4 years the sum retained by the Centre from the provincial share was reduced by ₹ 75 lakh a year over the previous year, and the full provincial share was restored to the Provinces in 1950-51.

Endnotes

1. It may be noted that Princely States enjoyed internal financial autonomy and therefore did not

form part of the structure of public finances of British India. They had separate budgets and separate sources of revenue. After Independence, the former Princely States were integrated into the fiscal and financial system of the country.

2. Gyan Chand, *The Essentials of Federal Finance: A Contribution to the Problem of Financial Re-adjustment in India* (Humphrey Milford, Oxford University Press, 1930), p. 42.
3. Government of India, *Report of the Indian Taxation Enquiry Committee*, 1924-25, Vol. I (President: Sir Charles Todhunter), p. 372.
4. *Report of the Fourth Finance Commission*, 1965, pp. 6-7.
5. Durga Das Basu, *Introduction to the Constitution of India* (New Delhi: Prentice-Hall of India Pvt. Ltd., 1987), p. 9.

Part III
Post-Independence History of Taxation

Part III (A)

Multiple and Punitive Taxation during Pre-reforms Period (1947 to 1990)

9

Integrated Direct Tax System

The Indian tax system has undergone major structural changes since Independence in 1947. It has become comprehensive and complicated over the years. It has successfully mobilised resources to finance developmental, welfare and administrative activities of public authorities. Besides being the main source of revenue, both for the Central and State Governments, it is an effective instrument to realise various socio-economic objectives of national policies. However, the tax system has been relying heavily on indirect taxes and suffering extensively from fiscal malady called tax evasion.

9.1 Review of Indian Tax System by Nicholas Kaldor, *1956*

In mid-1950s, British economist Nicholas Kaldor carried out, at the request of the Government of India, a review of the Indian tax system particularly with reference to personal and business taxation. He was asked to examine the Indian tax system in the light of the revenue requirements of the Second Five Year Plan (1956-57 to 1960-61) launched in the same year. It may be recalled that an extensive review of the Indian tax system had already been undertaken by the Indian Taxation Enquiry Commission (Chairman: John Matthai), 1953-54.

Kaldor made the first systematic estimates of income tax evasion in India. He estimated income tax loss through tax evasion at ₹ 200 to ₹ 300 crore for the year 1953-54. [1] The estimates of Kaldor were based on certain tentative figures relating to national income provided to him by the Central Statistical Organisation. Kaldor made it clear in his report that his estimates were tentative and should be interpreted with caution.

A tax on capital gains was in operation in India for a short period in respect of capital gains which arose during the period April 1, 1946 to March 31, 1948. Following the recommendations of Kaldor, the tax was revived in 1956 and made applicable on capital gains arising on or after April 1, 1956.

Following the recommendations of Kaldor, an *integrated direct tax system* was introduced in India in the mid-1950s. In 1957 and 1958, three new taxes were introduced, viz. wealth tax, expenditure tax, and gift tax. Estate duty was already in operation since 1953. The basic philosophy underlying the introduction of the system of integrated direct taxes was to prevent evasion and avoidance of direct taxes and thereby to reduce inequalities of income and wealth.

However, the yield from expenditure tax, gift tax, and estate duty was never of much significance in Central revenues. The meagre revenue collections from these taxes ultimately led to the abolition of expenditure tax in 1966, estate duty in 1985 and gift tax in 1998. Wealth tax continued to be in operation till 2014-15, though the revenue was negligible as compared to the total tax collections of the Central Government.

Main provisions of expenditure tax, estate duty, and gift tax at the time of their abolition are explained below. Wealth tax and its abolition are discussed chapter 11 of this book.

9.2 Expenditure Tax

Pursuant to the recommendations of Professor Nicholas Kaldor, a tax on personal expenditure was first imposed in India on April 1, 1958. The tax was introduced as an adjunct to the personal income tax as part of a scheme to evolve a self-checking system of direct taxes in India.

Expenditure tax was withdrawn by Finance Minister Morarji Desai in his budget for the year 1962-63 on account of insignificant revenue yield and its failure to restrain ostentatious expenditure, and promote savings. [2] It was reintroduced in the 1964-65 budget by Finance Minister T.T. Krishnamachari with the hope that the tax would help lessen inequalities of income and wealth. However, the tax was repealed again in the 1966-67 budget on the grounds of burden on administration and inconvenience to assesses. [3] Some of the features of the expenditure tax in the last year of its operation (1965-66) were the following:

Corporations were not subject to tax, neither was any taxpayer whose income from all sources did not exceed ₹ 36,000 in the base year (the base year was the same as that for income tax purposes, expiring on March 31). An individual taxpayer and his dependants were entitled to a simple standard expenditure allowance of ₹ 30,000. Also, there was a long list of expenditures exempt from tax: (a) expenditure incurred in earning income, (b) investment expenditure either in connection with a business or in the nature of personal investment in deposits, loans, shares, securities, insurance policies etc. (c) expenditures covering books, and works of art, (d) charitable expenditures, (e) expenditures by way of gifts, trust and settlements, (f) expenditures on Union, State and Local government taxes, and (g) cost of legal proceedings, expenditure on marriage, medical treatment, maintenance of parents, and education outside India, up to specified limits. [4]

That the tax proved a flop is evident from the small number of assessees falling within its ambit, and the meagre revenue collections. For example, in the first year when the expenditure tax was imposed, the total number of assessees was 7,774 as against 9,83,277 under the income tax. [5]

It is noteworthy that the revenue yield was poor in spite of the high rates of the tax which ranged from 10 percent on the first ₹ 10,000 of taxable expenditure to 100 percent on taxable expenditure above ₹ 50,000. The low coverage and low revenue yield of the tax were attributed to the following three factors:

1. High initial income exemption.
2. Generous standard expenditure allowance.
3. Complex and comprehensive series of exempt categories of expenditure. [6]

The introduction of expenditure tax proved abortive in Ceylon (now Sri Lanka) where it was also imposed in 1959, but withdrawn in 1963. The unsuccessful experiments of India, and Sri Lanka have served as a deterrent for other countries to impose expenditure tax.

In 1985, the Government of India appointed a Study Group on Taxation of Expenditure which discounted the practicability of administering a universal classical type of expenditure tax. It observed, "In a developing country, such as India, given the large share of cash transactions, the fact that a substantial number of taxpayers do not maintain proper accounts and the limited capability of the tax administration, the administration of a full-fledged expenditure tax would simply not be feasible". [7]

9.2.1 Expenditure Tax Act, 1987: In 1987, the government introduced, on a modest scale, a tax on luxury expenditure relating to hotel receipts. The Expenditure Tax Act, 1987 levied a tax at the rate of 20 percent (reduced to 10 percent by the Finance, Act, 1994) on expenditure incurred in hotels where the room charge for any unit of accommodation was ₹ 400 or more per day per individual (increased to ₹ 1,200 or more by the Finance Act, 1992). This tax was charged on expenditure incurred in a hotel on food or drink, accommodation, and other services. However, expenditure for which payment was made in foreign exchange or any expenditure incurred by a person enjoying diplomatic immunity was exempted from the levy of expenditure tax. The exemption granted in respect of payment made in foreign exchange was withdrawn by the Finance Act, 1992.

The scope of expenditure tax was extended to expenditure incurred in air-conditioned restaurants by the Finance (No. 2) Act, 1991. This tax was levied at the rate of 15 percent on the expenditure incurred in, or any payment made to such restaurants for the provision of food and drink. However, in a hurried move the Finance Minister announced the withdrawal of the levy of expenditure tax on air-conditioned restaurants in his 1992-93 budget speech.

In the above context, the Task Force on Direct Taxes (Chairman: Vijay Kelkar) observed, "The present tax on expenditure in hotels is in the nature of a consumption tax. It was introduced as a separate tax in the absence of a tax on services. Since tax on services has since been introduced, it is only appropriate that this levy is merged with the service tax". [8] Following the recommendations of the Task Force, expenditure tax was abolished effective from June 1, 2003.

9.3 Estate Duty

9.3.1 Justification for Estate Duty: The institution of inheritance is a major contributory factor for inequalities of income and wealth and their perpetuation in capitalist societies. To deal with this problem democratically, estate taxation, if designed properly, can become an instrument for improving the distribution of economic power.

Transfer of property has always been considered an appropriate base for taxation by governments which not only protect privately-owned properties but also supervise their transfers from one generation to another.

Taxation of transfer of wealth at death may take various forms. Tax imposed on the estate as a whole of the deceased at the time of its transfer to his heirs is called estate duty. Tax on each inheritance to which the estate gives rise is known as inheritance tax or succession duty. Estate duty can be avoided if property is transferred by gifts among living persons. To prevent such possibilities, estate tax is generally accompanied by gift tax on the donor. Similarly, inheritance tax is associated with gift tax on the donee. The basic philosophy underlying estate taxation is to curtail an individual's right to acquire property without his own efforts. However, estate taxation does not interfere with the right of a person to use his property during his lifetime.

The role of capital transfer taxes (death duty, inheritance tax, gift tax etc.) is all the more important in countries where real estates have appreciated precipitously in value. Taxation of estate is least objectionable on grounds of efficiency. As Nicholas Kaldor has opined, "Death duties unquestionably represent the least harmful method of making scale levies on capital, largely because in contemplation of death human beings are not perfectly rational, and taxes dependent on death do not in fact lead to the same kind of reaction on conduct as similar taxes which are expected during the taxpayers' lifetime". [9]

Estate duty is often avoided through the use of trusts. A testator may leave to his heir that portion of his assets which are tax free and keep the remainder which are taxable in a trust. He can make arrangements under which his wife and children receive income there from during their lifetime. Such lacunae in the tax law make trust arrangements advantageous for testators of enormous wealth. Trust arrangements can be curtailed, so far as tax implications are concerned, by limiting trusts to fixed values for each beneficiary or making trusts taxable.

Although bearing a sound social philosophy (to promote a more equitable distribution of wealth) and being least objectionable on efficiency grounds, implementation of estate taxation bristles with difficult technical, social, and economic problems. An appropriate solution of these problems is necessary, primarily on equity considerations.

1. To what extent does society desire to abridge a person's right to transfer property through bequest. The question pertains to exclusions, deductions, exemption limits, and rate progression. For example, if the society wishes to impose a ceiling on such transfers, it may impose a 100 percent duty on the value of the estate in excess of the ceiling limit.
2. Should the limits imposed on bequests apply irrespective of the family relationship of the recipient with the deceased? It would, of course, be unfair to treat the spouse and a distant relative of the deceased equally under the law of estate duty. In other words, tax treatment of estate should be lenient in case of close, and stricter in case of distant family relationship with the deceased. For this purpose differential rate structures may be prescribed depending on the closeness of the family ties between the testator and the donee.
3. Should an individual's right to pass on wealth be curtailed more severely as successive generations become beneficiaries? According to Italian economist Eugenio Rignano, the level of applicable rates may rise as the property passes through successive bequests. [10] The foregoing issues are value-laden and therefore defy universally acceptable solutions.

9.3.2 Estate Duty in India: Under the Government of India Act, 1935, estate duty was a provincial source of revenue. In the Constitution of independent India, the duty was bifurcated into: (a) estate duty on non-agricultural estates, and (b) estate duty on agricultural estates. The former was allocated to the Union Government and the latter to the State Governments.

Estate duty was introduced in India in 1953 when the Estate Duty Act of that year imposed a duty on the capital value of all property passing on the death of any person on or after October 15, 1953. The rationale for the tax was to curb the perpetuation of income and wealth inequalities through inheritance. However, following the recommendations of the Economic Administration Reforms Commission, 1981-83, estate duty was abolished with effect from March 16, 1985. The duty was abolished on the ground that it had failed in both its objectives, viz. to reduce the accumulation of dynastic wealth and raise resources for the Government. The Commission noted that 96.8 percent of the assessees in 1980-81 related to the estates whose principal value was less than ₹ 3 lakh. [11] In 1985-86, estate duty yielded a paltry sum of ₹ 23 crore (0.08 percent) out of a total Central tax collection of ₹ 28,671 crore in the same year. However, according to some experts abolition of estate duty was a retrograde fiscal step. Instead of improving and strengthening the duty, the baby was flung out with the bath water.

9.3.3 Main Provisions of the Estate Duty Act, 1953 at the Time of its Abolition in 1985: Section 5 of the Estate Duty Act was the charging section. It provided for the levy of estate duty on the *principal value* [12] of all property which passed or was deemed to pass on the death of a person. Estate tax, therefore, was charged directly on the value of property changing hands at death, irrespective of the destination of that property or its distribution among the beneficiaries. [13]

A. Properties Deemed to Pass on Death: By virtue of sub-section (3) of Section 3 of the Act, property passing on death included property deemed to pass on death. Under Sections 6 to 17, the following items of property were deemed by law to pass on the death of a person.

1. Property which the deceased was, at the time of his death, competent to dispose of (Section 6).
2. Property in which the deceased or any other person had an interest ceasing on the death of the deceased (Section 7).
3. All gifts made in contemplation of death (Section 8).
4. All gifts of property made within two years [14] of death or gifts which had not been made *bonafide* (Section 9). However, the following gifts were not deemed to pass on death: (a) gifts made in consideration of marriage up to maximum of ₹ 10,000 and (b) gifts which were proved to have been part of the normal expenditure of the deceased up to a maximum of ₹ 10,000.
5. Gifts made with a reservation of some right (Section 10).
6. Where an interest, limited to cease on death, had been disposed of within two years of decedent's death and which but for such disposition would have passed on the death under Section 5 (Section 11).
7. Property passing under any settlement made by the deceased where the settler reserves to himself an interest in the settled property or the right to revoke the

settlement or to reclaim the absolute interest in such property (Section 12).

8. Where a person, having been absolutely entitled to any property, had caused it to be transferred to or vested in himself and another person jointly so that the beneficial interest in some part of that property accrued by survivorship to the other person (Section 13).
9. Money received under a policy of life insurance, kept by a person for the benefit of a donee (Section 14).
10. Any annuity or other interest, purchased or provided by the deceased to the extent of the beneficial interest accruing or arising on his death (Section 15).
11. Any annuity or other interest which was attributable to property derived from the deceased (Section 16).
12. If the deceased had made a transfer of any property to a controlled company and received benefit from the company in the three years ending with his death, the assets of the company were deemed, for the purpose of estate duty, to be included in the property passing on his death in proportion to benefits accrued to him from the company (Section 17).

B. Property Exempt from Estate Duty: The provisions relating to exemptions from the charge of estate duty were contained in Part III (Sections 21 to 33) of the Estate Duty Act, 1953. The following were not included in the property passing on the death of the deceased.

1. All immovable property situated out of India [Section 21(1)(a)].
2. All movable property situated out of India at the time of death if the deceased was not domiciled in India [Section 21(1)(b)].
3. Property held by the deceased as trustee for another person subject to the condition that the deceased was not the sole trustee (Section 22).
4. Settled property in the case of which the interest of the deceased failed before becoming an interest in possession (Section 23).
5. Income of settled property acquired on death of the spouse if the settlement was effected before the commencement of the Act (Section 25).
6. Property passing by reason of a *bona fide* purchase for full or partial consideration in money (Section 26).
7. Settled property in respect of which, since the date of settlement, estate duty had been paid on the death of the deceased's spouse (Section 29). [15]
8. Certain pensions and annuities payable to the widow and other dependants of the deceased (Section 29A).
9. Gifts made by the deceased for a public charitable purpose in the vulnerable period (i.e. within a period of six months before death) to the extent of ₹ 2,500 [Section 33(1)(a)]. [16]
10. Gifts made by the deceased for any other purpose in the vulnerable period (i.e. within a period of two years before death), to the extent of ₹ 1,500 [Section 33(1)(b)].
11. Household goods to the extent of ₹ 2,500 [Section 33(1)(c)].
12. Book not intended for sale [Section 33(1)(d)].

13. Wearing apparel, but not including any precious stones or ornaments [Section 33(1)(e)].
14. Insurance policies taken out and moneys deposited for the purpose of eventual payment of estate duty subject to a monetary limit of ₹ 50,000 or the amount actually payable as duty, whichever was lower [Sections 31(1)(f) and (g)].
15. Moneys payable under one or more policies of insurance effected by the deceased on his life to the extent of ₹ 5,000 [Section 33(1)(h)]. [17]
16. Drawings, paintings, photographs etc. which were retained in the family of the deceased and dealt with or disposed of in accordance with the prescribed conditions and were not intended for sale [Section 33(1)(j)].
17. Moneys earmarked under policies of insurance or declaration of trusts or settlements by the deceased for the marriage of female relatives dependent upon him to the extent of ₹ 10,000 in respect of each such relative [Section 33(1)(k)].
18. Any one building in the occupation of a former ruler declared by the Central Government as his official residence [Section 33(1)(l)].
19. Estate of members of the armed forces killed in action, during operations against an enemy and of members of the police force, including border security force, killed in action in protecting the border [Sections 33(1)(m) and (mm)]. [18]
20. One house or part thereof exclusively use by the deceased for his residence, to the extent the principal value did not exceed rupees one lakh if such a house was situated in a place with a population exceeding ten thousand, and the full principal value in any other case [Section 33(1)(n)].
21. Property gifted by the deceased to his spouse, son, daughter, brother or sister at least five years before his death provided that the gift was chargeable to gift tax under the Gift Tax Act, 1958 [Section 33(1)(o)].
22. National Defence Gold Bonds, 1980, to the extent of an aggregate weight of fifty kilograms of gold [Section 33(1)(p)].

C. Aggregation of Properties for Rate Purposes: It should be noted that the properties mentioned in Sections 33(1)(a), 33(1)(b), 33(1)(f) and (g), 33(1)(h), and 33(1)(k) though not liable to estate duty were included in the principal value of estate for the purpose of determining the rate of duty. [19]

D. Deductions and Reliefs: The provisions relating to deductions in computing the principal value of the estate and reliefs from the duty payable were contained in Part VI (Sections 44 to 50B) of the Estate Duty Act, 1953. The following deductions were permissible.

1. Funeral expenses up to ₹ 1,000 (Section 44). [20]
2. All bonafide debts and encumbrances with some exceptions (Section 44).
3. Relief from estate duty where court fees had been paid for obtaining representation to estate of the deceased (Section 50).
4. Relief from estate duty where gift tax had been paid (Section 50A).
5. Relief from estate duty where tax has been paid on capital gains (Section 50B).

E. Quick Succession Relief: An estate which has been subjected to duty may change hands quickly on account of successive deaths and again become liable to payment of duty. In such cases, estate duty puts undue burden on families suffering deaths at short intervals. This problem is mitigated by providing quick succession relief in the law.

To prevent quick diminution of such estates, Section 31 of the Estate Duty Act, 1953 provided relief from duty on 'the same property' consequent upon deaths taking place in quick succession. The relief was provided on the basis of fixed percentages laid down in the section itself. The amount of estate duty payable on the second death in respect of the same property was reduced as under:

Where the second death occurs within:

3 months of the first death	100 percent
1 year of the first death	50 percent
2 years of the first death	40 percent
3 years of the first death	30 percent
4 years of the first death	20 percent
5 years of the first death	10 percent

It may be observed that duty payable was reduced on account of successive death occurring within 5 years and depended on the interval during which the estate changed hands. Reduction in duty was not allowed where a successive death occurred beyond a period of five years.

Further, in case the value on which the duty was payable on the second death exceeded the value of the property on which the duty was payable on the first death, the latter value was substituted for the former for the purpose of calculating the relief.

F. Rate Structure: Estates with a net capital value or principal value of ₹ 50,000 or less were exempt from duty. On estates of a higher value than ₹ 50,000 there was a progressive duty, ranging from 4 percent to 85 percent on estates with a net capital value of over ₹ 20 lakh. The progressive rates of estate duty were justified by the Committee on Direct Tax Laws (1978) in the following words, "The fact that income-tax and wealth-tax rates have been brought down does not necessarily imply that there is a case for similar reduction in the estate duty rates. With the deceased's property subject to first charge under section 74 of the Estate Duty Act, there is almost an assumption that there is a prior claim of the State over that of the legal heirs. Besides, the incidence of this levy is felt the least since inheritance is a mere bounty. Estate duty, which thus stands on a different footing, can play a more significant role in the national goal of achieving a socialistic pattern of society". [21]

9.4 Gift Tax

9.4.1 Gift Tax: An Introduction: Gifts from one person to another provide a convenient device to avoid or reduce liability under income tax, wealth tax, and estate duty. Thus, the objective of gift tax is to ensure that transfers of wealth which are effected during the lifetime of a person bear tax liability similar to the levy of estate duty on property passing on the death of a person.

After Independence in 1947, the Taxation Enquiry Commission, 1953-54, considered the proposal for the introduction of gift tax and concluded, "A gift tax is theoretically an attractive proposition, but it requires considerable experience of the operation of estate duty (levied in 1953) before it can be introduced. One of the pre-requisites for operating successfully a tax of this nature would be to introduce the submission by income tax assessees of a statement of assets and liabilities. As more experience is gained of this type of work, the feasibility of introducing a gift tax can be considered. Moreover, the rates of death duty are at present low. The value of the gift tax as a second line of defence for estate duty is greater if the rates of the latter are steeply progressive. We are, therefore, not in favour of introducing the gift tax at this stage". [22] The recommendation of the Commission was framed at a time when there was no wealth tax and estate duty was also in its infancy. The recommendation was influenced by the fact that all gift, *inter vivos*, made within two years of the death of a person were chargeable to estate duty at that time.

9.4.2 Main Provisions of Gift Tax Act, 1958 at the Time of its Abolition in 1998: A tax on *inter vivos* gifts was imposed in India under the Gift Tax Act, 1958 which came into force on April 1 of that year. The Act was enacted as part of an integrated scheme of taxation of income, wealth, expenditure, and gifts, recommended by Nicholas Kaldor. The legislation was intended also to supplement the imposition of estate duty with effect from October 15, 1953. Explaining the philosophy of gift tax in his 1958-59 budget speech, the then Prime Minister and the Minister of Finance Jawahar Lal Nehru had stated, "My first proposal is to introduce a tax on gifts which will fill a gap in the scheme of direct taxation and would not only make evasion or avoidance difficult but also spread the tax burden more equitably....the transfer of properties through gifts to one's near relations or associates is one of the commonest forms of avoidance of not only the estate duty but also of income tax, wealth tax and even the expenditure tax. The only way of effectively checking this practice is to levy a tax on gifts". [23]

The Gift Tax Act, 1958 (hereinafter called the Act) was amended from time to time by the annual Finance Act and other legislations pertaining to direct taxes. The law of gift tax is stated here as applicable for the assessment year 1998-99.

A. Persons Liable to Gift Tax: Section 3 of the Act was the charging section. It imposed a tax for every assessment year on the aggregate value of gifts made by any person (individual, Hindu undivided family, firm, company or other association of persons) during the previous year. The 'previous year' was the period of twelve months ending on March 31, immediately preceding the assessment year. However, the following persons were not liable to pay gift tax:

1. A company in which the public are substantially interested.
2. A charitable or religious institution whose income is exempt from income tax (under Sections 11, and 12 of the Income Tax Act).

B. Definition of Gift: Under Section 2(xii) of the Act, a gift was defined as a transfer by one person to another of any existing movable or immovable property made voluntarily and without consideration in money or money's worth and includes gifts referred to in Section 4. In other words, before a transfer of property became liable to gift tax, the following conditions must be satisfied: (a) the transfer was voluntary, (b) the transfer was of existing property, and (c) the transfer was without consideration in money or money's worth.

C. Deemed Gifts: Situations could arise when transfer of property could not be wholly covered within the above-mentioned definition of gift, despite the fact that such transfers passed an element of bounty or benefit in them. To bring such transfers within the purview of the Act, deeming provisions were inserted therein. Under Section 4 of the Act, the following transfers were treated as deemed gifts.

1. Transfers of properties which were not wholly without consideration, but in which the consideration was inadequate. The amount by which the market value of the property exceeded the value of consideration was deemed to be a gift.
2. If the property was transferred for a consideration which had not passed or was not intended to pass, the amount of consideration was deemed to be a gift by the transferor.
3. If there was a release, discharge, surrender or forfeiture or abandonment of any debt, contract, actionable claim or any interest in property in favour of another, the value of release, discharge etc. to the extent it was not found bonafide, was deemed to be a gift by the person responsible for the release, discharge etc.
4. Where transfers took the form of vesting of property in joint ownership to enable appropriations to be made by another for the benefit of a person other than the person who was absolutely entitled to the property, the value of such appropriations was deemed gifts.
5. Where an individual converted his self-acquired property into Hindu undivided family property by throwing it into the common stock of the family, it was deemed that the individual had made a gift.
6. If a person, who had an interest in property as a tenant for a term or for life, surrendered his interest in the property without consideration or without adequate consideration, the value of interest or the amount by which such value exceeded the consideration received was deemed to be a gift made by such person.

E. Gifts Exempt from Tax: The Act provided for various exemptions as enumerated in Section 3. Therefore, taxable gifts were defined as the total gifts made during the previous year, less the exemptions allowed under the Act. The following gifts were exempt from gift tax.

1. Gifts of immovable property situated outside India and in the State of Jammu and Kashmir.
2. Gifts made by a person resident outside India out of the moneys standing to his credit in a Non-resident (External) Account maintained in India.
3. Gifts of foreign currency made by an Indian citizen who was not resident in India to any of his relatives in India from a country outside India. The purpose of exemption was to encourage the remittance of foreign exchange into the country.
4. Gifts of notified Special Bearer Bonds, Capital Investment Bonds, Relief Bonds up to prescribed limits.

5. Gifts made to the Central Government, any State Government or any local authority.
6. Gifts to any institution or fund established or deemed to be established in India for charitable purpose and in respect of which deduction was available under Section 80G of the Income Tax Act.
7. Any gift to a temple, mosque, gurudwara, church or any other place as had been notified by the Central Government under Section 80G(2)(b) of the Income Tax Act.
8. Gifts up to a maximum of ₹ 1 lakh in value on the occasion of the marriage of any relation, male or female, dependant on the donor.
9. All gifts made under a will. Such gifts were subject to estate duty (abolished in 1985).
10. All gifts in contemplation of death. Such gifts were subject to estate duty (abolished in 1985).
11. Gifts made by an individual for the education of his children.
12. Gifts of a reasonable amount (subject to the satisfaction of the gift tax officer) by an employer by way of bonus, gratuity or pension to an employee, or to the dependants of a deceased employee.

F. Basic Exemption and Rate of Tax: Apart from the exemptions referred to above, no gift tax was payable by any person if the total value of the gifts made by him in any one previous year did not exceed ₹ 30,000 [Section 5(2)]. In other words, gift tax was payable on the excess of the aggregate value of such gifts over ₹ 30,000. Basic exemption was raised from ₹ 5,000 to ₹ 20,000 from the assessment year 1987-88, and further up to ₹ 30,000 from assessment year 1994-95.

Rates of gift tax were given in the Schedule to the Gift Tax Act. From the assessment year 1987-88, a flat rate of 30 percent was applicable.

G. Computation of Gift Tax: The following steps were followed to compute the gift tax liability:

1. The value of all the gifts made during the previous year was computed. There was no difficulty in the valuation of gifts so far as cash gifts were concerned. Problems of valuation arose in the case of gifts other than cash. In such cases, the value was taken to mean the amount which the property could fetch if sold in the open market on the date on which the gift was made.
2. Values of gifts falling under any one of the categories of gifts exempted under Section 5 of the Act were deducted.
3. From the resultant figure, basic exemption of ₹ 30,000 was deducted.
4. The balance represented the value of taxable gifts for which tax liability had to be calculated according to the rates applicable for a particular assessment year.

9.4.3 Why Was Gift Tax Abolished? At the time of its abolition, gift tax was debated by fiscal experts from three viewpoints: (a) as a revenue-earner, (b) equity promoter, and (c) as an anti-tax avoidance device.

Revenue adequacy is a well-recognised canon of taxation and is particularly relevant in India in view of the need for additional resource mobilisation. Right from its inception in 1958, the share of gift tax had hovered around 0.05 percent in the Centre's total tax collections. From revenue angle, gift tax was merely a paper tax much less worth the administrative efforts involved in operating it.

The meagre revenue yield made gift tax an ineffective tool of redistributive policy. Prior to the assessment year 1987-88, the rate structure was quite progressive ranging from 5 percent on the value of taxable gifts not exceeding ₹ 20,000 to 75 percent on the value of taxable gifts in excess of ₹ 20 lakh. The basic exemption limit was ₹ 5,000. However, from the assessment year 1987-88, the 5 percent to 75 percent rate-range was abolished and replaced by a 30 percent flat rate tax. Hence, whether one made a taxable gift of ₹ 40,000 or ₹ 40 lakh or even ₹ 4 crore, the rate of tax remained the same, i.e. 30 percent. Moreover, the gift tax legislation did not take into account the two basic indices of taxable capacity of a person, viz. income level and wealth holding. Whether a gift of say ₹ 40,000 was made out of a property of ₹ 50,000 or ₹ 50 lakh, the rate applicable remained the same. This violated the principle of vertical equity in taxation.

The utility of gift tax as an anti-tax avoidance device had also been reduced. Estate duty to which gift tax provided the second line of defence was abolished from March 16, 1985. It may be recalled that the Direct Taxes Enquiry Committee, 1971, while suggesting measures to check avoidance of gift tax had recommended aggregation of gifts made by a person from year to year and their integration with estate duty. It observed, "The principle of aggregation of gifts should be extended further so as to achieve complete integration with estate duty. For this purpose the principal value of the estate passing on death should be aggregated with the taxable gifts made during life-time. The estate duty will first be calculated on this aggregate amount, subject to such exemptions as may be available at the time, and then credit allowed for the gift tax paid during life time. This will secure equity between a person who makes gifts in his life-time and another who leaves his property in its entirety on his death to his heirs". [24]

Moreover, the maximum marginal rates of both income tax and wealth tax had been reduced considerably over the years, making splitting of income and wealth among family members less attractive.

9.4.4 Donor-Based Versus Donee-Based Gift Tax: In the 1990-91 budget, the then existing gift tax on donors was proposed to be substituted with a donee-based gift tax. The new provisions proposed a basic exemption of ₹ 20,000 for each year and the levy of gift tax on a graduated scale in case the gifts received in any year exceeded the exemption limit. The rates proposed were: 20 percent in the slab of ₹ 20,000 to ₹ 50,000; 30 percent in the slab of ₹ 50,000 to ₹ 2 lakh; and 40 percent on the value of gifts in excess of ₹ 2 lakh. The purpose of the change from donor-based to donee-based gift tax was stated by the Finance Minister as follows, "At present, gifts are taxed in the hands of the donor, but there is no limit on the amount which a donee can show as having been received by way of gifts. Because of this, the mechanism of gifts is used to split up capital and launder black money. Some instances have also come to notice recently where attempts have been made to explain away wasteful and ostentatious expenditure on marriage receptions and other functions as having been financed out of gifts. With a view to curbing such practices, I have decided to substitute the present gift tax on donors with a donee-based gift tax". [25] The Minister made it clear that the purpose of the donee-based gift tax was not to raise revenue but check tax evasion and conspicuous consumption. Accordingly, the Gift Tax Bill, 1990, was introduced in the Lok Sabha on March 31, 1990. However, the proposed changes in the Gift Tax Act could not be made when the Bill lapsed due to the dissolution of the Ninth Lok Sabha on March 13, 1991. Hence, gifts continued to be taxed in the hands of the donors.

9.4.5 Integration of Gift Tax and Income Tax: Since gift tax as a separate tax was not serving any useful purpose, it was often suggested that it should be merged with income tax. By treating gifts as a source of income and thus levying income tax on the donee, a separate legislation for gift tax could be dispensed with. The history of income tax reforms in India provided instances when certain incomes (windfall profits like lotteries and gambling wins, and realised capital gains) were brought under the purview of income tax. It was quite feasible to treat gifts received by a person as accretion to his income. The inclusion of gifts in the definition of income or expenditure was also supported by the Meade Committee which observed, "One way of taxing transfers of capital is to incorporate such transfers into the income tax or the expenditure tax itself. Thus, with a comprehensive income tax, gifts received could be taxed as part of the recipient's income and with an expenditure tax gifts made could be taxed as part of the donor's expenditure. Such an arrangement would cause the rate of tax to be adjusted progressively to the recipient's income level in the case of a comprehensive income tax and to the donor's expenditure level in the case of an expenditure tax. The arrangement would have the great advantage of enabling the whole of the apparatus of a separate transfer tax to be dismantled, although there would have to be some averaging arrangements to avoid the unfair effects of progressive tax rates on large lump sum receipts (under a comprehensive income tax) or large lump sum outgoings (under an expenditure tax)". [26]

However, the Indian Committee on Direct Tax Laws did not favour the integration of income tax and gift tax. It observed, "The present provisions for taxing income, wealth, and gifts separately are now well settled in the minds of the taxpayers. The inclusion of gifts as deemed income would be a revolutionary concept and would considerably remove the stability achieved over the past two decades of the operation of the Gift Tax Act. Various other considerations would also result in the income tax law which would outweigh the advantages of integration. We are, therefore, not in favour of treating gifts as income under the Income Tax Act and recommend the continuation of the Gift Tax Act in its present form". [27]

Responding to the realities of the situation, the Finance Minister in his 1998-99 budget discontinued the levy of gift tax on gifts made after September 30, 1998. To ensure that there were no leakages of income tax revenue through the mechanism of gifts, the gifts were made taxable under the Income Tax Act itself in the hands of the recipients. However, replying to the debate on the Finance Bill in the Lok Sabha on July 17, 1998, the Finance Minister announced exemption from all taxes of gifts made on or after October 1, 1998. In other words, his earlier proposal to tax the value of gifts as income of recipient was withdrawn.

Endnotes

1. Nicholas Kaldor, *Indian Tax Reform: A Survey, 1956*, p. 105.
2. Government of India, Ministry of Finance, *Speeches of Union Finance Ministers, 1947-48 to 1984-85,* p. 216.
3. Ibid., p. 275.
4. James Cutt, *Taxation and Economic Development in India* (New Delhi: Vikas Publications, 1969), p. 197.
5. Government of India, *Report of Direct Taxes Administration Enquiry Committee* (Chairman: Mahavir Tyagi), 1958-59, p. 8.
6. James Cutt, *op. cit.*, p. 200.
7. Government of India, Ministry of Finance, *Study Group on Taxation of Expenditure* (Final Report), 1987, p. 121.
8. Government of India, Ministry of Finance and Company Affairs, *Report of the Task Force on Direct Taxes* (Chairman: Vijay Kelkar), December 2002, p. 178.
9. Nicholas Kaldor, *An Expenditure Tax* (London: George Allen and Unwin Ltd., 1955), p. 95.
10. Quoted in Richard A. Musgrave and Peggy B. Musgrave, *Public Finance in Theory and Practice* (McGraw-Hill, International Student Edition, 1980), p. 496.
11. Government of India, Economic Administration Reforms Commission, *Report on Tax Administration, 1981-83*, p. 33.
12. There was no specific definition of *principal value* in the Estate Duty Act, 1953. The Direct Tax Laws Committee (1978) had recommended the following definition: The term *principal value of the estate* may be defined to mean the aggregate of market values of all property which passes or is deemed to pass on the death of a person as reduced by the debts and encumbrances and after allowance of the admissible deductions. See, Government of India, Ministry of Finance, *Final Report of Direct Tax Laws Committee* (Chairman: C.C. Chokshi), September, 1978, p. 216.
13. The incidence of estate duty depended on the domicile of the deceased person and location of the property. In case the deceased was domiciled in India, duty was attracted on all properties passing on his death except immovable properties situated outside India. However, if the deceased was not domiciled in India, the duty was payable on all properties passing on death which were situated in India.
14. 6 months in the case of gifts made for charitable purposes.
15. While Section 25 dealt with settlements effected before the commencement of the Act, Section 29 related to cases in which estate duty had been paid on the death of any one party to a marriage irrespective of when the settlement was made.
16. The Direct Tax Laws Committee had recommended the limits under Sections 33(1)(a) and 33(1)(b) to be raised to ₹ 5,000 and ₹ 3,000 respectively. It had also recommended the period of two years mentioned in Section 33(1)(b) to be raised to five years to bring it in line with its another recommendation for increasing the period for gifts under section 9 from two years to five years. See, *Final Report of the Direct Tax Laws Committee (1978), op. cit.*, p. 224.
17. The Direct Tax Laws Committee (1978) had recommended this exemption to be raised to ₹ 10,000. It should be noted that provident funds were not being treated on par with insurance moneys for exemption under Section 33(1)(h) of the Estate Duty Act whereas in the Income Tax Act, 1961, all long-term savings in the form of insurance policies and provident funds

were treated almost alike for tax concessions. The Committee, therefore, found no justification for leaving out provident fund deposits from the scope of exemption under the estate duty law and therefore recommended that moneys payable from provident funds should also be covered by exemption under Section 31(1)(h) of the Estate Duty Act within the same consolidated monetary limit of ₹ 10,000 (as recommended by it). See, *Final Report of Direct Tax Laws Committee (1978), op. cit.*, p. 225.

18. The Direct Tax Laws Committee (1978) had recommended the enlargement of this exemption to the cases of civil servants and members of National Cadet Corps, Territorial Army, Home Guards etc. whose employment in the national cause is equally hazardous. For details, see *Final Report of Direct Tax Laws Committee (1978), op. cit.*, p. 225.
19. As per Part IV, Section 34(1)(a) of the Estate Duty Act, 1953.
20. The Direct Tax Laws Committee (1978) had recommended this limit to be raised to ₹ 2,500. See, *Final Report of Direct Tax Laws Committee (1978), op. cit.*, p. 230.
21. See, *Final Report of Direct Tax Laws Committee (1978), op. cit.*, p. 242.
22. Government of India, Ministry of Finance, *Report of the Taxation Enquiry Commission* (Chairman: John Matthai), 1953-54, Volume II, p. 246.
23. Government of India, Ministry of Finance, *Speeches of Union Finance Ministers, 1947-48 to 1984-85,* p. 168.
24. Government of India, Ministry of Finance, *Final Report of the Direct Taxes Enquiry Committee* (Chairman: Justice K.N. Wanchoo), December 1971, p. 87.
25. Government of India, Ministry of Finance, *Budget Speech of Finance Minister, 1990-91,* Part B.
26. Institute for Fiscal Studies, *The Structure and Reform of Direct Taxation: Report of a Committee Chaired by Professor J.E. Meade* (London: George Allen and Unwin, 1978), pp. 512-513.
27. *Final Report of Direct Tax Laws Committee (1978), op. cit.,* p. 106.

10

Income Tax

After Independence in 1947, Taxation Enquiry Commission (TEC), 1953 [1] dealt at length with the administration of income tax. TEC made several recommendations regarding income tax, some of which dealt with the broad structure of taxation while others related to maters of detail like inclusion and exclusion of certain categories of income from taxation, grant of concessions to promote objectives of economic policy and so on.

10.1 Constitutional Provisions

Taxation of income in India may be classified into two broad categories: (a) taxation of non-agricultural income, a Central subject, and (b) taxation of agricultural income, a matter for State legislation. The two relevant entries in List I (Union List) of the Seventh Schedule of the Constitution which empower the Parliament to levy income tax are: Entry 82, "taxes on income other than agricultural income", and Entry 85, "corporation tax". According to Article 366(6) of the Constitution "corporation tax means any tax on income, so far as that tax is payable by companies".

The states are empowered to make laws with respect to taxes on agricultural income vide Entry 46 of List II (State List) of the Seventh Schedule of the Constitution. Therefore, agricultural income is exempt from Central income tax. However, from the assessment year 1974-75, agricultural income is taken into account to determine the rate of tax on non-agricultural income if agricultural income exceeds ₹ 5,000. Although the power to impose tax on agricultural income is vested in State Governments, in practice very few States have imposed this tax and wherever it is imposed the revenue is negligible.

For the purpose of taxation of non-agricultural incomes, the present enactment is the Indian Income Tax Act, 1961 which is amended from time to time by the annual Finance Act and other legislations pertaining to direct taxes. The Act which came into force on April 1, 1962, replaced the Indian Income Tax Act, 1922, which had remained in operation for 40 years. Furthermore, a set of rules known as Income Tax Rules, 1962 have been framed for implementing the various provisions of the Act. Entities chargeable to tax under the Act are of two types: (a) non-corporate entities and (b) corporate entities. Non-corporate entities mainly consist of individuals and firms and their taxation is called personal income tax. Besides being the main source of direct tax revenue for the government, income tax is an effective instrument to realise various socio-economic objectives of national policies.

Prior to the Constitution (Eightieth Amendment) Act, 2000 the proceeds from income tax were shareable with the states under Article 270(1) of the Constitution. The Finance Commission [2] recommended the formula for the distribution of income tax revenue between the Centre and the states and the distribution of states' share among the states themselves. Thus, income tax played an important role not only in Central finances but also in the finances of the state governments. The said amendment substituted a new Article for Article 270 under which States are now given a percentage share of all Central taxes and duties. However, the surcharge levied for purposes of the Union under Article 271 is excluded from the divisible pool.

10.2 High Rates of Income Tax

Rates of income tax in India were quite high, almost punitive, till mid-1970s. For example, in 1973-74, the maximum marginal rate of individual income tax was as high as 97.7 percent which proved counter-productive from revenue angle.

The Report of the Direct Taxes Enquiry Committee (DTEC) [Chairman: Justice K.N. Wanchoo] [3], 1971, was a milestone in the area of income tax rates. DTEC made a number of far-reaching suggestions for unearthing black money, preventing evasion and avoidance of taxes, and reducing arrears. One important recommendation of DTEC related to reduction in the rates of direct taxes which in its view were mainly responsible for tax evasion because they made tax evasion profitable and attractive. Following the recommendations of DTEC, the government initiated a series of rate reductions in individual income tax. The maximum marginal rate of tax for individual assessees was reduced from 97.7 percent in 1973-74 to 77 percent in 1974-75, and further down to 66 percent in 1976-77. It is noteworthy that DTEC had recommended a maximum marginal rate of 75 percent. [4]

The downward trend in the rate of income tax was temporarily reversed during the brief Janata Government rule at the Centre. The top marginal rate of income tax was increased from 66 percent in 1976-77 to 69 percent in 1977-78, and further up to 72 percent in 1979-80. However, the policy of low direct tax rates started by the Congress Government in 1974 and carried forward in 1976 was further reinforced after it came back to power at the Centre in 1980. After a series of revisions, the maximum marginal rate of individual income tax was 54 percent (including employment surcharge of 8 percent) for the year 1990-91 when economic reforms were initiated in India.

10.3 Income Tax Evasion

Among the host of causes of tax evasion and hence the generation of black money, the level of tax rates is probably the most crucial. It is widely believed that higher the rate of tax, the greater is the tendency to evade taxes. High tax rates make tax evasion more tempting. Tax evaders readily take greater risks if they know that in the event of success the reward is high. Per contra, it can be expected that low tax rates improve tax compliance and broaden the tax base.

Taxation Enquiry Commission (TEC), 1953 found staggering levels of tax evasion. To quote, "It is observed from statistics in connection with the 'Disclosure Drive' that income as originally included in the returns sent to the income tax department by assessees who made disclosures was grossly understated, the difference between the income as originally returned and that disclosed later to the department being, on the average, as much as 600 per cent. Such other statistics as have been made available to us by the Central Board of Revenue also give evidence of the fact that evasion is prevalent on a considerable scale". [5] It maintained that improvement and strengthening of the enforcement machinery was the only way to tackle evasion effectively.

10.4 Abolition of Distinction between Earned and Unearned Income

Earned income (or employment income) is derived from actual work or service performed and includes wages, salaries, and income from professions. Unearned income (or capital income) is derived from investments, rents etc.

The Indian Taxation Enquiry Committee (Chairman: Sir Charles Todhunter), 1924-25 examined, for the first time, the desirability of differentiation between earned and unearned incomes for the purpose of income tax. The Committee, however, rejected the idea, maintaining that it was premature in the context of the Indian conditions. It was in 1945 that a distinction between earned and unearned incomes was introduced when assessees were allowed to exclude from their earned incomes a fixed proportion subject to a maximum limit.

A notable recommendation of TEC pertained to the withdrawal of the concession relating to earned income beyond a certain level of income which it suggested should be ₹ 24,000. Agreeing with this recommendation that earned income relief should not be allowed on higher brackets of income, the government, as a first step, reduced the allowance in the 1955-56 budget by stages on incomes in excess of ₹ 25,000, the concession ceasing when the level of ₹ 45,000 was reached.

Under the recast scheme, an allowance of 20 percent subject to a maximum of ₹ 4,000 was granted to earned incomes not exceeding ₹ 25,000. For incomes in excess of this amount the allowance of ₹ 4,000 was reduced at the rate of 20 percent of the excess over ₹ 25,000 so that for an earned income of ₹ 45,000 the allowance was reduced to nil.

From 1957-58, the relief was given in the form of a lower surcharge on earned income than on unearned income. The surcharge was fixed at 5 percent of the tax on earned incomes up to ₹ 1 lakh and 10 percent on incomes in excess of that sum while for unearned incomes, a uniform surcharge of 20 percent was imposed.

However, the distinction between earned and unearned incomes introduced in 1945 under which the earned income was treated leniently was completely abolished from April 1, 1968. This decision was widely criticised as a retrograde fiscal measure.

10.5 Declining Share of Direct Taxes

Income tax has been the only major source of direct tax revenue in India since Independence. The tax structure at the Central level evolved around indirect taxes till the year 1990-91. The ratio between direct and indirect taxes in gross Central taxes consistently declined from 43.4:56.6 in 1950-51 to 32.6:67.4 in 1960-61, to 27.1:72.9 in 1970-71, to 22.7:77.3 in 1980-81, and to lowest ever 19.2:80.8 in 1990-91. Resultantly, indirect taxes came to occupy a dominant place in Central finances.

In his Budget Speech for 1985-86, the Finance Minister made a commitment to move towards a long-term fiscal policy co-terminous with the Seventh Five Year Plan (1985-86 to 1989-90). In December 1985, the Government of India announced its Long-Term Fiscal Policy (LTFP) which set out the broad direction and strategy for fiscal reforms, mainly taxation, to further the objectives of growth and social justice.

The declining share of direct taxes was a cause of concern for the government. LTFP while seeking to correct the imbalance between direct and indirect taxes maintained, "While the predominance of indirect taxes in the present situation is unavoidable, it cannot be gainsaid that a certain balance has to be maintained between direct and indirect taxes. Taxes like the personal income tax have an important role in the tax structure and cannot be substituted by taxes on commodities. It is not easy to tailor commodity taxes to the circumstances of the taxpayers in the same way as is possible with the personal income tax. Hence, although reliance on indirect taxation cannot be avoided in the foreseeable future, it is necessary to make a transition to a system whereby income tax makes a larger contribution to revenue. Such transition is not possible without a distinct improvement in the buoyancy of the income tax in response to growth in incomes. An important objective of fiscal policy must be to reverse the decline in the share of direct taxes over the long term". [6]

In the wake of reforms initiated in the early 1990s, rates of both corporate and personal income tax were substantially reduced. Following better compliance, the decline in the relative share of direct taxes was reversed. Direct taxes as a percentage of Centre's total tax collections rose from 19.2 percent in 1990-91 (pre-reform period) to 36.2 percent in 2000-01. The figure stood at highest ever of 55.7 percent in 2010-11 and was estimated at 51.5 for the year 2022-23 (Table 10.1).

10.6 Instability of Income Tax Law

During the pre-reforms period, there was considerable instability in the income tax law of India, owing mainly to introduction, withdrawal, and reintroduction of exemptions and concessions for various purposes. Income tax law was riddled with uncertainties and statutory amendments were as unpredictable as they were frequent. In this regard the Direct Tax Laws Committee (Chairman: C.C. Chokshi), 1977 [7] remarked, "The instability of our tax laws is another of their worst features. The laws are riddled with uncertainties and statutory amendments are as unpredictable as they are frequent. Surely, after more than half a century of the working of income tax Acts of 1922, and 1961, it should be possible to have an enduring tax structure". [8]

Frequent amendments led to uncertainty and confusion among taxpayers and tax collectors. The problem still prevails to some extent.

In short, income tax system in India during pre-reforms period (1947 to 1990) was characterized by high tax rates, large-scale tax evasion, and a plethora of exemptions and concessions.

Table 10.1: Gross Central Tax Revenue, Breakdown between Direct and Indirect Taxes with Percentage Shares: Selected Years

(₹ crore)

Year	Gross Central Taxes*(3+4)	Direct Taxes	Indirect Taxes	Col. 3 as % of Col. 2	Col. 4 as % of Col. 2
1	2	3	4	5	6
1950-51	405	176	229	43.4	56.6
1955-56	485	171	314	35.2	64.8
1960-61	895	292	603	32.6	67.4
1965-66	2,061	598	1,463	29.0	71.0
1970-71	3,206	869	2,337	27.1	72.9
1975-76	7,609	2,205	5,404	29.0	71.0
1980-81	13,179	2,997	10,182	22.7	77.3
1985-86	28,670	5,620	23,050	19.6	80.4
1990-91	57,577	11,030	46,547	19.2	80.8
1995-96	1,11,224	33,564	77,660	30.2	69.8
2000-01	1,88,603	68,305	1,20,298	36.2	63.8
2005-06	3,66,151	1,62,337	2,03,814	44.3	55.7
2010-11	7,93,072	4,38,515	3,54,556	55.7	44.3
2015-16	14,55,648	7,34,661	7,20,987	50.5	49.5
2020-21	20,27,104	9,44,863	10,82,241	46.6	53.4
2022-23	27,57,820	14,20,000	13,37,820	51.5	48.5

* Before transferring States' share in Central taxes.

2022-23 = Budget estimates.

Source: Rearranged data from Government of India, Ministry of Finance, *Indian Public Finance Statistics, 2017-2018*, Table 1.7; *Budget Papers 2022-23*. Columns 5 and 6 calculations own.

See also chapters 4 and 16 of this book.

Endnotes

1. Government of India, *Report of the Taxation Enquiry Commission* (Chairman: John Matthai), 1953-54, Volumes I, II and III.
2. Under Article 280 of the Constitution, Finance Commission is appointed by the President every quinquennium, or earlier if necessary. The main responsibilities of the Finance Commission are the following: (a) to evolve a scheme of transfer of financial resources from the Centre to the States so as to ensure financial equilibrium at the two levels of Government during the period of its award, (b) to design formulae to allocate resources so transferred among the states, (c) to determine the principles and quantum of grants-in-aid to States which are in need of such assistance and (d) to recommend measures needed to augment the Consolidated Fund of a state to supplement the resources of the panchayats/municipalities in the state on the basis of the recommendations made by the Finance Commission of the state.
3. The Report of the Direct Taxes Enquiry Committee (DTEC) [Chairman: Justice K.N. Wanchoo], 1971, was a milestone in the area of income tax rates. The Committee made a number of far-reaching suggestions for unearthing black money, preventing evasion and

avoidance of taxes, and reducing arrears. One important recommendation of the Committee related to reduction in the rates of direct taxes which in its view were mainly responsible for tax evasion because they made tax evasion profitable and attractive. The rates of individual income tax were quite high till the year 1973-74. However, following the recommendations of the DTEC, the Government initiated a series of rate reductions in individual income tax.

4. Government of India, Ministry of Finance, *Final Report of Direct Taxes Enquiry Committee,* (Chairman: Justice K. N. Wanchoo) December 1971, para 2.52.
5. *Report of the Taxation Enquiry Commission (1953-54), op. cit.*, Volume II, p. 189.
6. Government of India, *Long Term Fiscal Policy*, 1985, p. 23.
7. The Direct Tax Laws Committee was appointed by the Government of India on June 25, 1977. It was specifically directed to: (a) recommend measures to simplify and rationalise the laws relating to income-tax, surtax, wealth-tax, gift-tax and estate duty, and to alter those laws with a view to making them readily comprehensible to taxpayers, reducing litigation and thus sub-serving the interest of the national economy, (b) suggest ways and means of improving the administration of those laws and expediting assessment, appellate and other proceedings under those laws, (c) examine the advisability of consolidating the four laws relating to income-tax, surtax, wealth-tax and gift-tax into one Act and (d) prepare draft of the Bills for being presented before Parliament.
8. *Final Report of the Direct Tax Laws Committee* (Chairman: C.C. Chokshi), 1978, para 1-0, 10.

11

Wealth Tax

In his Budget Speech to the Parliament on February 28, 2015, the Finance Minister announced the abolition of wealth tax. Main provisions of wealth tax at the time of its abolition are explained below.

11.1 Rationale for Wealth Tax

Wealth tax is advocated on both benefit and ability-to-pay considerations. Protection of life and property has traditionally been the primary function of the government, and to perform it considerable cost is incurred on the law enforcement machinery and the judicial administration. The main beneficiaries of these services are people with fabulous wealth who as a rule should contribute towards the expenses on such services. Pavement sleepers hardly need the services of the state as a protector of property. Another dimension of the benefit argument is that public services like roads, street lighting, community centres, public parks etc. increase the value of real estates, conferring unearned benefits on the owners of such estates. It can, therefore, be argued that property owners should pay for these services.

In terms of ability-to-pay, possession of property is a measure of economic well-being and therefore of taxable capacity, quite apart from the income earned from that property. A tax on capital itself may seem undesirable when capital income is subject to income tax (as is generally the case). However, the coverage of capital income under the income tax is usually incomplete in view of liberal exemptions, tax avoidance, and evasion. Moreover, an income tax system does not include non-earning assets. Therefore, taxation of wealth is essentially a supplement to taxation of income. Hence, taxation of wealth is justified on equity criterion. It may be argued that wealth tax is unjust in cases where property does not yield money income directly. In this context Professor Kaldor has opined, "If a property does not yield money income, it must either yield an equivalent psychic income to the owner or it must be held in the expectation of a certain appreciation in value which makes it at least as attractive to the holder as other property on which a current money return is obtained". [1]

Yet another argument for taxation of wealth is social control over the most unjust and dangerous form of economic inequality. To quote Musgraves, "Alternatively, the taxation of wealth may be approached not as a matter of charging for benefits received or ability-to-pay, but as a form of social control. The social consequences of inequality in the distribution of wealth, as is easily seen, differ from those in the distribution of consumption, so that society may wish to deal with them separately. For this purpose, a progressive tax on wealth, rather than on income, is the proper instrument". [2] Situations may arise when certain taxpayers have taxable wealth but very low current incomes. One way to resolve this problem is to exempt from wealth tax liability all those taxpayers whose annual income from all sources does not exceed a specified limit.

In spite of being a potentially important source of revenue and economic control, the administration of wealth tax is difficult, particularly in developing countries. Imposition of wealth tax requires the preparation of an annual balance sheet of assets and liabilities of the taxpayer. For an honest exercise of this sort, an assessee should first declare, truthfully, all taxable assets with their proper current value. He must also make a genuine claim for deductible debts. Honesty of the sort required is an exception rather than the rule. Thus, tax officials for most of their part are busy detecting taxable assets, grappling with undervaluation of properties and verifying claims of deductible debts. Some of these problems (e.g. valuation of assets) are encountered also in connection with estate duty, capital gains tax, and local property tax. Valuation of assets for purposes of one tax is generally used as a basis for computing tax liability under another tax. However, the continuous rise in prices (leading to appreciation of real estates), the underdeveloped nature of money markets (causing difficulty in the valuation of shares), and the ingenuity of tax evaders leave the tax authorities groping in the dark without much success.

11.2 Wealth Tax Act, 1957: Main Provisions

An annual tax on net wealth was introduced in India with the enactment of the Wealth Tax Act, 1957, which came into force from April 1 of that year. The rationale behind the imposition of wealth tax lied essentially in furthering the equity objective of tax policy. Since ownership of wealth is the main source of economic inequalities in India, a tax on wealth was intended to reduce its concentration in a few hands to promote vertical equity.

Wealth Tax Act, 1957 (hereinafter called the Act), was amended from time-to-time by the annual Finance Act and other legislations pertaining to direct taxes. A set of Wealth Tax Rules also existed to enforce the provisions of the Act.

11.2.1 Persons Chargeable to Wealth Tax: Section 3 of the Act was the charging section. It provided for the levy of wealth tax for every assessment year in respect of net wealth, as on the valuation date, of individuals, Hindu undivided families, and all companies having net wealth exceeding ₹ 30 lakh. Wealth tax on companies was discontinued from the assessment year 1960-61. The Finance Act, 1983, however, revived the levy of wealth tax on closely-held companies from the assessment year 1984-85. The Finance Act, 1992, extended the scope of wealth tax to all companies.

11.2.2 Net Wealth and Residential Status: The wealth tax liability was affected by residence and citizenship of the assessee. In the case of an individual, the incidence of the tax depended upon his residential status and nationality. Thus, for an Indian citizen who was also 'resident' in India, the net wealth included wealth in India as well as wealth outside India, but the foreign wealth was chargeable to wealth tax at half the average rate. However, if an Indian citizen was 'not ordinarily' resident, or was 'non-resident', the foreign wealth was completely exempt. In the case of an individual who was not a citizen of India, only his wealth in India was taxable. Furthermore, if the foreign national happened to be a non-resident, the wealth tax payable by him on his Indian wealth was reduced by 50 percent thereof (Section 6 of the Act). For the purpose of wealth tax, residential status was the same which an individual enjoyed under the Income Tax Act, 1961.

11.2.3 Meaning of Net Wealth: Wealth tax in India was a levy made with reference to the net wealth which, as defined in Section 2(m) of the Act, broadly corresponded to the excess of assets over liabilities. It means provision was made for the deduction of debts from the assets owned by the assessee on the valuation date. All debts owned by the assessee, which had been incurred in relation to assets chargeable to tax, were deductible. As in the case of income tax, wealth tax was charged on a global basis, i.e. all pieces of wealth were pooled together and a flat rate tax was applied. In other words, all components of wealth tax were treated alike for the purpose of the tax.

Unlike income tax, there was no previous year for wealth tax. Wealth tax was imposed on net wealth possessed by an assessee on the valuation date and the value of his assets was determined as on that date. Valuation date meant the last day of the previous year, i.e. March 31 [Section 2(q)]. For example, for the assessment year 2014-15, the valuation date was March 31, 2014. Valuation of assets, for determining the net wealth of a taxpayer, was an important and difficult subject under the wealth tax law. Valuation was easy in the case of quoted shares and for assets like cash and bank balances. However, serious problems arose in most other cases partly because the value of assets changed from year-to-year. Under the Act, the value of an asset was defined (Section 7) as the price it would fetch if sold in the open market on the valuation date. A wealth tax officer was empowered to make the estimate of market value subject to the various rules made in this regard. Since the tax was imposed on net wealth which represented the excess of assets over debts, it is necessary to understand the concepts of 'assets' and 'debts' as used in the Act.

11.2.4 Meaning of Assets: The term 'assets' was described in Section 2(e) of the Act. The definition of 'assets' was drastically narrowed by the Finance Act, 1992. It meant: (a) a guest house, (b) a residential (or commercial) house, (c) a farmhouse situated within 25 kilometres from the local municipal limits, (d) motor cars, (e) jewellery, bullion etc., (f) yachts, boats, and aircrafts, (g) urban land (of certain description), and (h) cash in hand in excess of ₹ 50,000.

It is noteworthy that the term 'assets' did not include, *inter alia*: (a) a house meant exclusively for residential purposes and allotted to a whole-time employee, (b) residential house, jewellery, bullion, motor cars used as stock-in-trade, and (c) yachts, boats, and aircrafts used for commercial purposes. In other words, assets held as stock-in-trade were not taxable.

From the assessment year 1997-98, commercial properties other than those occupied by the assessee for the purpose of any business or profession carried on by him were also included in the term 'assets' and were consequently taxable.

11.2.5 Deemed Assets: As already noted, wealth tax was chargeable on the net wealth of an assessee. Ordinarily speaking, this would mean assets belonging to the assessee form part of his net wealth. However, the Act provided for the inclusion of certain assets in the net wealth of an individual though such assets did not legally belong to the individual on the valuation date. In other words, such assets were deemed to belong to the taxpayer. These provisions corresponded to those contained in Section 64 of the Income Tax Act, 1961, which deals with the clubbing of income. The purpose of these provisions was to check tax avoidance by the assessees. The following assets, *inter alia,* were included as belonging to the assessee while computing his net wealth under Section 4 of the Act.

1. Assets held by the spouse of an individual where such assets were transferred by the individual without adequate consideration.
2. Assets held by a minor child, not being a married daughter, of such individual. However, assets acquired by a minor child out of his income derived from manual work etc. were not included in the net wealth of his parent.
3. Assets held by a person to whom such assets were transferred by the individual without adequate consideration for the immediate or deferred benefits of such individual, his or her spouse.
4. Assets held by a person to whom such assets were transferred by an individual under a revocable transfer.
5. Assets held by an individual's son's wife to whom such assets were transferred by such individual without adequate consideration.
6. Assets held by any person to whom such assets were transferred by an individual for the benefit of his son's wife.
7. If an individual threw his self-acquired property into the common stock of the Hindu undivided family of which he was a member, the said property was included in his net wealth.
8. An individual, being a partner in a firm, could gift some money by crediting the amount in the account of the donee and by debiting his own account in the account books of the firm. In such cases, if the physical possession of the money was not given to the donee and the same continued to be invested in the business, and the gift was made only by making entries in the books of account without actually delivering the money to the donee, the value of such gift was included in the net wealth of the individual making the gift.

11.2.6 Assets Exempt from Wealth Tax: Section 5 of the Act provided for exemption of certain assets from the charge of wealth tax. Prior to the assessment year 1993-94, the list of exempted assets was quite lengthy and served to explain leakages in the base of wealth tax. The exempted assets were broadly divided into two categories: (a) assets which were totally exempt and therefore left out totally in computing the net wealth, and (b) assets which enjoyed only partial exemption. In the case of partial exemption, a ceiling was prescribed and the value of the assets in excess of the prescribed limit was included in the net wealth of the assessee for wealth tax purposes.

The Finance Act, 1992, drastically pruned the list of taxable assets for the purpose of wealth tax. Correspondingly, the list of exemptions/deductions allowable under Section 5 was also restricted. Thus, from the assessment year 1993-94, only the following assets were exempt from being included in the net wealth of an assessee:

1. Any property held by any assessee under trust for any public purpose of charitable or religious nature in India.
2. Interest of an assessee in the property of any Hindu undivided family of which he was a member. It may be noted that Hindu undivided family itself was liable to wealth tax.
3. Any one building in the occupation of an ex-ruler which was declared by the Government as his official residence.
4. Recognised heirloom jewellery of an ex-ruler.
5. Value of assets brought by persons of Indian origin.

11.2.7 Basic Exemption and Rate of Tax: Wealth tax liability was computed by applying the rate schedule to net wealth (i.e. taxable wealth). The rates of wealth tax were given in Schedule 1 of the Act. Till the financial year 2014-15, wealth tax was charged at the flat rate of 1 percent in the case of all assessees having taxable wealth exceeding ₹ 30 lakh.

11.3 Critical Comments

11.3.1 Shrinkage of Base: Prior to the enactment of the Finance Act, 1992, the term *assets* as described in Section 2(e) included property of every description, movable and immovable, such as cash, bank balances, shares, jewellery, and other assets. The term 'assets' was of widest import and sufficiently comprehensive.

However, consequent upon the recommendations contained in the Interim Report of the Tax Reforms Committee, 1991, [3] the various provisions of the wealth tax law were drastically restructured by the Finance Act, 1992. The Committee had recommended that in order to encourage the taxpayers to invest in productive assets such as shares, securities, bonds, bank deposits, mutual funds etc., these financial assets should be exempted from wealth tax. Wealth tax should be levied on individuals, Hindu undivided families, and all companies only in respect of non-productive assets such as residential houses, jewellery, bullion, motor cars, yachts, and aircrafts which were not used for commercial purposes. Hence, the definition of the term 'assets', was significantly narrowed from the assessment year 1993-94. In short, the basis of taxation was shifted from wealth to unproductive assets. Following pressure that a residential house is a universal necessity and should not be subjected to tax, the Finance Act, 1993, exempted the value of one house from the levy of wealth tax.

11.3.2 Lowering of Top Marginal Rate: The maximum marginal rate of wealth tax, applicable to net wealth above ₹ 15 lakh, was quite high at 8 percent till the year 1975-76. It was drastically reduced to 2.5 percent the following year (1976-77). In a reversal of policy of low rates, it was increased to 3.5 percent in 1977-78, and further up to 5 percent in 1979-80. In 1985-86, it was again lowered to 2 percent and made applicable to net wealth over ₹ 20 lakh.

The Tax Reforms Committee, 1991, suggested that wealth tax should be charged at the flat rate of 1 percent with a basic exemption of ₹ 15 lakh instead of the then existing ₹ 5 lakh. These recommendations were accepted and incorporated in the Finance Act, 1992. Later on the basic exemption was increased of ₹ 30 lakh. The trends in the maximum marginal rate of wealth tax beginning with the year 1973-74 are given in Table 11.1.

Table 11.1: Trends in the Maximum Marginal Rate of Wealth Tax in India

Financial Year	Top Rate of Wealth Tax (percent)	Applicable to Net Wealth
1973-74 to 1975-76	8.0	Over ₹ 15 lakh
1976-77	2.5	Over ₹ 15 lakh
1977-78 and 1978-79	3.5	Over ₹ 15 lakh
1979-80 to 1984-85	5.0	Over ₹ 15 lakh
1985-86 to 1991-92	2.0	Over ₹ 20 lakh
1992-93 to 2008-09	Flat rate of 1 percent on wealth exceeding ₹ 15 lakh	
2009-10 to 2014-15	Flat rate of 1 percent on wealth exceeding ₹ 30 lakh	

Sources: Government of India, *Finance Acts* (various years).

The scope of wealth tax, both in terms of base and rate, was very narrow. It had only decorative value for the statute book. In view of the meagre revenue and problems of administration and compliance, the Task Force on Direct Taxes (Chairman: Vijay Kelkar), 2002 recommended the abolition of wealth tax. In his Budget Speech to the Parliament on February 28, 2015, the Finance Minister announced the abolition of wealth tax.

Endnotes

1. Nicholas Kaldor, *Indian Tax Reform: Report of a Survey* (Government of India, Ministry of Finance), 1956, p. 22.
2. Richard A. Musgrave and Peggy B. Musgrave, *Public Finance in Theory and Practice,* (McGraw-Hill, International Student Edition, 1980), p. 472.
3. Government of India, Ministry of Finance, *Interim Report of the Tax Reforms Committee,* (Chairman, Raja Chelliah), December, 1991, chapter 7.

12

Excise Duties

Prior to tax reforms initiated in 1991, excise taxation in India was an interesting example of the multitude of rates which were subject to frequent revisions. Numerous considerations contributed to the complexity of excise rates. The excise system was leaky (riddled with extensive exemptions) and characterized by multiplicity of specific and *ad valorem* rates. The labyrinthine intricacies of the tariff often led to confusion and litigation amongst the taxpayers and revenue authorities.

Excise duties were an important source of indirect tax revenue for the Central Government. They were levied on a wide range of products of the industrial sector of the economy. Central excise duties were assessed and collected through a vast network of offices scattered all over the country. There were various procedures to assess and collect excise duties.

12.1 Different Procedures to Collect Excises

12.1.1 Physical Control System: This procedure, based on personal verification of production by excise officers, was the chief procedure to realise excise duties till it was replaced by a new system called self-removal procedure from June 1, 1968. Under the physical control method, excise control was exercised by the officers of the excise department who were posted at the factory to keep watch over the operations in the various departments of the factory to prevent illegal disposal of the manufactured articles. The physical control procedure was based on personal verification of production, storage, and clearance of excisable goods.

The manufacturers, however, were unhappy with this direct interference in the manufacturing process. Therefore, ever since Independence in 1947 they had been demanding abolition of the physical control scheme and its replacement by a system based on audited accounts. Taxation Enquiry Commission (TEC), 1953-54, favoured the retention of the physical control system. It observed, "It seems to us reasonable for the Government to ensure that for the period intervening between production and clearance the goods should be kept in a proper place and under adequate supervision. The procedure followed in India in this regard is also practically the same as that obtaining elsewhere. Physical supervision is considered to be necessary in such cases in almost every country". [1]

The organised sector, however, continued to build up pressure for the replacement of the physical control system and ultimately the self-removal procedure was introduced with effect from June 1, 1968. A few commodities were still subject to the physical control system including sugar, chewing tobacco, and matches.

12.1.2 Self-Removal Procedure (SRP): Under this liberal system, introduced in place of the physical control system, an assessee was allowed to take clearances on his own assessment of the duty liability without prior permission of physical checks by excise officers. This procedure was applicable to most of the commodities under the excise net. An assessee was, however, required to get his classification list approved by the excise authorities before effecting any removal. In the classification list the assessee detailed the description of the goods produced so that they could be categorised in terms of the rate of duty applicable to them.

In the case of *ad valorem* duties, the assessee was further required to submit a price list showing the prices charged along with discounts and deductions, if any. In essence, the SRP was a record-based system of duty collection relying on mutual trust and belief. Unfortunately, heavy evasion of excise duty took place under this scheme. Excise evasion under this liberal scheme was generally resorted to by following such malpractices as incorrect accounting of goods, undervaluation of goods, and flouting the conditions subject to which any goods could be exempted from duty.

12.1.3 Compounded Levy Scheme: This was another procedure for the benefit of small-scale sector and for administrative convenience. Levying of excise duties on small-scale sector was a major problem of the excise system. In many cases, small-scale sector accounted for a significant portion of the output of an industry and it became necessary to subject it to excise taxation. However, the procedures adopted for collection of excise from big firms were often found expensive and time-consuming when applied to small firms. This necessitated the adoption of special procedures suitable for small-scale sector.

Under the compounded levy scheme introduced in 1954, a lump sum payment was made on the basis of some installations, e.g. the number of looms in case of textile units. Once the compounded levy was paid, the producer became free from all excise formalities except to maintain a record of looms in operation. The scheme was applicable to small units producing *khandasari* and cotton fabrics produced on power looms. This system afforded considerable advantages to the small producers because they were saved from the cumbersome normal excise procedures and also by the fact that the fiscal burden under compounded levy was generally lower than the burden under normal procedures.

12.2 Commodity Coverage

As already noted, excise taxation in India was fairly selective in terms of commodity coverage during the pre-Independence period. However, the need for resources required for planned economic development made it necessary to rely on excise taxation for additional funds. This was particularly so in view of the extremely narrow base for direct taxation and the dwindling relative revenue significance of customs duties owing to euphoria for import restrictions and substitution. The scope for extension of excise coverage improved considerably as development efforts were intensified for the production of industrial goods that enjoyed a relatively large and stable domestic market.

The Taxation Enquiry Commission (TEC), 1953-54, after having studied the then existing excise system, made important recommendations in terms of commodity coverage. It recommended the extension of excise coverage to sewing machines, vegetable oils, woollen textiles, biscuits, paper, dry batteries, electric lamps, aerated waters, electric fans, glass and glassware, paints and varnishes, and ceramics. In the opinion of the TEC these industries had developed sufficiently as a result of protection and it was necessary to impose excises on them to raise the much needed revenue for financing development programmes.

Consequent upon the recommendations of the TEC, the history of excise taxation in India since 1954 was one of increasing commodity coverage. Cement, footwear, rayon or artificial silk fabrics, and soap were added to the excise system in 1954. In 1955, excise duties were imposed on paints and varnishes, paper, woollen fabrics, electric batteries, electric light bulbs, and electric fans. In 1956, the excise net was extended to vegetable non-essential oils, rayon or synthetic fibres and yarn, and motor cars.

With the start of production of diesel oil and other fuel oils at the new refineries in Bombay, excise duty was imposed on a variety of petroleum products for the first time in 1956. These included refined diesel oil, diesel oil, and furnace oil. In 1959, excise duties were imposed on asphalt, bitumen, and tar.

The early 1960s witnessed another big expansion in the coverage of excise taxation in India. In 1960, eleven additional goods were subjected to excise duties including aluminium, pig iron, silk fabrics, and motor vehicles. In 1962, the number of additional products brought under the excise system was sixteen and included, *inter alia*, soda ash, caustic soda, cosmetics and toilet preparations, glass and glassware, copper and copper alloys etc. In 1962, ten more products including gases, rubber products, plywood, jute manufactures, and iron and steel products were covered under the excise net.

In 1968, duties were imposed on radio-parts, steel furniture, leather cloth, and chocolates. The biggest expansion was witnessed in 1971 when 25 additional products including linoleum, ready-made garments, vacuum flasks, and pressure cookers were brought under the excise net. The process of covering more and more items under the excise system reached its pinnacle when Tariff Item No. 68 was introduced in 1975. Tariff Item No. 68 was a catch-all item which encompassed all goods not elsewhere specified in the excise tariff. This residual tariff item was abolished with the introduction of a harmonised system of commodity classification introduced from February 28, 1986. The large assortment of commodities under this head got scattered under proper heads in the new nomenclature of excise tariff.

12.3 Central Excise Reorganisation Committee

This Committee (Chairman: A.K. Chanda) was constituted by the Government of India on November 2, 1960 with the following terms of reference:

1. To examine generally the organisational and administrative set up of the Central Excise Department and advise the government on such reorganisation as may be necessary for achieving maximum efficiency at minimum cost.
2. To review the Central Excise Act and Rules and procedures and recommend the steps required for their rationalisation. Simplification and improvements wherever necessary so as to better adapt the machinery to the changing conditions.

3. To make any other recommendations germane to the objectives of the investigation.

The Committee noted the use of incentives in different forms, including preferential rate of, or exemptions from excise duties, to give impetus to the growth of the village and small scale industries. However, it prescribed two conditions if small scale industries were to make their full contribution to the national economy. Firstly, these industries should be largely complementary and not competitive with organised industries and, secondly, they must attempt at becoming self-reliant and self-supporting by adopting improved techniques and more efficient forms of organisation.

12.4 Rationalisation and Simplification of the Tax Structure, 1968

In 1968, the Government of India appointed Mr. S. Bhoothalingam to examine the structure of direct and indirect taxes in India. In his report he recommended, *inter alia*, a general excise duty at the rate of 10 percent *ad valorem* on all manufactured products. [2] However, this recommendation was not accepted by the government.

12.5 Indirect Taxation Enquiry Committee (ITEC), 1978

ITEC (Chairman: L.K. Jha) was set up by the Government of India on July 19, 1976 to review the existing structure of indirect tax system. It was assigned the following terms of reference:

1. To review the existing structure of indirect taxes–Central, State and Local—in all its aspects.
2. To examine the role of indirect taxation in promoting economic use of scarce resources.
3. To examine the structure and levels of excise duties, the impact of these duties on prices and costs, the cumulative effect of such duties, their incidence on various expenditure groups, the scope for widening the tax base and increasing the elasticity of the system.
4. To examine the feasibility of adopting some form of value added tax in the field of indirect taxation where appropriate and, if found feasible, to suggest the appropriate stage to which it should be extended having regard to Indian conditions, i.e. whether the stage of coverage should be manufacturers, wholesalers or retailers.
5. To examine whether and how far it would be advisable to assist any particular industry or particular sectors of an industry by grant of concessions in indirect taxes; in doing so, the Committee will doubtless take into account all the normal canons of taxation, and the balance of administrative convenience. In those cases where these devices are found to be advisable, to suggest norms for the same.
6. To examine the structure and levels of import duties from the point of view of import trade control, protection to indigenous industry and pricing of indigenous products and suggest changes, if necessary.
7. To advise the government on the steps to be taken to implement the recommendations made, including changes in the administrative and organisational set up.

8. To suggest changes, if any required, in the Constitution and in the related taxation statutes, for the implementation of the changes suggested in the tax structure and having regard to the revenue needs of both the Centre and the States.
9. To consider the interaction and the proper balance between indirect and direct taxes in the tax structure while examining the role of indirect taxation in mobilising resources.
10. To make any other recommendations germane to the enquiry.

Computations of the ITEC revealed poor elasticity of the indirect tax system, except import duties. For the Union excise duties, accounting for nearly half of Centre's total tax collections, it estimated the buoyancy and elasticity coefficients at 1.31 and 0.75 respectively for the period 1963-64 to 1974-75.

ITEC undertook a comprehensive study of the incidence of indirect taxes for the year 1973-74. It was based on NSS data of consumer expenditure collected in the 28th round (October 1973 to June 1974). Taking into account all indirect taxes which amounted to 11.2 percent of national income in 1973-74, the ITEC arrived at the following main conclusions, "of this 11.2 percent, 1.65 percentage points could be said to have fallen on the government sector and on the investors, and the rest to have been shifted to the private consumers. The portion falling on the consumers is estimated to have amounted to 10.54 percent of household consumption expenditure. This is an average of the burden on rural and urban households, which differed considerably in percentage terms. While the burden on rural households amounted only to 8.0 percent of their consumption, that on the urban households amounted to 18.0 percent. The rural sector accounted for 77 percent of private consumption, and bore 57 percent of the indirect taxes allocable to consumers. The share of rural sector in total population is estimated to have been 80.1 percent in that year". [3]

ITEC worked out indirect taxes paid as percent of consumer expenditure by different per capita expenditure groups ranging from the poorest group with a monthly per capita expenditure not exceeding ₹ 15 to the highest expenditure group with a monthly per capita expenditure above ₹ 100. The Committee revealed a progressive distribution of the tax burden in terms of percentage of total expenditure at the all-India level. It increased progressively from 2.96 percent for households with per capita monthly expenditure not exceeding ₹ 15 to 21.96 percent for the group with per capita expenditure of ₹ 100 and above. Thus, even the poorest section of the society was found to be paying about 3 percent of its expenditure as taxes to the Government.

ITEC further revealed that the incidence of indirect taxes on different per capita expenditure groups in both rural and urban households was progressive but more so in urban than in rural area. In rural area, the lowest expenditure group (₹ 0-15) paid 2.91 percent of its expenditure as indirect taxes and the highest expenditure group (₹ 100 and above) paid 16.17 percent. In urban area, the proportion varied from 3.63 percent (for ₹ 0-15) to 30.19 percent (for ₹ 100 and above). The higher burden of taxes on urban households was explained by differences in the pattern of consumption between rural and urban households and also by the higher proportion of non-cash expenditures of rural households.

ITEC study concluded also that per capita indirect tax payment per annum for urban and rural households was ₹ 174.50 and ₹ 57.30 respectively in 1973-74, giving an approximate ratio of 3:1.

Apart from the combined burden of indirect taxes, ITEC studied also the incidence of individual taxes on various expenditure groups. It showed the relative incidence of Central indirect taxes vis-à-vis State indirect taxes as also the incidence of Central excise duties. It was revealed that Central taxes accounted for a larger share of incidence in both urban and rural sectors. Out of 8.03 percent, Central taxes accounted for 4.99 percentage points in rural areas and in urban areas their share was 12.03 percentage points out of a total tax burden of 17.96 percent of expenditure. The Committee observed that Central indirect taxes were more progressive than State taxes.

The share of Central excises hovered around half of the total incidence of indirect taxes. Their burden on the lowest expenditure group (₹ 0-15), middle expenditure group (₹ 43-55) and the highest expenditure group (₹ 100 and above) was estimated to be 1.47 percent 3.31 percent and 11.55 percent of expenditure respectively at all-India level; 1.42 percent, 2.92 percent and 7.87 percent for rural sector; and 2.42 percent, 4.94 percent and 16.78 percent for urban sector. The incidence of Central excises was quite progressive.

In a first attempt of its kind in India, ITEC worked out the incidence of indirect taxes on major types of goods separately. The goods subject to taxes were classified into three main groups according to the nature of use, viz.: (a) consumption goods, (b) intermediate goods, and (c) capital goods. It revealed that out of the total incidence of 10.54 percent of consumption expenditure for all households at all-India level, the share of consumption goods was 5.34 percentage points, amounting to half of the total incidence. Intermediate goods accounted for 4.53 percentage points and the remaining 0.63 percentage point was accounted for by capital goods. In sharp contrast to this pattern, the incidence of Central excises according to type of goods showed a totally different distribution. Intermediate goods claimed the largest share of the incidence of Central excises i.e. out of a total incidence of 5.34 percent of consumption expenditure attributable to Central excises in respect of all households at all-India level, the incidence of Central excises on intermediate goods accounted for 2.95 percentage points which was 55 percent of 5.34 percent.

The problem of multiplicity of rates was also considered by ITEC which recommended a set of four excise rates. It observed, "Instead of a pattern of which some product groups are very heavily taxed while others have remained either totally exempt or have been taxed at very low rates, the attempt should be to tax all consumer products, including those now falling under Tariff Item No. 68, at rates of 10, 20, 30 or 40 percent (cumulative), though some exceptional products may need to be taxed at lower or higher rates on special consideration". [4]

By suggesting a 10 to 40 percent range, the Committee virtually favoured a ceiling on excise rates. The Government disfavoured any drastic regrouping of the then existing rates. In his 1979-80 budget speech the Finance Minister observed, "A major restructuring of the excise tariff has to be ruled out in view of the need for resources and on other pragmatic considerations. Also, there is reason to apprehend that a major departure from the present pattern of excise taxation may upset the balance between different sectors of production". [5]

ITEC recommended also the introduction of Value Added Tax (VAT) at the manufacturing stage, called MANVAT, to tackle the problem of cascading effect of excise taxation.

12.6 Committee on Tax Measures to Promote Employment, 1979

This Committee (Chairman: V.M. Dandekar) was constituted by the Government of India in May 1979 to study the impact of tax concessions on the techniques of production used in industry and make recommendations for reform in order to encourage the adoption of labour-intensive methods and enlarge opportunities for employment.

Following were the terms of reference of the Committee:

1. To identify provisions in Central tax laws which have an influence on the employment of labour in the economy;
2. To examine the impact of these provisions on employment and the techniques of production in industry, agriculture and other areas of economic activity;
3. To suggest appropriate changes in Central tax laws so as to promote employment and adoption of labour-intensive methods of production having due regard to administrative feasibility and other objectives of public policy such as economic growth and self-reliance; and
4. To make recommendations regarding any other related matter.

The Committee made estimates of the annual cost of protecting or subsidising employment through concessions in excise duties. It found that the annual cost of protecting or subsidising employment through concessions in excise duties was ₹ 523 per full-time worker in the handloom industry, ₹ 881 in khandasari, and ₹ 2,669 in the cottage sector of the match industry. [6] It recommended several changes in Central tax laws so as to promote employment and adoption of labour-intensive methods of production.

12.7 Technical Study Group on Central Excise, 1984

The Group (Chairman: J. Datta) was set up by the Government of India on September 22, 1984 to undertake a comprehensive review of the then existing tariff nomenclature.

The Group was assigned the following terms of reference:

1. To recommend to the Government of India the lines on which the Central Excise Tariff (First Schedule to the Central Excises and Salt Act, 1944) should be revised, with particular reference to: (a) the need for simplification and rationalisation of the tariff and assessment procedures with a view to reducing the areas of conflict between the taxpayers and the tax collectors, (b) facility in collection of data regarding incidence of excise duty for policy formulation and (c) alignment, to the extent possible, with the Tariff Code of Customs and other statistical classification used by the government in regard to industrial production, industrial licensing, import licensing etc.

2. To review the pattern of exemptions and reliefs, particularly those aimed at encouraging small-scale and cottage industries.
3. To make recommendations for necessary legislative and administrative changes with a view to implementing the recommendations made by the Group and, especially to examine whether the First Schedule to the Central Excises and Salt Act, 1944 should be separately enacted as Central Excise Tariff Act.

The Group drafted a comprehensive and elaborate tariff nomenclature broadly patterned on Harmonised System Nomenclature (HSN), fully corresponding up to 2-digit level (i.e. Chapter level) in respect of 82 of the effective 96 chapters in the HSN. It also suggested that the new tariff should be provided for by a separate Act to be called the Central Excise Tariff Act in place of the then existing system of tariff being governed by the First Schedule of the Central Excises and Salt Act, 1944.

The recommendation of the Group as regards the new tariff nomenclature was accepted by the Government and a new Central Excise Tariff Act, 1985, was passed for the purpose. The excise tariff based on the internationally accepted harmonised commodity description and coding system came into effect from February 28, 1986, ushering a new era in excise taxation. The Schedule of the Central Excise Tariff Act, 1985, described the excisable commodities and the rate of duty leviable on them. The new tariff was spread over 91 chapters and covered around 700 four-digit headings and 1,400 six-digit headings.

12.7.1 Rate Structure: The Group favoured a drastic reduction in the number of duty rates to simply duty collection and compliance. The group recommended a band of five duty rates: middle rate, two rates below it and two above. Besides this, it also suggested a zero rate category. The middle rate (M) was defined to represent overall average incidence of excise duties. The two rates below this middle rate (L1 and L2) were suggested for adoption for inputs and important items of real mass consumption. The two rates in the upper scale (H1 and H2) could be applied to a few inputs, consumer durables and items consumed largely by the rich. The zero rate was recommended for products which deserve exceptional treatment on economic or social or administrative considerations.

The Group attempted only a broad and vague exercise of rate levels in terms of middle, below the middle, and above the middle rates of duty without specifying, even on a tentative basis, the duty rates in numerical terms. By leaving the actual fixation of rates to fiscal authorities, the Group left the exercise wide open.

12.7.2 New Excise Tariff Nomenclature: The year 1986 was a landmark in the evolution of excise taxation in India. In that year a new internationally accepted harmonised system of commodity classification was introduced in place of the then existing antiquated system introduced by the British. The history of excise tariff classification dates back to the year 1944 when the Central Excises and Salt Act, 1944 was passed, consolidating separate enactments for different goods. This Act of 1944 covered 11 tariff items which were arranged in alphabetical order.

In 1960, the tariff items, the number of which had soared to 30, were rearranged in accordance with the sections of the Standard International Trade Classification (SITC).

By 1986, the excise tariff schedule covered 137 tariff items and if account is taken of the sub-items, the number was well over 355 main classifications. The description of tariff commodities was based on the definitions of the Indian Standard Institution, and the descriptions and explanatory notes of the Customs Co-operation Council Nomenclature (CCCN). The domestic trade parlance was also relied upon.

As already noted, on September 22, 1984, the Government set up a Technical Study Group to undertake a comprehensive review of the then existing tariff nomenclature. The Group drafted a comprehensive and elaborate tariff nomenclature broadly patterned on Harmonised System Nomenclature (HSN), fully corresponding up to 2-digit level (i.e. Chapter level) in respect of 82 of the effective 96 chapters in the HSN. It also suggested that the new tariff should be provided for by a separate Act to be called the Central Excise Tariff Act in place of the then existing system of tariff being governed by the First Schedule of the Central Excises and Salt Act, 1944.

The recommendation of the Technical Study Group as regards the new tariff nomenclature was accepted by the Government and a new Central Excise Tariff Act, 1985, was passed for the purpose. The excise tariff based on the internationally accepted harmonised commodity description and coding system came into effect from February 28, 1986, ushering a new era in excise taxation. The Schedule of the Central Excise Tariff Act, 1985, described the excisable commodities and the rate of duty leviable on them. The new tariff was spread over 91 chapters and covered around 700 four-digit headings and 1,400 six-digit headings.

12.8 Long Term Fiscal Policy (LTFP), 1985

With regard to excise duties, LTFP envisaged the extension of the Proforma Credit Scheme [7] and observed, "The basic approach will be to move towards an extension of the present system of proforma credit to all excisable commodities with the exception of a few like petroleum, tobacco, and textile products. This programme would amount to a modified system of VAT or MODVAT for short. The programme will be implemented in a phased manner over a period of years, taking due account of the revenue implications, the need to revise administrative procedures and the lessons from experience gained in the early stages of the reform." [8] In pursuance of the proposal made in the LTFP, he Government introduced a modified system of value added tax or MODVAT with effect from March 1, 1986.

See also chapters 5 and 17 of this book.

Endnotes

1. Government of India, Ministry of Finance, *Report of the Taxation Enquiry Commission* (Chairman: John Matthai), 1953-54, Volume II, p. 323.
2. Government of India, Ministry of Finance, *Final Report on Rationalisation and Simplification of Tax Structure* (Chairman: S. Bhoothalingam), 1968, 8.
3. Government of India, Ministry of Finance, *Report of the Indirect Taxation Enquiry Committee,* (Chairman: L.K. Jha), Part II, 1978, p. 89.
4. Ibid., p. 174.

5. Government of India, Ministry of Finance, *Speeches of Union Finance Ministers, 1947-48 to 1984-85*, p. 459.
6. Government of India, Ministry of Finance, *Report of the Expert Committee on Tax Measures to Promote Employment* (Chairman: V.M. Dandekar), 1980, pp. 91, 113 and 117.
7. There were provisions in the Central Excises and Salt Rules, 1944, under which certain inputs were exempted from taxation to minimise the cumulative effect of excise levies. Thus, Rule 56-A of the said Rules, introduced in 1962, allowed the manufacturers of certain notified finished excisable goods to bring excise-paid components (for example compressors for refrigerators) to take credit for the said duty in the Proforma Credit Account to get adjustment of duty on the final excisable good.
8. Government of India, *Long Term Fiscal Policy*, 1985, p. 38.

13

Customs Duties

Customs duties are probably the most ancient form of taxation. They are as old as international trade itself. Just as domestic production flows provide the base for excise taxation so also international trade flows are the basis for customs duties. Customs duties are payable on goods exported from or imported into a country. Import duties are usually levied with *ad valorem* rates and their base is determined by the domestic value of the imported goods calculated at the official exchange rate. Similarly, export duties are imposed on export values expressed in domestic currency. Customs duties are imposed to raise revenue for the government.

Apart from revenue function, import duties act as policy instrument to provide protection to domestic industry, conserve and ration scarce foreign exchange, and frame external trade policy of the Government. Other measures to protect indigenous industries from foreign competition include import licensing, import quotas, and outright import ban.

Import duties are the main source of customs revenue in India. Therefore, customs policy has revolved round import tariff. Export duties have negligible revenue significance and therefore are mentioned towards the end of chapter 19 of this book.

13.1 Early Post-Independence Period

Soon after Independence, the government decided to follow a restrictive import policy, particularly in view of the rapid depletion of sterling balances. In his very first budget (1947-48) of independent India, the Finance Minister outlined the salient features of this restrictive policy in the following words, "Broadly speaking, that policy consists of dividing imports into three categories: free, restricted, and prohibited. Imports of food, capital goods, the raw material of industry and certain essential consumer goods are free and no exchange restrictions are placed upon their imports. Consumer goods which are not absolutely essential are licensed on a quota basis, while others which in the context of the economy of this country must be regarded as totally unessential and luxury imports have been altogether prohibited". [1]

During the early post-Independence period, customs policy remained in turmoil owing to a series of domestic and international happenings. India's commitments under the General Agreement on Tariffs and Trade (GATT) were given effect to in 1948, the rupee was devalued in September 1949, and the Korean War broke out in 1950. Being a signatory to GATT, India could not raise, above a certain level, import duties on a wide variety of goods, but enjoyed reciprocal concessions from its trade partners. Imports of articles which enjoyed concessions under GATT constituted 19 percent of the value of total imports while the value of exports which received concessions was 79.6 percent of total exports in 1952-53. The concessions obtained included items like mica, cashewnut, and various jute goods. The concessions granted pertained mainly to consumer goods and machinery. Since the actual rates of import duty on machinery, which formed the bulk of imports, were already low than the rates fixed by GATT, the effective concessions were chiefly on consumer goods. Although the Fiscal Commission, 1949-50, supported India's adherence to GATT in view of the need for international co-operation, the country later on felt the need to withdraw from GATT *bindings* when the domestic production base was strengthened and diversified. Following re-negotiations in 1971 and 1973, a host of items *bound* under GATT were freed to provide protection to domestic industries.

After the outbreak of the Korean War, important changes were introduced in the tariff structure under the Finance Act, 1951. The general surcharge of one-fifth on import duties (levied in 1942) was increased to one-fourth. The rate of surcharge on liquors which was fixed at 100 percent in 1948 was raised to 155 percent.

In pursuance of its general policy of gradually replacing quantitative restrictions by higher import duties, the Government raised import duties on a number of items including articles made of paper, cutlery etc., in the 1955-56 budget. Simultaneously, import quotas were liberalised. The already high level of import duties, particularly on luxury articles, did not leave much scope for raising additional revenue from this source, a fact lamented by the Finance Minister in his 1957-58 budget (final) speech.

13.2 Customs Reorganisation Committee, 1957

In January 1957, the Government of India appointed the Customs Reorganisation Committee (Chairman: F.C. Badhwar) which was asked "to conduct a comprehensive enquiry into customs procedures and organisation and to make recommendations for their improvement".

The following were the terms of reference to the Committee;

1. To examine in detail the procedure: (a) for the clearance of goods and passengers' baggage through the customs at the sea ports, airports and land customs stations, (b) for the administration of import, export and exchange control regulations, (c) for ensuring uniformity of classification of goods and methods of valuation, (d) for the grant of customs refunds and drawbacks and (e) other matters of customs procedure generally.
2. To examine the liaison between the customs on the one hand and the trade, the Port Trust/Commissioners, the Import and Export Trade Control authorities, and the Post and Telegraph Department, on the other;
3. In the light of examination made under items (1) and (2) above, and having regard to the safety of Government revenue, the adequate enforcement of prohibitions and restrictions, and the legitimate interest of the trade and of passengers, to recommend the modifications required in the various procedures for making them more effective simpler and speedier;
4. To examine the administration of the existing Customs Department as a whole with reference to the adequacy and disposition of staff provided at various levels, their working conditions, the exercise and delegation of responsibility and methods of

recruitment and training.

5. In the light of the examination referred to in item 4 above, to recommend necessary improvements.
6. To make any other recommendations germane to the objective of the investigation.

The Committee found that a major cause of disputes and delays in the clearance of imported goods was the faulty and inadequate classification system for determining customs tariff. It observed, "The complexity of the Customs Tariff will be evident from the fact that the whole range of goods constituting the country's foreign trade are grouped under 576 tariff items only as compared with 4850 classification heads in the 'Statistical Indian Trade Classification' which has recently been adopted for purposes of recording the country's trade statistics. Whilst the range and variety of imported goods have been continuously expanding in the post-war period, there has been little or no corresponding revision or elaboration of the customs tariff schedule". [2]

The Committee was also critical of too many rates of duty. It commented, "we should similarly point out the existence in the Indian Customs Tariff of too wide a range of *ad valorem* rates of duty which must inevitably add to the difficulties in the day to day application of the tariff, particularly when tariff descriptions carrying different rates could apply to the same article. Almost all multiples of 5 up to 100 are to be found in these rates". [3]

The Committee recommended, *inter alia*: (a) thorough revision of the Customs Tariff by aligning it closely with the Import Trade Control Licensing Schedule, and (b) removal of anomalies in rates of duty for similar categories of goods.

13.3 Rationalisation of the Import Duty Structure

The worsening foreign exchange crisis reached its climax when in 1965 foreign exchange reserves touched the critically low level of less than ₹ 100 crore. Moreover, the Customs Reorganisation Committee, 1957, had criticised the multiplicity of tariff rates. The Committee on Rationalisation and Simplification of Tax Structure, 1968, also favoured few rates of import tariff. It opined, "Except for a few 'luxury' items like watches, jewellery, alcoholic beverages and perfumes, there is need only for three or four rates of duty". [4]

Consequently, a drastic rationalisation of the import duty structure was undertaken in 1965, resulting in the introduction of a set of three rates of import duty: 40 percent on basic raw materials, 60 percent on semi-processed and intermediate goods, and 100 percent on finished consumer goods.

In spite of the rationalisation exercise of 1965, duty changes were made frequently depending upon the emerging situation. The three rates of import duty were scaled down following devaluation of the rupee in June 1966 to prevent the cost of imports going up to the full extent of the devaluation. However, in view of the difficult balance of payments position, the rates of import duty were gradually restored in due course to pre-devaluation levels. Rationalisation of import tariff was again attempted in 1971 when the following four rates of import duty were introduced: 30 percent, 40 percent, 60 percent, and 100 percent.

13.4 New Customs Tariff Nomenclature

As in the case of excise duties, a major problem in the administration of customs duties pertained to disputes and delays relating to interpretation of definitions of dutiable goods. The enactment of the new Customs Tariff Act, 1975, was a landmark in the history of customs tariff in India. The revised nomenclature for customs tariff was recommended by the Tariff Revision Committee set up in 1964. Though the Government accepted the recommendations of the Committee, the Bill to implement the revised nomenclature could only be passed in 1975 and came into effect from August 2, 1976. The Act of 1975, which replaced the Indian Tariff Act, 1934, is based on the Customs Co-operation Council Nomenclature (originally known as Brussels Tariff Nomenclature). The First Schedule of the Act contains import tariff while the Second Schedule deals with export tariff. As a further measure to rationalise and modernise customs administration, the Parliament passed the Customs Tariff Amendment Act, 1985, to adopt the Harmonised Commodity Description and Coding System. The new commodity classification became operative from February 28, 1986. Similarly, India adopted the GATT Valuation Agreement (Valuation Code) on August 16, 1988. The GATT Valuation Code lays down broad principles for valuation of goods for levy of customs duty.

13.5 Indirect Taxation Enquiry Committee, 1978

The Indirect Taxation Enquiry Committee (Chairman: L.K. Jha), 1978, examined at length the structure of import duties and recommended its rationalisation on the following lines: "(a) a levy adequate to give the degree of protection deemed necessary for particular products, (b) a revenue element, which would generally be the countervailing duty, being equal to the excise duty leviable on the same or similar domestic product, and (c) a regulator element which will be used on such factors as reinforcing import restrictions, preventing excess profits on account of scarcity of products in domestic market, and generally to regulate imports from the angle of conserving foreign exchange". [5]

13.6 Long-Term Fiscal Policy, 1985

The need for import tariff rationalisation was underlined in the Long Term Fiscal Policy (LTFP), 1985, also. The official document noted that the prevailing tariff rates were high and the tariff system was very complicated. Therefore, it stressed the need to reduce the rates and simplify the system. For carrying out these reforms, the LTFP distinguished between the following broad categories of imports:

1. Capital goods.
2. Raw materials.
3. Other intermediate goods including components.
4. Essential consumer goods like foodgrains, edible oils, and life saving drugs.
5. Non-essential consumer goods.

Understandably, essential goods were preferred to either remain exempt or bear low rates of import duties while non-essential items were singled out to either remain banned or subjected to high import tariff. Regarding the first three categories of goods the LTFP observed, "Ideally, in the long-run, there is a strong case for subjecting all capital goods, raw materials, components and other intermediate products to the same rate of nominal tariff. This system, if it could be implemented, would have several important advantages. First, the substitution of the present multiplicity of nominal tariff rates by a single rate would constitute an enormous simplification for both trade and industry as well as for the customs administration. Second, this would vastly reduce incentives for misclassification of imports to evade taxes. Third, a single nominal rate of import duty would assure a uniform rate of effective protection (that is, protection of value added) at different stages of production of intermediate and capital goods. This would encourage the economy to specialise in those activities in which it has competitive strength". [6]

However, the LTFP cautioned that a major deviation from the present pattern of import tariff is not immediately feasible. Domestic industries have grown under different levels of protection and are in different stages of maturity. The rationalisation of import tariff has to be phased over a long period providing some differentials in import tariff short of a uniform system of duties.

Consequent upon the rationalisation of import tariff on capital goods by the Finance Act, 1987, the rate of import duty on general machinery was reduced to 85 percent *ad valorem.* Import duty on components for machinery was fixed at 15 percent below the applicable rate on complete machines. This differential, in line with the recommendations of the LTFP, was intended to encourage the domestic production of capital machines instead of their total imports. Imports of capital goods for certain preferred sectors were allowed at relatively low rates of duty. For example, duty on equipment for fertiliser plants was 15 percent *ad valorem* and on machines, equipment, and tools for gem and jewellery 25 percent *ad valorem.* Electronics industry emerged as a preferred sector for fiscal incentives. The Finance Act, 1988, fixed a uniform concessional import duty of 60 percent *ad valorem* in respect of 280 items of machinery for the electronics sector. By the same Act, the duty on moulds, tools, and dies required by the electronics industry was reduced from 60 percent to 30 percent *ad valorem* with the underlying purpose of indigenisation and development of electronics and computers.

In short, guidelines suggested by the LTFP for reform of import tariff were never implemented comprehensively. In a half-hearted manner, some rationalisation of rates was effected in the case of components of capital goods, drug intermediates, and electronic goods.

See also chapters 6 and 19 of this book.

Endnotes

1. Government of India, Ministry of Finance, *Speeches of Union Finance Ministers: 1947-48 to 1984-85,* p. 8.
2. Government of India, *Report of the Customs Reorganisation Committee,* (Chairman: F.C. Budhwar), 1957-58, p. 12.
3. Ibid., p. 13.
4. Government of India, *Final Report on Rationalisation and Simplification of Tax Structure,*

(Chairman: S. Bhoothalingam), 1968, p. 14.

5. Government of India, Ministry of Finance, *Report of the Indirect Taxation Enquiry Committee,* (Chairman: L.K. Jha), Part II, 1978, p. 139.
6. Government of India, *Long Term Fiscal Policy,* p. 41.

14

Sales Tax

The problems relating to taxation of inter-State sales were considered by the Drafting Committee of the Constituent Assembly. It proposed incorporation of provisions in the Constitution restricting the powers of the State Governments in respect of the levy of sales tax in the course of foreign trade, inter-State trade, and on essential commodities. In spite of opposition from some States, these provisions were finally incorporated in the Constitution as Article 286 (explained below).

14.1 Constitutional Provisions for the Regulation of Taxation of Inter-State Sales

Under Entry 54 of List II (State List) in the Seventh Schedule of the Constitution, the States were given the power to levy "a tax on sales or purchases of goods other than newspapers". This provision was quite similar to Entry 48 of List II in the Seventh Schedule of the Government of India Act, 1935. However, under the Constitution, the States' power to levy sales tax was subject to a number of restrictions. These restrictions on the sale or purchase of goods as mentioned in Article 286 of the Constitution were the following.

1. No law of a State shall impose a tax on the sale or purchase of goods where such sale or purchase takes place: (a) outside the State, or (b) in the course of import of goods into, or export of goods out of, the territory of India.
2. Except in so far as the Parliament may by law otherwise provide, no law of a State shall impose a tax on the sale or purchase of any goods where such sale or purchase takes place in the course of inter-State trade or commerce.
3. No law made by the legislature of a State imposing a tax on the sale or purchase of any such goods as have been declared by Parliament by law to be essential for the life of the community, shall have effect unless it has been reserved for the consideration of the President and has received his assent.

In simple words, the States were prevented from taxing the following transactions: (i) sales or purchases in the course of foreign trade; (ii) sales of goods delivered in another State for consumption purpose; and (iii) sales in the course of inter-State trade and commerce.

Furthermore, the power of States to levy the tax on commodities declared to be *essential* by the Parliament was made subject to the prior approval of the President.

14.2 Consequences of Constitutional Restrictions on Sales Tax

The first restriction resulted in considerable loss of revenue to States, which were levying sales tax on exports. The main losers in this category were Bombay, Bihar, Madhya Pradesh, Orissa, and Assam. Nevertheless, this was the least controversial provision of Article 286.

The second and third restrictions, the benefits of which applied equally to registered dealers, unregistered dealers, and consumers, led to large scale evasion and avoidance of tax and hence loss of revenue to the States in general. As the Taxation Enquiry Commission, 1953-54, observed, "Traders in one State started to sell direct to unregistered dealers and consumers in another. Similarly, consumers of valuable commodities tried to get these from dealers in another State rather than buy the articles from their local dealers.

The practice grew for sales of goods within a State itself to be shown in the books of accounts as having been made to fictitious dealers outside the State and the goods having then been resold by those dealers to consumers within the State. For valuable commodities like motor vehicles, jewellery, watches, etc. this practice became very common.

On transactions that could be shown to be in the course of inter-State trade, the *exporting* State was prohibited under Article 286 from levying the sales tax; and if the goods delivered as a result of these transactions were shown to be received by individual consumers or unregistered dealers neither could any tax be levied on them by the *importing* State. Thus, many of these transactions escaped sales tax altogether". [1]

The loss of revenue was more for States with single-point system as compared to States having multi-point sales taxation. This was so because the restriction was not applicable to sales in the State prior to the last point of sale for export to another State.

The Constitutional restrictions led to uneconomic diversion of trade and production centres. The problems which the constitutional provisions sought to solve got further compounded *albeit* with a different nature. To quote, "The Constitutional restrictions on sales taxation greatly increased the scope for evasion. While the problem before the Constitution had been multiple taxation (by different States) on the same act of inter-State sale, the problem after the Constitution was that inter-State sales frequently escaped taxation altogether". [2]

14.3 Essential Goods Act, 1952

As already noted, in addition to the above restrictions, Article 286 also prevented the States from levying tax on sales or purchases of goods declared by the Parliament to be essential for the life of the community, except with the previous assent of the President. For this purpose, the Parliament enacted the Essential Goods (Declaration and Regulation of Tax on Sale or Purchase) Act, 1952, and various commodities were declared as essential including cereals and pulses, fresh and dried fruits, fresh milk, meat, fish, salt, hides and skins, iron and steel, coal, fertilisers, petroleum products, and books.

As to the desirable purpose of the Act, the Taxation Enquiry Commission, 1953-54, noted, "It is obvious that the object of restricting the power of the states to levy a tax on the sale or purchase of 'essential goods' is to achieve some degree of uniformity in the tax burden on those goods, and not necessarily or in all cases to eliminate altogether the sales tax on such goods. When the Bombay Government sought the assent of the President to tax some of the 'essential goods' under their new multi-point tax system, the assent was given on condition that the tax burden on these goods should not in any event exceed the previous tax burden under the single-point system. This seems to indicate that the policy underlying the restriction is one of freezing the existing tax levied on these goods and of ensuring that new proposals to tax them are confined within reasonable limits". [3]

In spite of its desirable objectives, the enactment of the Essential Goods Act, 1952, led to various problems and criticism from some State Governments. Since the legislation was not retrospective, the States which had been levying sales tax on *essential goods* prior to the passage of the Essential Goods Act, continued to levy the tax. However, those States which sought to levy the tax after the passage of the Act had to obtain the consent of the President. This evoked sharp resentment among the State Governments.

The resentment among the States was further fuelled by the fact that the Central Government itself was levying relatively high rates of excise/customs duties on some of the so-called *essential goods*.

14.4 Constitution (Sixth Amendment) Act, 1956

In view of the problems arising from constitutional restrictions on the taxation of inter-State sales, the Taxation Enquiry Commission, 1953-54, recommended as follows, "In essence, the sales tax must continue to be a State tax. However, power and responsibility of the State must end and that of the Union begin when the sales tax of one State impinges administratively and fiscally on the consumers of another State. Inter-State sales tax should be the concern of the Union". [4]

Consequently, the Constitution was amended by the Sixth Amendment Act of 1956. Under this Amendment, the Parliament was empowered to impose 'taxes on the sale or purchase of goods other than newspapers, where such sale or purchase takes place in the course of inter-State trade or commerce'. This new provision in the Constitution was made by inserting Entry 92A in List I (Union List) in the Seventh Schedule. Simultaneously, Entry 54 in List II (State List) was made subject to the provisions of the new Entry 92A of List I. Also, Article 269 of the Constitution was amended which added a new clause (1)(g) which permitted taxes on the sale or purchase of goods in the course of inter-State trade to be levied and collected by the Government of India but assigned to the States. [5] Again, clauses (2) and (3) of Article 286 of the unamended Constitution were substituted by new clauses to make it read as follows.

(1) No law of a State shall impose or authorise the imposition of a tax on the sale or purchase of goods where such sale or purchase takes place: (a) outside the State, or (b) in the course of import of goods into or export of goods out of the territory of India. [6]

(2) Parliament may by law formulate principles for determining when a sale or purchase of goods takes place in any of the ways mentioned in clause (1). [7]

(3) Any law of a State shall in so far as it imposes or authorises the imposition of a tax on the sale or purchase of goods declared by Parliament by law to be of special importance in inter-State trade or commerce, be subject to such restrictions and conditions in regard to the system of levy, rates and other incidents of the tax as Parliament may by law specify. [8]

The new Article 286(2) gave Parliament the powers to define a sale outside a State. The new Article 286(3) was different from the old Article 286(3) in the following respect: In the old provision, Parliament had the authority to restrict State taxation of commodities declared by Parliament to be *essential for the life of the community*. In the new provision, Parliament was empowered to restrict State taxation of goods declared to be of special importance in inter-State trade only. [9]

14.5 Central Sales Tax (CST) Act, 1956

Consequent upon the Constitution (Sixth Amendment) Act, 1956, the Central Sales Tax (CST) Act, 1956 was enacted which came into force on January 5, 1957. The following three main objectives of the CST Act were stated in the Preamble:

1. To formulate principles for determining when a sale or purchase of goods takes place in the course of inter-State trade or in the course of import into or export from India.
2. To provide for the levy, collection, and distribution of taxes on sale of goods in the course of inter-State trade or commerce.
3. To declare certain goods to be of special importance in inter-State trade and specify the restrictions to which State laws imposing taxes on the sale and purchase of such goods of special importance shall be subject.

14.5.1 Main Provisions of CST Act: The regulations contained in the CST Act provided, *inter alia*, for a degree of uniformity by prescribing a maximum rate of sales tax on certain goods considered important for the whole country. According to Section 3 of the CST Act, a sale or purchase of goods was deemed to take place in the course of inter-State trade if it: (a) occasions the movement of goods from one State to another, or (b) is effected by a transfer of documents of title to the goods during their movement from one State to another.

Section 14 of the Act declared certain goods to be of special importance in inter-State trade and commerce. These were coal, cereals, cotton, cotton yarn, cotton fabrics, crude oil, hides and skins, iron and steel, jute, oilseeds, pulses, rayon and artificial silk fabrics, sugar, tobacco, woollen fabrics. The list of *declared goods* originally covered by the Act in 1956 was expanded twice, once in 1957 to include textiles, sugar, and tobacco, and again in 1976 to include cereals (like wheat, paddy, rice etc.), crude oil, and pulses.

Section 15 of the Act laid down the rate structure. The rates were different depending upon the classes of goods and the status of the person to whom the goods were sold. Thus, goods were either *declared goods* (goods of special importance) or *non-declared goods* while a person was either a registered or a non-registered dealer. Based on these classifications, the rates of sales tax were prescribed by the Central Government though the tax was administered (i.e. assessed, collected and appropriated) by the State Governments by virtue of the powers delegated to them by the Central Government under Article 258(1) of Constitution.

The maximum prescribed rate of sales tax on *declared goods* inside a State was 2 percent of the sale price and was not leviable at more than one stage. [10] Thus, although sales tax on intra-State sales was levied by the States, taxation of intra-State sales of *declared goods* (goods of special importance) was subject to certain restrictions in terms of the nature of the levy (not to be levied at more than one stage) and the rate of tax (not more than 2 percent).

In the case of inter-State sale of such goods to registered dealers, the rate of tax was the same as applicable to the sale of such goods inside the exporting State. In respect of sale of *declared goods* to non-registered dealers (including consumers) the CST was chargeable at twice the rate applicable to the same goods inside the State, i.e. 8 percent. Where *non-declared* goods were sold in the course of inter-State trade to a registered dealer, the ceiling rate was 4 percent [11] or the rate applicable to internal sales of the concerned goods, whichever was lower. [12] However, on inter-State sale of *non-declared goods* to non-registered dealers, the rate of CST was 10 percent or the rate applicable to the sale of such goods inside the exporting State, whichever was higher. [13]

The Act further specified that when a sales tax had been levied inside a State on any *declared goods* and such goods were sold in the course of inter-State trade, the tax so levied would refunded. Provision also existed that goods which were generally and unconditionally exempt from the sales tax within a State would also be exempt from CST in the course of inter-State trade.

14.5.2 Working of CST Act: It is clear as to why some kind of Central control was necessary on sales tax for larger national interest. Had Punjab and Haryana been free to levy sales tax on foodgrains at will, the people of food deficit States would have suffered. Similarly, uncontrolled imposition of sales tax by West Bengal, and Bihar on iron and steel, and coal would have impeded the growth of engineering industry in Gujarat and Maharashtra.

CST Act authorized a State to tax residents of other States. Lest this power should be misused to export undue tax burden to the other States, the original scheme devised in 1956 kept the rate of CST low at 1 percent ensuring some reasonable revenue for the exporting States. However, over the years the rate of CST was raised by stages to 4 percent. This trend benefited industrially advanced States (like Maharashtra, Gujarat, Tamil Nadu, and West Bengal) at the cost of industrially backward States. Since manufactures were the main items of inter-State trade, the developed States were able to export a part of their taxation to other States. In effect, it amounted to transfer of financial resources from poorer States to well-off States, much against the declared objective of regional balanced development and equitable distribution of resources among the States. Moreover, the high rate of CST hindered the free flow of trade and commerce within the country.

There were suggestions that the rate of CST should be reduced to the original level of 1 percent to safeguard the interests of poorer States. However, these suggestions met with stiff resistance from most State Governments. At the New Delhi Conference of Chief Ministers held on September 16-17, 1980, there was a unanimous opinion that the rate of CST should not be brought down from 4 percent to 1 percent. [14] However, it was agreed to constitute a panel of Chief Ministers to consider, *inter alia*, additions to the list of *declared goods*. The Conference also expressed unanimity over the need for uniform sales tax laws in the country because various variants of the sales tax posed problems for the collecting authorities as well as for the taxpayers. The Chief Ministers' Conference decided to request the Law Commission to undertake, on a high priority basis, the drafting of a model sales tax law for consideration by the States.

Originally, the rate of CST was 1 percent, which was increased first to 2 percent, then to 3 percent and with effect from July 1, 1975 to 4 percent. Later on it was reduced from 4 percent to 3 percent with effect from April 1, 2007 and from 3 percent to 2 percent with effect from June 1, 2008. These reductions were done as a precursor to the introduction of GST, as CST was inconsistent with the concept and design of GST. CST was an origin-based tax and hence inconsistent with GST (a value added tax) which is destination-based tax with inherent input tax credit refund.

CST was a state-level tax, applied to inter-state sales of goods, based on the origin principle. The tax law (including the base, rates, and the procedures) was enacted by Parliament, but the entire revenue accruing under the levy of CST was collected and kept by the State in which the sale originated. The Act excluded taxation of imports and exports. It was a perfect example of absolute harmonization, with the States enjoying the risks and rewards of ownership of the tax.

CST was subsumed under GST when the latter came into force on July 1, 2017.

14.6 Additional Duties of Excise (Goods of Special Importance) Act, 1957

Another landmark in the evolution of sales tax in India was the year 1956 when, following a voluntary agreement between the Centre and the States at a meeting of the National Development Council (NDC) held in December, 1956, it was decided to replace sales tax on textiles, tobacco, and sugar by additional duties of excise and to distribute revenues derived therefrom among the States. The agreement provided also that the share accruing to each State shall not in any case be less than the revenue realised from the levy of sales tax on these goods for the financial year 1956-57 in that State. The Council's decision was implemented through the Additional Duties of Excise (Goods of Special Importance) Act, 1957, the First Schedule of which prescribed the rates of additional duties of excise and the Second Schedule the scheme of distribution of the net proceeds among the States.

The Act did not debar States from the levy of sales tax on the specified commodities, but it did provide that if in any year any State levied and collected a tax on the sale or purchase of such commodities, no sum would be paid to that State in that year by way of share out of the net proceeds of the additional duties of excise, unless the Central Government by special order decided otherwise. The commodities covered under the scheme (textiles, tobacco, and sugar) were declared goods of special importance in inter-State trade so that no State could find it worthwhile to opt out of the voluntary agreement not to impose sales tax on these goods. [15] The revenue derived from additional duties of excise, levied and collected by the Centre, was distributed among the States in accordance with the formula prescribed by the Finance Commission. The Fourth Finance Commission described it as a *tax rental arrangement.* [16]

14.6.1 Rationale of the Scheme: The scheme of additional duties of excise in lieu of sales tax had the following advantages:

1. It minimized tax evasion by levying the tax at first point and saving industry, trade, and consumers from administrative complexities involved in the collection and payment of sales tax.
2. It helped in maintaining uniformity in the prices of widely consumed goods throughout the country.
3. Such an arrangement contributed to the development of an integrated market by facilitating movement of goods across State borders.
4. Rationalisation of commodity taxation at the national level became easy.
5. Cost of collection is reduced.

14.6..2 Views of the State Governments: While the business community demanded extension of this scheme to other commodities, the States generally remained disinclined in this regard. The distrust between the Centre and the States regarding the operation of this scheme by the Central Government was an irritant in Centre-State relations. States had argued that: (a) sales tax was the only elastic source of revenue available to them and in view of its regional applicability it was also the only effective instrument for shaping their economic policies, (b) replacement of it by Central levy encroached on their constitutional rights leading to erosion of their financial autonomy, and (c) if taxes were levied and collected by a State itself then it was more conscious of its responsibilities towards the taxpayers. Subventions from the Centre may lead to reckless spending, causing fiscal indiscipline.

As regards the working of the scheme, the dissatisfaction of State Governments was borne out of their belief that revenue potential of additional duties of excise was not fully exploited by the Centre. Their complaint was that the growth of revenue from additional excise duties on textiles, sugar, and tobacco lagged behind the growth in revenue from basic excise duties on the same commodities. The States complained that once sales tax on the three commodities was replaced by additional excise duties, the Centre did not feel the need for consultation with the States for reviewing the working of the scheme. They claimed that the growth rate of their sales tax revenue was much higher than the growth rate of the yield from additional excise duties.

14.6.3 Decisions of the National Development Council (NDC): Following complaints from the States, the whole issue was reconsidered by the NDC in its meeting held on December 28, 1970. The Council decided to continue the scheme with the following conditions: (a) that the incidence of additional duties would be stepped up to 10.8 percent of the value of clearances within a period of two or three years, (b) that a ratio of 2:1 between basic and additional excise duties would be achieved and maintained, (c) that specific duties would be converted into *ad valorem* duties except in regard to unmanufactured tobacco. It was also agreed that a Standing Review Committee consisting of representatives of the Central and State Governments with the Economic Adviser, Planning Commission, as convenor, would be set up and the same would meet at least once a year to review the working of the new arrangement and make such recommendations as may be necessary for its further improvement.

As a follow up action, specific duties were replaced by *ad valorem* rates and significant enhancements were made in additional excise duties in the Central budgets for the three consecutive years 1971-72 to 1973-74. The Standing Review Committee met for the first time in February 1981 and appointed a sub-committee which recommended that the incidence of 10.8 percent should be achieved in three stages: 8.5 percent by 1984-85; 9.75 percent by 1987-88; and 10.8 percent by 1989-90. The Ninth Finance Commission was informed by the Union Finance Ministry that the incidence achieved by the end of 1988-89 was 10.7 percent. The Commission hoped that the committed level of 10.8 percent would actually be achieved by the end of 1989-90. In a significant move, the Commission recommended that during its award period (1990-95), if in any year the incidence of additional excise duties fell short of the level of 10.8 percent of the value of clearances, the shortfall would be made good by the Centre by providing an equivalent amount by way of grants-in-aid to be distributed among the States in the same manner as recommended for sharing the proceeds of additional excise duties. [17] As regards the ratio between basic excises and additional excises, the Centre fulfilled its obligations by achieving the stipulated 2:1 ratio by 1981-82.

14.6.4 Expert Committee on Replacement of Sales Tax by Additional Excise Duty, 1983: As already noted, sales tax on textiles, tobacco, and sugar was replaced by additional duties of excise in 1957. The scheme of additional excise duties was proposed to be extended to some more commodities in 1980. At a conference of the Chief Ministers convened by the Centre on September 16-17 of that year, it was resolved to bring *vanaspati*, and life-saving drugs under additional excise duties in lieu of sales tax. It was also decided to constitute a committee of Chief Ministers to consider what other items could be added to the list for additional excise duties. However, the non-Congress(I) States viz. Kerala, Tamil Nadu, Tripura, and West Bengal did not agree with the resolution passed at the Chief Ministers Conference.

The matter was further examined at another conference of Chief Ministers held in February 1981, which recommended the appointment of an expert committee by the Central Government to look into this matter. Shri Mohanlal Sukhadia assumed charge as the Chairman of the committee on January 9, 1982. However, after his sad demise on the February 2, 1982, Shri Kamlapati Tripathi was appointed as the Chairman of the Committee by the Government of India by its Resolution dated March 1, 1982. The expert committee headed by Mr. Kamlapati Tripathi submitted its report [18] in January 1983.

It recommended the replacement of sales tax by additional excise duty on *vanaspati*, drugs and medicines, cement, paper and paper board, and petroleum products. The recommendations were considered in a conference of Chief Ministers held on November 2, 1983. However, the six Chief Ministers of the non-Congress(I) States, viz. Andhra Pradesh, Jammu and Kashmir, Karnataka, Tamil Nadu, Tripura, and West Bengal opposed the Centre's initiative to implement the recommendations. The recommendations of the Tripathi Committee were further discussed at a conference of Chief Ministers held in New Delhi on February 9-10, 1989. However, no progress could be made in this regard and the matter remained in limbo ever afterwards.

Opposition of non-Congress(I) States was based on the belief that implementation of the scheme would erode their revenue position. However, a close perusal of the recommendations of the Tripathi Committee suggested that it evolved elaborate formulae for protecting the financial interests of the States.

In the case of three commodities, namely paper and paper board, *vanaspati*, and drugs and medicines, it suggested that the annual growth rate of the amount to be collected by way of additional excise duty in lieu of sales tax would be related to the future annual growth rate of sales tax revenue of all the States.

For petroleum products and cement, which were substantially subject to administered prices, the Committee recommended and worked out linkages between the amount to be collected by way of additional excise duty from year-to-year and value of consumption on which normal sales tax would be leviable.

In spite of these safeguards, the apprehension of some States that their resource position would be adversely affected reflected their lack of confidence in the Centre in implementing the scheme sincerely. Thus, an important tax reform became a casualty of the distrust between the Central and the State Governments.

It is pertinent to mention here that during the first two decades of Independence (1947-67), the Congress party ruled, with some exceptions, both at the Centre and in the States. This political homogeneity facilitated taxation agreements between the two tiers of the Government, e.g. the agreement reached in 1957 regarding substitution of sales tax by excise duties on sugar, textiles, and tobacco. Since 1967, the politics of confrontation pursued by different political parties ruling at the Centre and in the States has hindered the process of rationalisation and harmonisation of commodity taxation. In fact, reform of commodity taxation is closely interwoven with the political process.

Additional duties of excise in lieu of sales tax were subsumed under GST when the latter came into force on July 1, 2017.

14.7 Constitution (Forty-sixth Amendment) Act, 1982 and Consignment Tax

Consequent upon the Sixth Amendment of the Constitution, the Central Sales Tax (CST) Act was passed in 1956. Section 14 of the Act declared certain goods to be of special importance in inter-State trade while Section 15 of the Act laid down the rate structure.

However, the CST Act left out of its ambit the consignments (or despatches or stock-transfers) from a company to its branch located in a different State. Since no sale was involved, it was called in-house transaction by a company. The loophole came in handy for unscrupulous parties to evade sales tax by showing virtual sales as consignments from one State to another. By this method, the payment of CST was avoided. Only local sales tax became payable. Therefore, through the Constitution (Forty-sixth Amendment) Act, 1982, the Parliament was empowered to levy 'taxes on the consignment of goods (whether the consignment is to the person making it or to any other person), where such consignment takes place in the course of inter-State trade or commerce'. This was done by inserting Entry 92B in List I (Union List) of the Seventh Schedule and simultaneously amending Article 269 by inserting sub-clause 269(1)(h). Consignment tax was a levy on inter-State transfer of goods.

The States had been pressing the Centre to levy the tax, the net proceeds of which were entirely assignable to States under Article 269. The proposed tax was intended to check avoidance of CST. The Commission on Centre-State Relations, 1988, also impressed upon the Government to "bring in suitable legislation in this regard without further loss of time". [19]

Though the necessary legislation was still to be enacted, industrial and commercial circles expressed grave concern about the deleterious effects of the impending levy. Trade circles maintained that consignments were necessary in view of seasonal fluctuations in the demand for goods as well as frequent transport bottlenecks. Commercial practices like *branch transfer* or *transfer on consignment basis* also helped manufacturer-supplier to reduce avoidable costs of holding high levels of inventory.

The levy has till date not been effectuated and consignment tax has virtually remained still-born in India.

It is noteworthy that as per the Central Goods and Services Tax (CGST) Act, 2017, supply of goods by a principal to his agent even without consideration, is treated as a supply and shall be liable to GST, and thus consignment sales have become taxable under GST.

14.8 Problems Created by Sales Tax

As already noted, under Entry 54 of List II (State List) in the Seventh Schedule of the Constitution, the States were given the power to levy "a tax on sale or purchases of goods other than newspapers". Enjoying this Constitutional right, different State Governments levied sales tax on a wide range of commodities at different rates with diverse procedures and rules for its collection. The Central Government also entered the field in so far as it prescribes the ceiling rate of sales tax on goods in inter-State trade. In the case of three important commodities, viz. textiles, sugar, and tobacco, additional duties of excise were imposed in lieu of sales tax, the proceeds of which were distributed among the States.

Perhaps no other tax impinged on so large a number of interests as sales tax. Firstly, it impacted the consumers who ultimately bore its burden. Next, there were the dealers from whom it was collected, and in many cases the producers also came in its ambit in case it was levied at the manufacturer's level. Then there were the State Governments, always anxious to extend its scope and retain their hold on it. Furthermore, the Central Government decided the rate of sales tax on goods of special importance in inter-State trade. Consequently, the operation of sales tax created a host of problems which may be summarised as follows.

1. Different States adopted different variants of the sales tax due to a number of reasons including administrative convenience, ad hoc measures to increase tax revenues, and to attract enterprise in their respective areas. Sales tax in a State could take the form of a single point, double-point and/or multi-point levy. However, single-point was the main type of sales tax imposed on most commodities in all States. In most States, a significant part of sales tax revenue originated from first-point levy, i.e. at the manufacturer's level.

Some States also levied surcharges on sales tax as an ad hoc measure to augment their resources.

2. The rate structure of sales tax was further complicated in view of different lists of exemptions/concessions, numerous nominal rate categories, and different administrative procedures in each of the States. These variations caused disparities in the effective rate of sales tax on similar commodities in different States. Agricultural commodities like cereals and pulses were either exempted or subjected to low rate of sales tax, ranging from 2 to 3 percent. For most commodities, the rate of single-point levy varied between 4 to 8 percent. However, in the case of luxury items (like motor cars and refrigerators), the rate could go up to even 15 percent in some States. The rate of multi-point levy hovered around 4 percent.
3. Sales tax was a levy on commodities which, in most cases, were also subject to excise duties. As excise duty and sales tax were levied by different layers of Government, it became difficult to determine judiciously the impact of these levies on production, investment, and the consumers. No attempt to rationalise commodity tax system could succeed if the Centre and States acted independently without co-ordination among themselves.
4. A closely related problem was the taxation of inputs and capital goods, by the Central and State Governments, through excise duties and sales tax respectively. Apart from generating cascading effect, sales tax on inputs benefited comparatively richer States at the cost of poorer States. To quote, "The (sales) taxation of inputs also means that its burden falls on consumers outside the State. While procedures exist for refund of excise duties on a product when it is exported outside the country, the sales tax paid on inputs is not rebated. In consequence, the more developed States which have attained high levels of agricultural or industrial production are able to derive additional resources, by taxing consumers in other States, while the resource mobilisation capacity of the less developed States, which have to depend on most of their needs being met by imports from other States, is weakened". [20] This reverse flow of funds was further strengthened by the frequent hikes in the rate of Central sales tax (CST).

   Originally at 1 percent, CST rate steadily increased to 4 percent, thereby imposing undue burden on the importing States and defeating, in the process, the very objective of Central Sales Tax Act of 1956.

   To tackle the problem of cascading effect associated with the taxation of intermediate goods, reforms at the Central level provided instant credit of excise duty paid on inputs under the modified value added tax (MODVAT) scheme. Although State laws did provide relief through exemptions in regards to sales tax when inputs are sold to manufacturers, such concessions were limited and lacked uniformity. This lacuna in the sales tax system hindered reform of indirect tax system in India.
5. In order to attract trade and industry to their respective areas, some States indulged in a kind of *rate war* (competitive reductions in sales tax rates). It is true that some

States lacked infrastructural facilities and to compensate for that sales tax concessions came handy to attract industries, but this shortcut eroded the resource-base of the States, so vital for the development of infrastructure which alone could guarantee their speedy development on permanent footing.

6. Differential rates of sales tax on the same set of commodities in different States often led to uneconomic diversion of trade as well as production centres. It was not uncommon for people of one State making purchases in other States to avoid or reduce sales tax liability. Apparently, purchases from lower tax States to those where rates were higher were beneficial so long as the cost of transporting goods was lower than the tax differential. Purchase of truck chassis in Daman (a Union Territory levying a low rate of 3 percent) by the residents of a far off State of Jammu and Kashmir was a popular case in point.
   Similarly, rate differentials caused flight of capital and enterprise from high to low tax rate States thereby distorting natural selection of production centres based on geographical advantages, leading to unnecessary transportation of raw materials and finished goods and hence cost escalations. Such a misallocation of resources undermined economic efficiency and thereby retarded developmental efforts.
7. Sales tax had another disadvantage in that it discouraged horizontal integration and on the contrary encouraged vertical integration in industries. Firms tried to produce their own components in order to avoid sales tax. This tendency harmed the growth of ancillary units which were mainly in the small-scale sector.

14.9 Alternative Remedies Suggested

To deal with the foregoing weaknesses of the sales tax system, fiscal experts put forward various suggestions from time-to-time. Some of these were as under:

14.9.1 Sales Tax as Central Levy: It was argued that through a constitutional amendment, the levy of sales tax could be made a Central subject and thereafter a rationalised system of indirect taxation of domestic production and consumption could be administered by the Centre. This was a drastic suggestion which did not find favour with statesmen. The Taxation Enquiry Commission (TEC), 1953-54, was quite categorical in rejecting this suggestion. Emphasising the impracticability of centralisation of sales tax the Commission observed, "On account of its yield and flexibility, sales tax has come to occupy a large and indispensable place in the State financial systems. Centralisation of the tax must be ruled out. Difficulties which confront the tax administrations vary considerably in character and composition from State to State and taken together present a large and almost bewildering variety of problems". [21]

The views of the TEC appeared to be valid considering the fiscal arrangements and political equations in the country. Thus, a constitutional amendment to make sales tax a Central subject was ruled out.

14.9.2 Complete Substitution of Sales Tax by Excise Duty: It was suggested, particularly by the business community that in place of sales tax corresponding enhancements could be made in Central excises the proceeds of which could be earmarked for distribution among the States. This would facilitate rationalisation of commodity taxation and also reduce the cost of collection apart from saving the business community from harassment from the differing sales tax practices of the various States.

Was a complete substitution of sales tax by excise duties possible? Probably not! Like sales tax, excise duties could not become universal in scope because of administrative reasons. For instance, the Centre had the legal power to impose excises on agricultural products but it refrained from doing so. Similarly, small and tiny units of the industrial sector were left out because of administrative reasons.

However, what was small for excise duty was large for the purpose of sales tax. The Indirect Taxation Enquiry Committee, 1977, estimated that nearly ₹ 500 crore of sales tax was being collected on goods not subject to excise duties such as agricultural products, articles of jewellery which for administrative or other reasons could not be reached by excises. It concluded, "The consequence of a simple abolition of sales tax from the angle of resource mobilisation would be a substantial loss of revenue to compensate for which something like a 50 percent increase in excise duties on the average would be necessary, given the present base of excise taxation". [22]

Since excise duties were of all-India nature, they could not take into account regional variations in the levels of income and patterns of consumption. However, different rates of sales tax in individual States permitted consideration of regional factors. Moreover, if sales tax was levied at the retail stage, the value base of the tax was large and even low rates of tax could yield sufficient revenues.

14.9.3 Partial Substitution of Sales Tax by Excise Duty: The approach towards substitution of sales tax by excise duties could have been selective. Some arrangements already existed in this regard in the form of additional duties of excise in lieu of sales tax on three important commodities, namely textiles, tobacco, and sugar. The extension of this arrangement to certain other commodities as recommended by Tripathi Committee has already been discussed in section 14.6.4 of this chapter.

See also chapters 7 and 20 of this book.

Endnotes

1. Government of India, Ministry of Finance, *Report of the Taxation Enquiry Commission, 1953-54* (Chairman: John Matthai), Volume III, p. 26.
2. Walter Mahler, *Sales and Excise Taxation in India*, New Delhi: Orient Longman Ltd., 1970, p. 154.
3. *Report of the Taxation Enquiry Commission,* 1953-54, Volume III, *op. cit.*, p. 30.
4. Ibid., p. 519.
5. Under Article 258(1), the Union has the power to delegate to any State Government any of its executive functions (including the power to assess and collect sales tax on inter-State trade). Thus, the power to levy and collect sales tax on inter-State trade belongs to the Centre [Article 269(1)(g)] though it has delegated the power to collect it to the States.
6. Clause (1) of Article 286 was amended by Section 13 of the Constitution (One Hundred and First Amendment) Act, 2016 in the following manner: (a) for the words "the sale or purchase of goods where such sale or purchase takes place", the words "the supply of goods or of services or both, where such supply takes place" shall be substituted; (b) in sub-clause (b), for

the word "goods", at both the places where it occurs, the words "goods or services or both" shall be substituted.

7. Clause (2) of Article 286 was amended by Section 13 of the Constitution (One Hundred and First Amendment) Act, 2016 in the following manner: for the words "sale or purchase of goods takes place", the words "supply of goods or of services or both" shall be substituted.
8. Clause (3) of Article 286 was omitted by Section 13 of the Constitution (One Hundred and First Amendment) Act, 2016.
9. Clause (3) of Article 286 was further amended by the Constitution (Forty-sixth Amendment) Act, 1982. In its present form it is as follows. Any law of a State shall in so far as it imposes, or authorises the imposition of: (a) a tax on the sale or purchase of goods declared by Parliament by law to be of special importance in inter-State trade or commerce; or (b) a tax on the sale or purchase of goods, being a tax of the nature referred to in sub-clause (b), sub-clause (c) or sub-clause (d) of clause (29-A) of Article 366, be subject to such restrictions and conditions in regard to the system of levy, rates and other incidents of the tax as Parliament may by law specify.
10. In 1956, when the Central Sales Tax Act was passed the rate was fixed at 1 percent. Subsequently, it was raised to 2 percent, 3 percent, and 4 percent in 1958, 1966, and 1975 respectively. It was reduced to 3 percent and 2 percent in 2007 and 2008 respectively.
11. Originally, the rate was fixed at 1 percent in 1956. It was raised to 2 percent, 3 percent, and 4 percent in 1963, 1966, and 1975 respectively.
12. It means the States were free to fix the rate of sales tax on the internal sales of non-declared goods but there was a ceiling rate of 4 percent on the sale of such goods in inter-State trade. For example, if the rate of sales tax on internal sale was 6 percent, it was 4 percent for inter-State trade, being lower of the two.
13. In other words, the rate of CST was a minimum of 10 percent. For example, if general sales tax was charged at the rate of 5 percent on the sale of colour television in a State, the rate of CST on the same could be 10 percent, being higher of the two rates. In 1956, the minimum rate was fixed at 7 percent but was raised to 10 percent by the Central Sales Tax (Amendment) Act, 1963.
14. To prepare for the implementation of national level Goods and Services Tax (GST), Central Government began a phased reduction of Central Sales Tax (CST). The Central Government brought down the level of CST over a few years from 4 percent to 2 percent as a precursor to rolling out GST. This was because CST, an origin-based tax, was inconsistent with value added taxes, which are destination based—the two should not co-exist.
15. Internal as well as inter-State sales tax on goods of special importance was governed by the Central Sales Tax Act, 1956. The rate of CST was 4 percent at that time (1957).
16. India's federal system of government creates a dual polity based on divided governmental functions and taxation powers. Taxation laws of the Central Government extend to the whole of the country while those of State Governments are applicable within their respective jurisdictions. A tax belonging to the States may be imposed with a varying base and/or rate in different States. Even the procedures and rules for its collection may differ from State to State. The lack of uniformity in the imposition of State tax laws can cause difficulties for traders and consumers and thus hinder inter-State trade. To overcome these problems, arrangements could be made to transfer from the States, the legal right to levy the tax, to the Centre with the proviso that revenue collected would be assigned to the States. This is known as *tax rental arrangement*.
17. *Second Report of the Ninth Finance Commission,* December 1989, p. 34.

18. Government of India, Ministry of Finance, *Report of the Expert Committee on Replacement of Sales Tax by Additional Excise Duty,* (Chairman: Kamlapati Tripathi), January 1983.
19. Government of India, *Report of the Commission on Centre-State Relations,* (Chairman: Justice R.S. Sarkaria), 1988, Part I, p. 293.
20. Government of India, Ministry of Finance, *Report of the Indirect Taxation Enquiry Committee,* (Chairman: L.K. Jha), 1977, Part I, p. 50.
21. *Report of the Taxation Enquiry Commission,* 1953-54, Volume III, *op. cit.*, p. 519.
22. *Report of the Indirect Taxation Enquiry Committee,* 1977, Part I, *op. cit.*, p. 49.

Part III (B)

Moderate and Rationalized Tax System in the Post-reforms Period (Since 1991)

15

Approach to Tax Reforms

It may be recalled that the external payments crisis of 1991, which led to the initiation of economic reforms in India, was the result of deteriorating fiscal situation during the latter half of 1980s. This period was marked by high and persistent fiscal deficits, accompanied by large revenue deficits. This had led to a significant enlargement of government borrowings from financial intermediaries and increased financing of government deficit through automatic monetisation which aggravated price rise. When the Indian economy faced an unprecedented macroeconomic crisis in 1991, fiscal consolidation constituted a major objective of the policy response. This consolidation was to be achieved through reduction in the size of budget deficit and public debt in relation to gross domestic product (GDP). For this purpose, it became necessary to: (a) enhance tax and non-tax revenue, (b) curtail current expenditure growth, (c) restructure public sector undertaking, including disinvestment, (d) improve fiscal-monetary co-ordination, and (e) deregulate financial system.

Apart from these reforms aimed at fiscal consolidation, a number of institutional measures were also taken during the 1990s. Public sector restructuring and disinvestments were undertaken with a view to increase the efficiency of the public sector undertakings and also to provide additional resources to the government.

The financing of fiscal deficit was another area which saw significant changes as a part of budgetary reforms. With the discontinuation of *ad hoc* 91-day Treasury Bills in April 1997, automatic monetisation of deficits was eliminated. Greater reliance on borrowing at market-related interest rates since 1992 led to a substantial lowering of statutory pre-emption of institutional resources for the government. This also facilitated development of the market for government securities, which witnessed remarkable changes since the latter half of the 1990s.

15.1 Tax Reforms Committee, 1991

Restructuring of the tax system constituted a major component of fiscal reforms initiated since 1991. The main focus of the tax reforms has been on simplification and rationalisation of both direct and indirect taxes with the objective of augmenting revenues and removing anomalies in the tax structure. Government's concern with tax reforms was reflected in the appointment of a number of committees to review the tax system. Among these, Tax Reforms Committee (Chairman: Raja Chelliah), 1991 was the most prominent. [1] It was asked to examine the structure of both direct and indirect taxes with the following terms of reference:

1. Ways of improving the elasticity of tax revenues, both direct and indirect, and increasing the share of direct taxes as a proportion of total tax revenues and of GDP.

2. Making the tax system fairer and broad-based, with necessary rate adjustments, particularly with regard to commodity taxation and personal taxation.
3. Rationalisation of the system of direct taxes with a view to removing anomalies, improving equity and sustaining economic incentives.
4. Identifying new areas for taxation.
5. Ways of improving compliance of direct taxes and strengthening enforcement.
6. Simplification and rationalisation of customs tariffs with a view to reducing the multiplicity and dispersion of rates and to eliminate exemptions which have become unnecessary.
7. Reducing the level of tariff rates, keeping in view the need for mobilising resources to facilitate fiscal adjustment and the objective of promoting international competitiveness.
8. Simplification and rationalisation of the structure of excise duties for better tax compliance and administration.
9. Scope of extending the modified value added tax (MODVAT) scheme.
10. Any other matter related to the above points or incidental thereto.

Based on the recommendations of various committees, tax reforms since 1991 have brought the tax system much closer to international tax practices. In fact, tax reforms are a part of the package to liberalise and globalise the Indian economy. Tax reforms undertaken by the government in tandem with economic reforms since 1991 have helped to rationalise and simplify the tax system considerably. The rates have been moderated and many exemptions and concessions have been weeded out.

The post-1991 period has witnessed a sharp decline in the rates of income tax, excise duties [now subsumed under goods and services tax (GST)] and customs tariff. The theory that high rates of duty lead to higher revenue collection has been discarded in favour of lower rates with fewer exemptions and concessions. GST is the latest addition in the fiscal armoury of Central and State Governments.

15.2 Task Forces on Direct and Indirect Taxes, 2002

At the time of presenting the first batch of supplementary demands for grants to Parliament in July 2002, the Finance Minister proposed the setting up of two task forces to recommend measures for simplification and rationalization of direct and indirect taxes. Accordingly, two task forces were set up in September 2002 under the chairmanship of Vijay Kelkar, Adviser to Minister of Finance and Company Affairs. These Task Forces made important recommendations on toning up tax administration to put in place a system that is simple, effective and at par with international standards.

15.2.1 Task Force on Direct Taxes: It was assigned the following terms of reference:

1. Rationalisation and simplification of the direct taxes with a view to minimizing exemptions, removing anomalies and improving equity.
2. Improvement in taxpayer services so as to reduce compliance cost, impart transparency and facilitate voluntary compliance.

3. Redesigning procedures for strengthening enforcement so as to improve compliance of direct tax laws.
4. Any other matter related to the above points.

The main recommendations on direct taxes related to raising of exemption limit of personal income tax, rationalization of exemptions, abolition of concessional treatment to long-term capital gains, and abolition of wealth tax.

15.2.2 Task Force on Indirect Taxes: It was specifically asked to review the customs and central excise law and procedures and recommend their simplification to reduce cost of compliance and facilitate voluntary compliance. In respect of indirect taxes, the main recommendations related to widening of the tax base, removal of exemptions, expansion in the coverage of service tax etc.

As regards duty exemption for the small scale sector, it recommended that duty exemption should be extended to only small units with a turnover of ₹ 50 lakh. Duty exemption limit for the larger units should be gradually brought down to ₹ 50 lakh as per the following time frame: from ₹ 100 lakh to ₹ 75 lakh by the year 2004-05 and from ₹ 75 lakh to ₹ 50 lakh by the year 2005-06.

Task Force on Indirect Taxes laid down a broad approach to customs tariff reforms in India. It envisaged a zero duty for essential items, 10 percent duty for raw materials, inputs and intermediate goods and 20 percent for final goods by 2004-05. Following introduction of value added tax (VAT) by the states, these duties were proposed to be further reduced to 5 percent for basic raw materials, 8 percent for intermediate goods, 10 percent for finished goods and 20 percent for consumer durables by 2006-07. However, in order to reap efficiency gains from further opening up of the economy, systemic changes in customs procedures and trade facilitation based on modern best practices, which rely on self compliance, may be necessary.

As regards customs exemptions, it recommended removal of all exemptions except in case of:

1. Life-saving goods.
2. Goods of security and strategic interest.
3. Goods for relief and charitable purposes.
4. International obligations including contracts.

15.3 Fiscal Responsibility and Budget Management (FRBM) Act, 2003

The need for improvements in budgetary practices led to the enactment of the Fiscal Responsibility and Budget Management (FRBM) Act, 2003 which ushered the Indian economy in an era of fiscal consolidation based on fiscal policy rules.

FRBM Act is an important legal expression to ensure the conduct of prudent and accountable fiscal policy. It enjoins upon the central government to take appropriate measures to limit annual fiscal deficit in the budget up to prescribed limits. However, it allows the government to exceed the limits on grounds of national security, acts of war, national calamity and other specified reasons.

Highlighting the importance of FRBM, Act, the *Economic Survey*, 2006-07 noted,

"FRBMA is an important institutional expression to ensure fiscal prudence and support for macroeconomic balance. With the enactment of the FRBMA, the traditional annual budgeting moved to a more meaningful medium-term fiscal planning framework. According to the Rules, revenue deficit is to be reduced by an amount equivalent to half percent or more of the estimated GDP at the end of each financial year and eliminated by March 31, 2009. Fiscal deficit is to be reduced by an amount equivalent to 0.3 percent or more of the estimated GDP at the end of each financial year and reduced to no more than three percent of the estimated GDP by the financial year ending on March 31, 2009". [2]

Similarly, all state governments have adopted a rule-based framework for fiscal correction and consolidation by enacting fiscal responsibility legislations of their own. Introduction of rule-based budget management practices has enabled the governments at different levels to take prudent and informed decisions. Besides, these enactments are seen as a demonstration of India's resolve to maintain macroeconomic stability. The emphasis of fiscal management has shifted from short-term considerations to a longer time horizon for the conduct of fiscal policy.

15.4 Abolition of Wealth Tax

An annual tax on net wealth was introduced in India with the enactment of the Wealth Tax Act, 1957, which came into force from April 1 of that year. The rationale behind the imposition of wealth tax lied essentially in furthering the equity objective of tax policy. Since ownership of wealth is the main source of economic inequalities in India, a tax on wealth was intended to reduce its concentration in a few hands to promote vertical equity.

The scope of wealth tax, both in terms of base and rate, was very narrow. It had only decorative value for the statute book. In view of the meagre revenue and problems of administration and compliance, the Task Force on Direct Taxes (Chairman: Vijay Kelkar), 2002 recommended the abolition of wealth tax. In his Budget Speech to the Parliament on February 28, 2015, the Finance Minister announced the abolition of wealth tax. It was a significant measure to reform the tax system.

For details, see chapter 11 of this book.

15.5 Taxation of Services

Service sector is very wide in its range. It includes, *inter alia*, health care, education, social security, leasing, entertainment, credit rating agencies, telecommunications, transport, publicity and advertising, insurance, banking, legal and financial services.

The Central Government had no specific powers to tax services when it introduced service tax on select services in 1994. It was done under its residual powers of taxation vide Entry 97 of List I (Union List in the Seventh Schedule). The collection of service tax was entrusted to the excise department.

However, the Constitution (Eighty-eighth Amendment) Act, 2003 put service tax in the Union List by inserting Entry 92C in that List. Furthermore, service tax was put under Article 268A of the Constitution which specifies that the principles of collection and appropriation of taxes on services would be determined by Parliament. In other words, revenue from service tax was outside the purview of the Finance Commission.

Before its subsumation under GST, service tax was levied on as diverse services such as credit rating on the one hand and mechanised slaughter houses on the other. The standard rate of service tax was 14 percent when it was merged with GST with effect from July 1, 2017.

For details, see chapter 18 of this book.

15.6 State Level Sales Tax/VAT

Prior to tax reforms initiated in early 1990s, sales tax was characterised by a multiplicity of tax rate and exemptions, lack of uniformity across States, large number of exemptions and concessions, and differing procedures for tax collection. It was a nightmare for a business entity doing business in more than one State.

In mid-1990s, most states had agreed to phase out the incentive related exemptions and implement floor rates of sales tax. As part of the nation wide efforts to redesign commodity taxation and the implementation of central value added tax (CENVAT) at the level of the centre, many states modified their sales tax regimes to launch a state level value added tax (VAT) under the scheme prepared by the Empowered Committee for this purpose.

At a meeting of the State Finance Ministers with the Union Finance Minister on June 18, 2004, it was decided that all States would introduce a uniform VAT from April 1, 2005 to replace sales tax. After missing many deadlines, VAT was finally introduced in all the States. Broadly speaking, the experience of implementing VAT was quite encouraging. The new system was received well by all the stakeholders, and the transition was quite smooth.

To pave way for the introduction of GST, sales tax/VAT was abolished by section 17 of Constitution (One Hundred and First Amendment) Act, 2016.

For details, see chapter 20 of this book.

15.7 Introduction of Goods and Services Tax (GST)

After an arduous journey of 12 years—beginning with the mention of Goods and Services Tax (GST) by the then Finance Minister P. Chidambaram in his Budget Speech for 2005-06 on February 28, 2005—GST finally became operative on July 1, 2017. The historic tax reform saw various ups and downs during this period.

GST is a tax on goods and services with comprehensive and continuous chain of set-off benefits up to the retailer level. It is essentially a tax only on value addition at each stage, and a supplier at each stage is permitted to set-off, through a tax credit mechanism, the GST paid on the purchase of goods and services. Ultimately, the burden of GST is borne by the end-user (i.e. final consumer) of the commodity/service.

GST is a comprehensive indirect tax levy on manufacture, sale and consumption of goods as well as services at the national level. GST is an indirect tax for the whole of India to make it one unified common market. GST is designed to give India a world class tax system and improve tax collections. It has ended the long-standing distortions of differential treatment of manufacturing sector and services sector. GST has facilitated seamless credit across the entire supply chain and across all states under a common tax base.

Signifying the spirit of co-operative federalism, GST is a historic and game-changing tax reform. Domestically, it will help improve governance, strengthen tax institutions, facilitate *Make-in-India by making-one-India*, and impart buoyancy to the tax base. Implementation of GST left behind an inefficient, complicated and fragmented indirect tax system.

For details, see chapter 21 of this book.

Endnotes

1. Other committees which examined the tax system of India, included, *inter alia*, the following: (a) Advisory Group on Tax Policy and Tax Administration for the Tenth Five Year Plan (2002-03 to 2006-07) (Chairman: Parthasarathi Shome), 2001; Inter-ministerial Working Group on Customs Tariff (Chairman: Arvind Virmani), 2002; Task Force on Direct Taxes (Chairman: Vijay Kelkar), 2002; Task Force on Indirect Taxes (Chairman: Vijay Kelkar), 2002; White Paper on State-Level Value Added Tax (Chairman: Asim Kumar Dasgupta), 2005; Rationalisation of Customs and Excise Duties on Edible Oils and Oilseeds (Chairman: Ashok Lahiri), 2006.
2. Government of India, Ministry of Finance, *Economic Survey*, 2006-07, p. 18.

16

Income Tax

Tax reforms undertaken by the government in tandem with economic reforms initiated from early 1990s have helped to rationalise and simplify the tax system considerably. The rates have been moderated and many exemptions and concessions have been weeded out. Care has been taken not to re-introduce the concessions and exemptions as they tend to erode the revenue productivity of the taxes and create inequities and inefficiencies which the reforms sought to alleviate.

Prior to tax reforms, rates of income tax were quite high, almost punitive. For example, in 1973-74, the maximum marginal rate of individual income tax was as high as 97.7 percent. When high rates proved counter-productive from revenue angle, the government initiated a series of rate reductions with the result that the present (financial year 2022-23) top rate for individual taxpayers is 30 percent.

16.1 Moderate Rates of Income Tax

Following the recommendations of Direct Taxes Enquiry Committee (DTEC) [Chairman: Justice K.N. Wanchoo], 1971, the government initiated a series of rate reductions in individual income tax. As a result, the maximum marginal rate of individual income tax was 54 percent (including employment surcharge of 8 percent), applicable from the financial year 1990-91.

Consequent upon the recommendations contained in the Interim Report of the Tax Reforms Committee (Chairman: Raja Chelliah), 1991, the number of income tax rates was reduced and the rates themselves were scaled down. The maximum marginal rate was fixed at 44.8 percent (including surcharge) from the financial year 1992-93. The Finance Act, 1994, abolished the surcharge of 12 percent and hence the maximum marginal rate of tax was 40 percent from the financial year 1994-95. From the same year it was made applicable on incomes above ₹ 1,20,000. It may be recalled that the top marginal rate of income tax applied to incomes above ₹ 1 lakh from 1967-68 to 1993-94. The ₹ 1 lakh of 1967-68 was approximately equivalent to ₹ 5.5 lakh of 1993-94. This showed the laxity of the administration in adjusting tax brackets for inflation. It is noteworthy that the Tax Reforms Committee had recommended 40 percent maximum rate inclusive of surcharge for income exceeding ₹ 2 lakh.

The maximum marginal rate of personal income tax was further reduced from 40 percent to 30 percent in the 1997-98 budget. In another significant move, it was made applicable to incomes above ₹ 1,50,000. After further revisions, the maximum rate stood at 30 percent for incomes above ₹ 10,00,000 for the financial year 2022-23.

16.2 Inflation Indexing for Capital Gains

A tax on capital gains was in operation in India for a short period in respect of capital gains which arose during the period April 1, 1946 to March 31, 1948. Following the recommendations of British economist Nicholas Kaldor, the tax was revived in 1956 and made applicable on capital gains arising on or after April 1, 1956. It is levied within the framework of Indian Income Tax Act, 1961. Section 14 of the Act prescribes five broad heads under which the income of an assessee is classified for purposes of computation of total income and the charge of income tax. These are: (a) salaries, (b) income from house property, (c) profits and gains of business or profession, (d) capital gains and (e) income from other sources.

Sections 45 to 55A of the Act relate to the taxation of capital gains. Since capital gains are not annual accruals from a given source but represent appreciation in the market value of assets over a period of time, they are treated on a different footing. The preferential treatment is given to long-term capital gains only.

Pursuant to the recommendations of the Tax Reforms Committee, 1991, the scheme of capital gains tax was drastically recast by the Finance Act, 1992 in the following manner.

1. The cut-off date for valuation of assets acquired in earlier years was shifted from April 1, 1974 to April 1, 1981.
2. A system of indexation was introduced for the first time under which long-term capital gains are now computed by allowing the cost of acquisition and the cost of improvement of the asset to be adjusted for general inflation.
3. A new section 112 was inserted in the Income Tax Act to provide that long-term capital gains would be subject to a flat rate of income tax. The rate of tax is 20 percent.

Presently, concessionary treatment to long-term capital gains is given through inflation indexing, relatively low flat rate of tax, and a set of exemptions.

16.3 Taxation of Partnership Firms

Prior to the financial year 1992-93, taxation of partnership firms was rather cumbersome. For example, the method of taxation differed according to whether the firm was registered or not under the Income Tax Act. Taxation of partnership firms was drastically modified through the Finance Act, 1992. The chief feature of these changes was to avoid double taxation of profits of firms. Thus, from the financial year 1992-93 a partnership firm is taxed as a separate entity. Like a company, it is liable to income tax however small its income may be. There is no distinction between registered and unregistered firms. Similarly, there is no distinction between firms carrying professions or business. The procedure for registration of firms has been abolished. A new procedure for the assessment of a firm as a firm has been prescribed in section 184 of the Income Tax Act. In order to be assessed as a firm, the partnership should be evidenced by an instrument of partnership, specifying the individual shares of the partners and a copy of the same certified in writing by all the partners should be filed along with the first return of the firm.

16.4 Large-scale Tax Evasion

As regards income tax evasion in the country, the Tax Reforms Committee (TRC), 1991 opined, "not more than 30-35 percent of legally taxable income is being disclosed, on the average". [1] In this context it observed, "it would be fair to say that the income tax department which is in-charge of all the Central Government direct taxes is in shambles. It cannot complain of lack of manpower, but the majority of personnel is constituted by inspectors and clerks who are not adequately trained and are paid fairly low salaries". [2] It is necessary to change the attitude of the people towards government and its laws. In this connection, the Committee observed, "...there is a widespread feeling among the electorate that there is considerable waste in government expenditure, that there is excess staff and that the tail to teeth ratio is unduly high. And with it all, it is generally felt that the public which pays the taxes gets poor service and members of the public are treated often not as masters who pay but as supplicants". [3] Moreover, salaried persons envy tax evasion opportunities available to self-employed professionals and retail traders, and are tempted to conceal their incomes from non-salary sources.

16.5 Estimated Income Schemes (Presumptive Tax) [4]

In its Interim Report, submitted in December 1991, the Tax Reforms Committee examined the problems and possibilities of taxing the small business sector. It suggested two new presumptive taxes on small businesses:

1. A fixed tax on businesses whose turnover was less than ₹ 5 lakh.
2. An estimated income scheme on small businesses with a turnover above ₹ 5 lakh but less than ₹ 25 lakh.

The schemes envisaged profit to be a certain percentage of turnover depending on the type of activity from which it was earned. The government introduced the first scheme through the Finance Act, 1992, but deferred its decision to introduce the second scheme.

The presumptive tax system for persons engaged in retail trade with an annual turnover up to ₹ 5 lakh was introduced on an experimental basis. The scheme was in operation initially for two financial years 1992-93 and 1993-94. It was continued after the expiry of these two years. The objective of the new simplified procedure for taxation was to widen the tax base by encouraging shopkeepers (including those engaged in vocations like tailoring, typewriting, photocopying, repair work etc.) and other small retail traders to pay taxes.

Unfortunately, the scheme of presumptive taxation did not gain popularity with small traders and self-employed entrepreneurs. In 1992-93, the first year of the operation of the scheme, 1,16,644 persons opted for the scheme and paid a total tax of ₹ 16.4 crore, as against the anticipated revenue collection of ₹ 140 crore. [5] This was by no means a significant addition to the existing 70 lakh individual assessees under the income tax net. The number of shopkeepers and other small traders was much higher. The scheme touched only the tip of the iceberg.

In the 1997-98 budget, the Finance Minister discontinued the presumptive scheme as it failed to yield the desired results. In its place, he introduced a new estimated income scheme for retail traders. The new scheme was applicable to persons engaged in the business of retail trade of any goods or merchandise having a total turnover of less than ₹ 40 lakh. The income of the trader was estimated at 5 percent of the total turnover.

In the meanwhile, government introduced through the Finance Act, 1994 two new schemes for estimating the income from the business of civil construction and plying or hiring trucks. The Finance Act, 1994 introduced Sections 44AD and 44AE in the Income Tax Act to provide for a method of estimating income from these businesses.

While the section for civil construction applied to all assessees whose gross receipts from the business did not exceed ₹ 40 lakh, the section for plying trucks applied to businessmen owning not more than 10 trucks. Under Section 44AD, the income from these businesses was estimated at 8 percent of the gross receipts paid or payable to an assessee. Income of truck owners was assessed at ₹ 3,500 p.m. per heavy vehicle and at ₹ 3,150 p.m. per medium and light vehicle.

16.6 Digitization of Income Tax Administration in India

In continuation with the government's emphasis on providing a more transparent, efficient and tax-payer friendly tax administration and improving taxpayer convenience, several initiatives have been launched by the Income Tax Department in recent years to promote the use of information technology (IT) and IT-enabled services for efficient and transparent administration of income tax.

Most of the processes and compliance requirements have been shifted to online platforms and the need for the taxpayers to physically visit the income tax office has been eliminated or minimized. Interaction with taxpayers is characterized by a spirit of trust and respect, relying more on voluntary compliance.

16.6.1 Honouring the Honest Platform: Government has consistently adopted reform measures aimed at the long-term benefits of a more transparent, efficient and taxpayer-friendly tax administration. A major step in this direction is the introduction of Honouring the Honest Platform. The platform for Transparent Taxation—Honouring the Honest was launched in August 2020 with the objective to impart greater efficiency, transparency and accountability, and to eliminate physical interface between taxpayers and tax officers.

The key features of the platform are: (a) usage of technology, data analytics and artificial intelligence and (b) recognizing taxpayers as partners in nation-building. The Platform stands on 3 pillars of tax administration reforms namely faceless assessment, faceless appeal, and taxpayers' charter. The platform is designed to ensure fairness by adopting measures like random selection through system using data analytics and artificial intelligence, dynamic jurisdiction, automated random allocation of cases, team-based assessment/review, provision of draft assessment order/review and finalization of the order in different cities and no requirement of physical interface between taxpayers and the department.

16.6.2 Faceless Assessment Scheme 2020: The Faceless Assessment Scheme, 2019 (earlier called the E-assessment Scheme) [6] was based on the idea that automated random allocation of cases across income tax teams with dynamic jurisdiction and elimination of face-to-face contact between the income-tax authorities and the taxpayer can lead to an efficient, non-discretionary, unbiased single window system of assessment. In 2020, the scope of Faceless Assessment Scheme 2019 was broadened by bringing all the pending assessment cases across the country within the purview of the scheme and declaring that any order passed outside the scheme shall be invalid. Faceless Assessment Scheme, 2020 abolished the earlier system of tax administration and assessment based on territorial jurisdiction. It provides for assessment by randomly chosen virtual teams with dynamic jurisdiction.

The scheme establishes a National Faceless Assessment Centre (NFAC) in Delhi, headed by Principal Chief Commissioner of Income Tax, as the sole point of contact between the department and the taxpayer. All notices or communications to and from the taxpayer, and internal communications related to assessment process within the department are routed through the NFAC. To further facilitate and streamline the process of assessment there are various Regional Faceless Assessment Centres which are vested with the power to make assessments.

16.6.3 Faceless Appeals Scheme 2020: Under Faceless Appeals Scheme, 2020, all income tax appeals are finalised in a faceless manner under the faceless ecosystem with the exception of appeals relating to serious frauds, major tax evasion, sensitive and search matters, international tax and Black Money Act. The scheme establishes a National Faceless Appeal Centre (NFApC) as the apex body for conduct of e-appeal proceedings in a centralized manner. Under the NFApC are Regional Faceless Appeal Centres (RFACs) to facilitate the e-appeal proceedings. NFApC is the only point of contact between the taxpayer and the underlying Appeal Units, and Appeal Units and NeAC/Assessing Officer. All internal and external communication takes place electronically and the assessee is not required to attend the proceedings personally or through an authorised representative.

16.6.4 E-filing of Returns, E-payment of Income Tax and Digital Signature: E-filing of income tax return is the process of electronically filing returns through internet which can be filed at any time at any place.

A new e-filing portal was launched in 2021 with improved features such as a new taxpayer-friendly portal integrated with immediate processing of income tax return (ITR), pre-filled returns, free of cost ITR preparation software, new call centre for taxpayer assistance including mobile app function.

This facility is provided to the taxpayers for making income tax payment through internet banking facility or through internet by using credit/debit cards. An assessee can make payment from his own account or from the account of any other person in an authorized bank. However, the challan must clearly indicate the permanent account number (PAN) of the assessee on whose behalf the payment if made

A person desiring to furnish his return of income electronically, may sign it digitally or manually. For signing the return digitally, he is required to obtain a digital signature.

A digital signature is the electronic signature issued by the certifying authority that shows the authenticity of the person signing the same.

16.6.5 Other Simplification Measures: To ease burden of senior citizens above the age of 75 years, they have been given exemption from filing income tax returns if they only have pension income and interest income. In their case the specified bank is responsible for computing their income and deduction of tax.

Certain non-resident persons have also been exempted from the requirement of furnishing of income tax returns, subject to fulfilment of prescribed conditions. The benefit of exemption is available from Assessment Year 2021-22 onwards. Relief has also been provided to NRIs regarding issues being faced on accrued incomes in their foreign retirement accounts.

To reduce the compliance on small charitable trusts running educational institutions and hospitals, relief by way of tax exemption to such trusts has been provided by the Finance Act 2021 by increasing the existing threshold of annual receipts from ₹ 1 crore to ₹ 5 crore. Certain improvements have also been introduced in the registration process for charitable trusts with the department including online process for filing of application, on-line processing of the applications and passing of the registration orders, online filing of donation statements by donee etc.

Faceless Penalty Scheme (FPS), 2021 was launched for greater efficiency, transparency and accountability to the procedure for imposition of penalty. The scheme makes it possible for taxpayers to submit replies and participate in the proceedings at their convenience.

16.7 Taxpayers' Charter

The taxpayers' charter for India comprises of commitments by the Income Tax Department and obligations of the taxpayers.

Traditionally, tax administrations paid limited attention to taxpayer service while performing the functions of regulator and enforcer of tax laws. However, due to an increased demand for better services to the tax payers, there has been a worldwide recognition of the rights of the tax payers, by publishing formal taxpayers' charters including behaviour expected from officials in the revenue department.

The introduction of taxpayers' charter by Government of India as a part of the Honouring the Honest platform is an important step in this direction, as it emphasizes the importance of fair, courteous and reasonable treatment of taxpayers. The taxpayers' charter includes the following as a part of Income Tax Department's commitment:

16.7.1 Taxpayers' Rights: As specified in the charter, these are as under:

1. Courteous, fair and reasonable treatment to taxpayers.
2. Treatment of taxpayers as honest unless the department has a reason to believe otherwise.
3. Fair and impartial appeal procedure and review mechanism.
4. Accurate and complete information for fulfilling tax compliance obligations under the law.
5. Timely decisions in every income tax proceeding (within the time prescribed under law).

6. Collection of the correct amount of tax due as per the law.
7. Respect for privacy of the taxpayer by following due process of law, and ensuring no more intrusive than necessary in inquiry, examination, or enforcement action.
8. Maintaining confidentiality by not disclosing any information provided by taxpayer to the department unless authorized by law.
9. Ensuring accountability for the actions of the tax authorities.
10. Provision to allow taxpayer to choose an authorized representative of his choice.
11. Provision for a mechanism to lodge complaint and ensure its prompt disposal thereof.
12. Fair and impartial system in resolving the tax issues in a time-bound manner
13. Publishing the service standards and report periodically by the tax department.
14. Reduced cost of compliance as the department shall duly take into account the cost of compliance when administering tax legislation.

16.7.2 Taxpayers' Obligations: As specified in the charter, these are as under:

1. Taxpayer is expected to honestly disclose full information and fulfil his compliance obligations.
2. Taxpayer is expected to be aware of his compliance obligations under tax law and seek help of department if needed.
3. Taxpayer is expected to keep accurate records required as per law.
4. Taxpayer is expected to know what information and submissions are made by his authorized representative.
5. Taxpayer is expected to make submissions as per tax law in a timely manner.
6. Taxpayer is expected to pay amount due as per law in a timely manner.

See also chapters 4 and 10 of this book.

Endnotes

1. Government of India, Ministry of Finance, *Interim Report of the Tax Reforms Committee,* (Chairman: Raja Chelliah), December 1991, p. 47.
2. Ibid., p. 37.
3. Ibid., p. 44.
4. Presumptive Tax: In every country, there are some soft-to-tax and hard-to-tax sources of income. Wages and salaries are properly recorded and therefore it is easy to assess and collect taxes on them through the Pay-As-You-Earn (PAYE) system. Similarly, income from securities paid through banks can easily be subjected to deduction at source.

   Contrarily, the three hard-to-tax classes of the non-corporate sector are: (a) unincorporated commercial and industrial units, (b) self-employed professionals, and (c) rich peasantry. The problem of taxing the first two categories relates to accounting difficulties while in the case of third category, it is essentially the lack of political will. Non-reporting and under-reporting of income is quite sizeable in these sectors. The growing small business sector is a tax haven. It is very difficult to enforce a reliable system of book-keeping to assess earnings of this sector. Pragmatically, a system of lump sum taxation may be tried in place of taxation of profits.

   Presumptive tax relates to the use of appropriate indicators of income, wealth etc. instead of the actual records of these tax bases. In the case of income tax, a presumptive tax is imposed on the basis of an estimated taxable income.

5. Government of India, *Economic Survey*, 1993-94, p. 26.
6. **E-assessment Scheme:** Finance Minister Arun Jaitley in his budget speech to the Parliament on February 1, 2018 announced, "We had introduced e-assessment in 2016 on a pilot basis and in 2017, extended it to 102 cities with the objective of reducing the interface between the department and the taxpayers. With the experience gained so far, we are now ready to roll out the e-assessment across the country, which will transform the age-old assessment procedure of the income tax department and the manner in which they interact with taxpayers and other stakeholders. Accordingly, I propose to amend the Income-tax Act to notify a new scheme for assessment where the assessment will be done in electronic mode which will almost eliminate person-to-person contact leading to greater efficiency and transparency". Government of India, Ministry of Finance, Budget Papers (2018-19), Speech of the Finance Minister, para 157.

17

Excise Duties

Prior to their subsumation under the GST, excise duties were an important source of indirect tax revenue for the Central Government. They were levied on a wide range of products of the industrial sector of the economy.

17.1 Present Constitutional Provisions Regarding Union Excise Duties

By virtue of powers vested in it under Entry 84 of List I (Union List) in the Seventh Schedule of the Constitution, the Central Government was authorised to impose, "duties of excise on tobacco and other goods manufactured or produced in India except: (a) alcoholic liquors for human consumption, (b) opium, Indian-hemp and other narcotic drugs and narcotics, but including medicinal and toilet preparations containing alcohol or any substance included in sub-paragraph (b) of this entry". [1, 2]

To pave the way for GST, section 17 of the Constitution (One Hundred and First Amendment) Act, 2016 substituted the following entry for the old Entry 84:

"84. Duties of excise on the following goods manufactured or produced in India, namely: (a) petroleum crude; (b) high speed diesel; (c) motor spirit (commonly known as petrol); (d) natural gas; (e) aviation turbine fuel; and (f) tobacco and tobacco products" (Table 17.1).

Table 17.1: Entry 84 of List I (Union List) in the Seventh Schedule of the Constitution

Before Constitution (One Hundred and First Amendment) Act, 2016	After Constitution (One Hundred and First Amendment) Act, 2016
Duties of excise on tobacco and other goods manufactured or produced in India except: (a) alcoholic liquors for human consumption; (b) opium, Indian hemp and other narcotic drugs and narcotics, but including medicinal and toilet preparations containing alcohol or any substance, included in sub-paragraph (b) of this entry.	Duties of excise on the following goods manufactured or produced in India, namely: (a) petroleum crude; (b) high speed diesel; (c) motor spirit (commonly known as petrol); (d) natural gas; (e) aviation turbine fuel; and (f) tobacco and tobacco products.

Petroleum and petroleum products have been constitutionally included as *goods* under GST. However, it has also been provided that petroleum and petroleum products shall not be subject to the levy of GST till notified at a future date on the recommendation of the GST Council. The present taxes levied by the Centre and the States on petroleum and petroleum products—excise duty/CENVAT by the Centre and sales tax/VAT by the States—will continue to be levied in the interim period. The five petroleum products which have been kept in abeyance for the purpose of GST are the following: (a) petroleum crude, (b) motor spirit (petrol), (c) high speed diesel, (d) natural gas, and (e) aviation turbine fuel.

Tobacco and tobacco products are subject to GST. In addition, the Centre has the power to levy Central excise duty on these products.

It is noteworthy that GST Council is entrusted to make recommendations to the Union and the States on taxes, cesses and surcharges levied by the Union, the States and the local bodies which may be subsumed in the goods and services tax [(Article 279A(4)(a)].

Apart from allocating taxation powers, the Constitution also provides for the sharing of certain taxes between the Centre and the States. Prior to the Constitution (Eightieth Amendment) Act, 2000, excise duties belonged to the category of taxes which *may* be divided between the Centre and the States (Article 272) and the subject matter of this division fell within the purview of the Finance Commission [Article 280(3)(a)]. In other words, the sharing of excise duties was permissive and therefore the States did not enjoy a constitutional right to claim a share out of the revenues from Central excises. However, successive Finance Commissions took the view that permissive sharing, contemplated under Article 272 was not only justified but even necessary in view of the growing financial needs of the States. Therefore, ever since April 1, 1952, the States got a share of the proceeds of Central excises. The Tenth Finance Commission fixed this share at 47.5 percent for the quinquennium 1995-2000. However, the Constitution (Eightieth Amendment) Act, 2000 substituted a new Article for Article 270 under which States were given a percentage share of all Central taxes and duties. However, the surcharge levied for purposes of the Union under Article 271 was excluded from the divisible pool. Moreover, Article 272 of the Constitution was omitted by the same amendment.

Pre-GST system of Union excise duties is explained in the rest of this chapter.

17.2 Various Types of Excise Duties

In accordance with the provisions of the Constitution, various types of excise duties and cesses were imposed by the Union Government on commodities covered by the Central Excise Act, 1944 and other Acts. Before they were subsumed under GST, the important duties in operation were the following.

17.2.1 Basic Excise Duty: Levied under Section 3 of the Central Excise Act, 1944, this was the main duty commonly known as basic excise duty. This duty was fixed with reference to the value, weight, volume, unit, length or area of the excisable goods. These details were given in the Schedule of the Central Excise Tariff Act, 1985.

17.2.2 Additional Duties in Lieu of Sales Tax: These duties were imposed under the Additional Duties of Excise (Goods of Special Importance) Act, 1957, which provided for the levy and collection of additional duties on sugar, tobacco, cotton fabrics, rayon or artificial silk fabrics and woollen fabrics produced or manufactured in India. These duties were in addition to the duties payable under the Central Excises and Salt Act, 1944, and replaced, by agreement with State Governments, the sales tax levied by them on these commodities. The net proceeds from additional excise duties were distributed among the States in accordance with the principles of distribution formulated and the recommendations made by the Finance Commissions from time to time.

17.2.3 Cesses: These were levied under separate enactments on certain commodities and the revenue was earmarked for specific purposes. For example, handloom cess was levied on fabrics to raise funds for developing *khadi* and other handloom industries and for promoting the sale of *khadi* and other handloom cloth. Cesses were also levied under various Acts on tea, jute, indigenous crude oil, paper, sugar, *bidis*, automobiles, vegetable oils, and television sets.

The Central Excise Act, 1944, was the main enactment under which duties were levied on different commodities. Under Section 37 of this Act, a set of rules known as the Central Excise Rules, 1944 were framed to implement the provisions of the Act. Another set of rules under the same section dealt exclusively with the valuation of the excisable commodities and was known as Central Excise (Valuation) Rules, 1975. The Act and the Rules were amended from time to time. Broadly speaking, the Act embodied the substantive law, and the Rules contained both substantive law and procedural matters.

Although the Central Government was empowered to levy duties on agricultural products also, it refrained to do so in view of the administrative difficulties involved. Therefore, the excise system remained confined mostly to the products of the industrial sector with the notable exceptions of tea and coffee.

17.3 Administration of Excise Taxation

There was an elaborate administrative machinery for the collection of excise duties. At the apex level was the Central Board of Excise and Customs (CBEC)—a statutory Board forming part of the Department of Revenue in the Ministry of Finance. The Board, consisting of a chairman and five members, was responsible for the proper collection of customs and Central excise duties, and framing and implementation of related fiscal policies under the control and direction of the Union Finance Minister.

Under CBEC there were 34 Commissionerates of Central excise at the field level, entrusted with the task of collecting Central excise duties. Each of the Commissionerates was headed by a Commissioner of Central Excise who was aided by a number of Additional Commissioners and Deputy Commissioners. A group of Commissionerates was headed by a Chief Commissioner.

For administrative convenience, each Commissionerate was divided into a number of divisions, each such division headed by an Assistant Commissioner. A division was further sub-divided into a number of ranges. Each range was headed by a Superintendent of Central Excise who, in turn, was assisted by a number of Inspectors.

In fact, the range was the basic unit in the administrative set up responsible for the proper assessment of Central excise duties and generation of the statistical information relating to revenue collection. The range was the primary unit which was in contact with the assessees and tried to ensure that the laws and procedures were properly followed by the production units.

To ensure that the goods were properly classified, assessable value correctly determined, and the duties correctly paid, each Commissionerate had an internal audit wing which was headed by an Additional Commissioner directly responsible to the Commissioner of Central Excise. The internal audit was in addition to the statutory audit conducted by the Comptroller and Auditor-General of India.

Each Commissionerate had an anti-evasion wing headed by an Additional Commissioner directly responsible to the Commissioner of Central Excise. The anti-evasion wing made checks on the basis of intelligence and information to ensure that duties were properly paid and there was no evasion of duties or leakage of revenue. In some Commissionerates, there was a separate Commissioner to look after the judicial and adjudication work. There were Commissioners who attended to appeals against orders passed by officers lower in rank to them.

Moreover, a number of supportive organisations under the CBEC undertook work of a specialised nature. Thus, there was the Directorate of Inspection headed by a Chief Commissioner which undertook the inspection of Central excise formations. The Directorate of Anti-Evasion had the responsibility to ensure all-India co-ordination of anti-evasion work. The National Academy of Customs, Excise and Narcotics was entrusted with the task of training officers. The Directorate of Publicity and Public Relations was responsible for printing and publicity. The Directorate of Statistics and Intelligence was responsible for compiling and updating statistical information.

17.4 Revenue Significance of Excise Duties

In the post-Independence period, the relative share of excise duties in Central Government's tax collections had increased precipitously. In 1950-51, excise duties accounted for a modest 16.8 percent of the total Central tax collections: ₹ 68 crore out of ₹ 404 crore. Within a span of 20 years, the proportionate share shot up to 54.9 percent in 1970-71. It declined to 49.3 percent in 1980-81 and further down to 42.6 percent in 1990-91. It stood at 36.3 percent in 2000-01 and 17.4 percent in 2010-11. It was estimated at 19.5 percent in the budget for 2016-17 (Table 17.2). A Government document noted the following reasons for this downward trend, "The buoyancy of excise has suffered because of a variety of factors including numerous exemptions and concessions which have given rise to substantial administrative and legal complexities. Recent years have witnessed an unprecedented increase in litigation". [3] It may be reiterated that most Union excise duties were subsumed under goods and services tax (GST) effective July 1, 2017.

Although excise duties were imposed on a large number of commodities, a substantial proportion of revenue was derived from a limited number of items. These high revenue yielding commodities included iron and steel, motor spirit, tyres and tubes, cigarettes, cement, plastics and refined diesel oil. It is noteworthy that many of the high revenue yielding items were commodities of mass consumption and therefore the burden of excise duties fell on all sections of society.

Tax Reforms Committee (Chairman: Raja Chelliah), 1991, identified many items which were outside the excise net but which could be considered for levying excise duty. Some of the identified items were butter and cheese, skimmed milk powder, spices, fertilisers, feature films, wood pulp, umbrellas, bicycles, toys and sports goods, buttons, and vacuum flasks.

Table 17.2: Trends in the Relative Revenue Significance of Union Excise Duties in Gross Tax Revenues* of the Central Government: Selected Years

(₹ crore)

Central taxes	1950-51	1960-61	1970-71	1980-81	1990-91	2000-01	2010-11	2016-17
A+B Gross tax revenues	404 (100.0)	888 (100.0)	3,206 (100.0)	13,179 (100.0)	57,576 (100.0)	1,88,603 (100.0)	7,93,072 (100.0)	16,30,888 (100.0)
A. Direct Taxes	174 (43.1)	290 (32.6)	870 (27.1)	3,004 (22.8)	11,025 (19.1)	68,306 (36.2)	4,45,962 (56.2)	8,47,097 (51.9)
B. Indirect taxes of which	229 (56.7)	599 (67.5)	2,337 (72.9)	10,175 (77.2)	46,552 (80.9)	1,20,297 (63.8)	3,47,110 (43.8)	7,83,791 (48.1)
Union excise duties	68 (16.8)	414 (46.6)	1,759 (54.9)	6,500 (49.3)	24,514 (42.6)	68,526 (36.3)	1,38,299 (17.4)	3,18,670 (19.5)

* Before transferring States' share in Central taxes.

Figures in parentheses are corresponding percentages of gross tax revenues.

Sources: Government of India, Ministry of Finance, *Explanatory Memorandum on the Budget of the Central Government* (various years); *Receipts Budget* (various years); and *Budget at a Glance*, 2016-17.

17.5 Excise Tariff Structure

Once the commodities for excise taxation were identified, the next step was to formulate a tariff structure for various commodities.

17.5.1 Statutory versus Effective Rates: Rates of excise duty approved by the Parliament were termed as statutory or tariff rates. However, the Government enjoyed the power to exempt, by notification, any excisable goods from the whole or any part of duty leviable on such goods. In exercise of this power, the Government determined and notified from time-to-time the effective rates of duty. The rationale for granting such powers to the executive was that during the period intervening two consecutive budgets, necessary adjustments might have to be made to regulate exports, consumption, and prices of different commodities. However, the delegation of this power to the executive led to frequent changes in excise rates, creating an unsettling atmosphere for trade and industry and problems for the administration.

Moreover, since the notifications were technically not rules, there was no obligation to place them on the table of the House. Consequently, the Parliament did not always have the information on the variations made in the rates approved by it. The determination of the operative or effective rates of duty by executive decisions led to abridgement of Parliamentary control over the excise system.

Under the Central Excise Tariff Act, 1985, the Government was empowered to enhance the rates of duty specified in the Schedule of the Act through notifications. The increase of duty was subject to certain limits and such powers were exercised only in emergent circumstances. The notifications bringing into force such increases were subject to approval by the Parliament. The said limits were: (a) in case where the rate of duty immediately before the issue of notification is nil, a rate of duty not exceeding 50 percent *ad valorem* may be specified, and (b) in any other case, the increase in the rate of duty shall not be more than twice the rate of duty in force immediately before the issue of notification.

17.5.2 Specific versus *Ad Valorem* Duties [4]: In the early days of the excise system of independent India, the emphasis was on specific rates due to administrative reasons. However, the emphasis shifted to *ad valorem* rates when the economy started experiencing frequent spells of inflation. The 1970s saw a big shift from specific rates of duty to *ad valorem* rates. While introducing the change in the 1969-70 budget, the Finance Minister observed, "...*ad valorem* duties are more rational than specific duties whose incidence declines during periods of rising prices and increases when prices fall. *Ad valorem* duties can also act as a spur to reduction in costs and prices". [5] He converted the then existing specific rates into *ad valorem* rates on cement, vegetable products, electric fans, lighting tubes and bulbs, soaps, soda, and sodium silicate. The change of duties on paper and cotton fabrics into *ad valorem* tax was effected in 1976 and on paints, varnishes, radios, and tape recorders in 1977.

However, beginning with the 1980s, the tendency to shift to *ad valorem* rates was not only halted but reversed in view of an unprecedented spurt in litigation which mainly pertained to disputes over classification and valuation of goods for purposes of excise levies. As a measure to combat tax avoidance and evasion, the basis of duty was changed from *ad valorem* to *ad valorem*-cum-specific rate or specific rate on a number of commodities. Important commodities where the shift took place (with year of change given in brackets) were: flat glass, aluminium metal (1982), paper, aerated waters, motor cars, cigarettes, sugar (1983), paper boards, tyres for buses and trucks (1984), gases, tubes and flaps of tyres, and colour television sets (1985).

The balance further tilted in favour of specific duties as the policy of conversion from *ad valorem* rates to specific rates continued right up to 1990-91. In this connection, the Tax Reforms Committee (Chairman: Raja Chelliah), 1991, observed, "As a result of this gradual shift to more and more specific rates over the years, the share of revenue from specific-rated items has increased from a level of about 46 percent of the total revenue in 1981-82 to 65 percent in 1986-87 and has currently (presumably 1990-91) reached a level of about 70 percent". [6] The Committee examined the advantages and disadvantages of *ad valorem* and specific rates of duty and concluded, "the advantages of having *ad valorem* duties far outweigh the administrative benefits derived by switching over to specific duties. In a system of comprehensive taxation with a wide coverage of MODVAT, it would be necessary to have by and large only *ad valorem* duties in order to ensure a rational system of taxation". [7] Following the recommendations of the Committee, a modest switch over to *ad valorem* rates was made in the 1992-93 Budget.

At the time of its subsumation under GST, excise duty was levied at specific rates on cigarettes, coffee, tea, sugar, beverages, mineral fuels, mineral oils, silk, man-made staple fibres, and iron and steel. *Ad valorem* rates of duty predominated for commodities including organic chemicals, pharmaceutical products, leather, footwear, ceramic products, tools and implements, machinery and mechanical appliances, electrical machinery and equipment, and miscellaneous manufactured articles. A few commodities, viz. cotton fabrics, paper and paper boards, were subject to *ad valorem*-cum-specific rates of duty.

17.6 Multiplicity of Excise Tariff

The excise rate structure was provided by the Schedule of the Central Excise Tariff Act, 1985, which included goods ranging from toys to nuclear reactors. The Schedule was divided into 20 sections covering 96 chapters. Goods falling under each chapter were divided and sub-divided into numerous headings and sub-headings. The statutory rate of duty applicable in respect of each item was shown against the appropriate commodity heading/sub-heading. These statutory rates were modified, if necessary, by Government notifications to determine effective rates of duty.

Prior to tax reforms initiated in 1991, excise taxation in India was an interesting example of the multitude of rates which were subject to frequent revisions.

Commodities such as sewing machines, water coolers, and bicycles, though on the tariff list, were completely exempt from the payment of duty. However, a host of other commodities were subject to a wide amplitude of excise rates. The rate of duty on necessities of life like food products (cheese, butter, vegetable oils), pharmaceutical products, and footwear ranged from 10 to 15 percent *ad valorem*. Rates of excise duty on semi-luxuries like washing machines, tape recorders, refrigerators, and colour televisions ranged from 25 percent to 40 percent *ad valorem*. Luxury items like cosmetics and air-conditioners suffered a high rate of duty ranging from 100 to 110 percent.

Most capital goods, classified under chapter 84 of excise tariff, were subject to duty ranging from 15 to 20 percent *ad* valorem. Some important items under this category were machine tools, cranes, agricultural machinery, textile machinery, printing machinery, calculating machines, automatic data processing machines, and other office machines.

Tobacco items were conspicuous by high rates of duty. Successive upward revision of excise duty on cigarettes was a notable feature of tobacco tariff in India. Upward revision of excise duty on cigarettes was almost an annual feature. No surprise that the commodity earned such nicknames as *annual hardy, old faithful* etc.

Broadly speaking, necessities of life were either exempt or paid a low rate of duty, semi-luxuries were moderately taxed, and luxuries and tobacco products stood out distinctly as high-rated tariff items. Capital goods were subject to a relatively low rate of duty.

17.7 Task Force on Indirect Taxes, 2002

Government of India had appointed two task forces on direct and indirect taxes in September 2002 under the chairmanship of Vijay Kelkar. These Task Forces made important recommendations on toning up tax administration to put in place a system that is simple, effective and at par with international standards (see section 15.2 of chapter 15 of this book). The Task Force on Indirect Taxes recommended the following excise duty structure (Table 17.3).

Table 17.3: Central Excise Duty Structure Recommended by the Task Force on Indirect Taxes

Rate (percent)	Description of the commodity
0	Life-saving drugs and equipments, security items, food items, necessities and the like, and agricultural products.
6	Processed food products and matches.
14	Standard rate for all items not mentioned against other rates.
20	Motor vehicles, air-conditioners and aerated water.
Separate rates for tobacco products and their substitutes (like *pan masala*)	

Source: Government of India, Ministry of Finance and Company Affairs, *Report of the Task Force on Indirect Taxes*, December 2002, p. 181.

17.8 Simplification of Excise Tariff

17.8.1 Triple Rate Excise Structure: Multiple rates of commodity taxes were long considered a weakness of the indirect tax system of India. Admitting the problems created by the multiplicity of rates, the Finance Minister in his 1999-2000 budget speech observed, "The multiple rates of indirect tax are generally recognised to be a major source of misclassification, tax evasion and avoidance and cumbersome litigation. The multiplicity also encourages inefficient allocation of resources. Over a 100 countries in the world now enjoy the benefits of a value added tax (VAT) with very small number of rates in each case". [8]

Thus, in a landmark move, the Finance Minister announced in his 1999-2000 budget a triple rate excise structure. In other words, the then existing 11 major ad valorem rates were reduced to 3, viz. a central rate of 16 percent, a merit rate of 8 percent and a demerit rate of 24 percent. This was done by: (a) merging the existing rates of 5 percent, 10 percent and 12 percent into the existing 8 percent rate, (b) creating a new rate of 16 percent by merging the existing 13 percent, 15 percent and 18 percent rates into it, and (c) fixing a new rate of 24 percent in substitution of the existing rate of 25 percent. The initiative of the Finance Minister to rationalise the rate structure of excise system was widely appreciated.

17.9 Excises on Inputs and the Introduction of Modified Value Added Tax (MODVAT) and Central Value Added Tax (CENVAT)

One perennial problem of the Indian excise system was the taxation of inputs (raw materials, components, and other intermediates) and the resulting cascading effect on the prices of final products. Prior to the Second Five Year Plan (1956-61), excise coverage was limited to consumer goods with the notable exception of steel ingots. However, the need for additional resources for successive Plans necessitated extension of the excise net to capital goods and raw materials. Various inputs like internal combustion engines, aluminium, cotton yarn, woollen yarn, fertilisers, chemicals, were brought within the excise ambit. The disadvantages of input excises are well-known. [9] However, levies on inputs formed an integral part of the excise system in India for reasons of sheer administrative convenience.

17.9.1 Pre-MODVAT Arrangements: Prior to 1986, excise duty was levied on both inputs used and the output produced. This meant that an amount paid as tax on the input was subject to taxation again at the output level (with limited set offs). This was applicable to each intermediate good in the manufacturing process. This *tax on tax* led to cascading of taxes. This problem was sought to be addressed by the VAT regime under which tax paid on the inputs was deducted from the tax payable on the output. Similarly, sales tax also had a cascading effect through the distribution chain.

Prior to the introduction of MODVAT in 1986, there were provisions in the Central Excises and Salt Rules, 1944, under which certain inputs were exempted from taxation to minimise the cumulative effect of excise levies. Thus, Rule 56-A of the said Rules, introduced in 1962, allowed the manufacturers of certain notified finished excisable goods to bring excise-paid components (for example compressors for refrigerators) to take credit for the said duty in the Proforma Credit Account to get adjustment of duty on the final excisable good.

The Indirect Taxation Enquiry Committee (Chairman: L.K. Jha), 1978, which made an in-depth study of the cascading effect of input excises, recommended a wider extension of Rule 56-A to products falling under different tariff items. The same Committee recommended also the introduction of value added tax (VAT) at the manufacturing stage, called MANVAT, to tackle the problem of cascading effect of excise taxation.

The Long Term Fiscal Policy Statement (December 1985) also envisaged the introduction of a modified system of VAT or MODVAT for short. The government introduced MODVAT with effect from March 1, 1986. It was introduced for a selected number of commodities and in a step-by-step manner for all commodities in terms of CENVAT in 2002-03.

17.9.2 MODVAT Scheme: Features and advantages of MODVAT scheme were as under.

MODVAT scheme provided for instant and complete reimbursement of excise duty and additional duty of customs (countervailing duty) paid on the components and raw materials when used in the manufacture of the final products. Articles which were not used as inputs in the manufacturing process were not eligible for credit under this scheme.

Initially, the MODVAT scheme covered 38 chapters of the schedule to the Central Excise Tariff Act, 1985. These chapters pertained to the products of chemical and allied industries, paints and packaging materials, plastics, glass and glassware, rubber products, base metals and articles of base metals, machinery and mechanical appliances including electrical equipment, motor vehicles, and certain miscellaneous manufactured products. In 1987, the scheme was extended to all the remaining chapters (except those relating to textiles, tobacco, and the petroleum sector). The extension covered food products, mineral products, leather and travel goods, footwear, paper and paper-board, wood and cork products, asbestos cement products, and precious metals. As long as the inputs and the final products were covered by the specified chapters, credit of duty on inputs was available. In 1994, MODVAT scheme was extended to tobacco, fibres, yarn and fabrics, and petroleum products (excluding motor spirit and high speed diesel oil) used as input.

MODVAT scheme was further expanded and rationalised in the sense that all inputs (excepting motor spirit and high speed diesel oil) and all capital goods were included in the eligible list of MODVAT scheme. However, the availability of MODVAT credit on capital goods was spread over a period of 2 years.

A. Features: The features of the MODVAT scheme were as follows:

1. The credit under MODVAT was available to a manufacturer of a final product only if the final product was dutiable. Where the final product manufactured by a manufacturer was exempt from excise duty then no credit of the duty paid on the inputs was available. Credit was allowed only after the evidence of payment of duty was received by the excise department.
2. Where the same input was used for different finished products, some of which were not dutiable, the credit of duty was allowed only for that part attributable to inputs which were used for the manufacture of dutiable finished products.
3. Credit of the duty paid on the inputs under the MODVAT scheme could be utilised for payment of duty on the final products in which the inputs were used.
4. Under the MODVAT scheme, credit of duty was not restricted to raw materials and components only but covered all specified inputs which were used in the manufacture of final products.
5. Machines, plant, equipments, apparatus, tools or appliances used in the manufacture of the final products were not covered by the term *inputs* for the purpose of MODVAT benefits.
6. Under the MODVAT scheme, inputs could be either procured from outside or manufactured within the factory. In either case, the duty credit was available to the extent of duty actually paid.

The Government had made it clear in its Long Term Fiscal Policy Statement (1985) that the proposed MODVAT scheme was to be broadly revenue-neutral. Thus, along with the introduction of MODVAT which considerably reduced the cost of final products, the rates of duty on final products were suitably revised upwards by the Finance Act, 1986, to retain the collection of excise duties at the earlier level. This was justified on grounds of resource mobilisation for the Five Year Plans.

B. Advantages: MODVAT scheme had the following advantages:

1. It aimed at making excise levies transparent so that the effective rate of taxation on a particular commodity could be known. This information was helpful in undertaking meaningful studies of excise incidence. The results of these studies could be used to control excise burden on different commodities to ensure the desired degree of progressivity in the excise levies.
2. It sought to avoid cascading effects associated with a traditional turnover tax. In particular, it worked as a cost-saving device through the availability of instant credit

of the duties paid on the inputs and the consequent reduction of the interest costs.

3. MODVAT scheme improved the competitive strength of the small-scale sector by allowing credit of duty which could be in excess of the duty actually paid on the inputs made by the small-scale units.
4. MODVAT scheme encouraged indigenisation because full set off was available when indigenous inputs were used. However, no credit of basic and auxiliary customs duties was permissible on imported materials and components. Although MODVAT scheme provided for set off of countervailing duty [10], this element of import duty was not very significant in comparison with other elements of import duty, viz. basic and auxiliary duties. As the scope of MODVAT was widened, the process of indigenisation gathered momentum.
5. MODVAT scheme was designed to encourage exports by making them more competitive in the international market. Since MODVAT allowed set off through different stages of production, the final duty became clear on final goods which could be exported without payment of duty under bond. The payment of duty drawback was swifter in view of the transparency of excise duty.
6. MODVAT checked excise evasion because credit of input duty could not be claimed unless actual production was declared to the excise authorities.
7. MODVAT scheme also helped to reduce the number of disputes—arising on account of classifications requiring lower or higher rates of duty—because the duty element on a large number of components became irrelevant for manufacturers in view of set off. Previously, a selective set off triggered disputes as regards the eligibility of an input for set off. The introduction of Harmonised System Nomenclature in 1986 further reduced the scope for ambiguities.

Some experts felt that MODVAT was old wine in a new bottle because the facility under it was practically the same as was available under Rule 56-A as mentioned above. In other words, MODVAT scheme was only an extension and liberalisation of the proforma credit facility already in operation. Though some degree of similarity did exist, the two schemes could not be termed identical. Rule 56-A scheme was restrictive and had several procedural formalities, e.g. a manufacturer had to intimate the Excise Department about the arrival of input materials for verification by the excise officials. Moreover, it was applicable on a commodity-to-commodity basis and involved discretion in taking decisions. MODVAT scheme was more comprehensive and rule-based and therefore curtailed the discretionary powers of the Excise Department. MODVAT credit on inputs could be availed on the basis of a duplicate copy of the invoice.

The Tax Reforms Committee (Chairman: Raja Chelliah), 1991, examined, *inter alia,* the scope of extending the MODVAT scheme and observed, "there is no alternative to gradually transforming the present excise tax system, consisting of two parts, namely: (a) MODVAT, and (b) excise on gross value basis with no set off for some sectors, into a genuine VAT at the manufacturing level. Manufacturing and such a VAT should include also the 'manufacture' of services although some services may be exempted on practical considerations". [11]

17.9.3 Introduction of CENVAT: As already noted, in his 1999-2000 budget, the Finance Minister had introduced three ad valorem rates of basic excise duty, namely 8 percent, 16 percent and 24 percent. Furthering the reform of excise taxation, the 2000-01 budget introduced a single rate CENVAT by converging the three ad valorem rates to a single rate of 16 percent. The 8 percent excise rate was abolished and most of the items under it were moved to 16 percent rate. Similarly, items that were mainly in the nature of raw materials or intermediates were moved from the 24 percent rate to 16 percent CENVAT. However, in addition to the 16 percent CENVAT rate, three rates of special excise, viz. 8 percent, 16 percent, and 24 percent were introduced. While the CENVAT rate was modvatable, the special excise duties were not, i.e. users could not avail of MODVAT credit of these duties. Some of the commodities on which special excise duties applied included white cement, glazed tiles, cosmetics, air conditioners, aerated water and chewing tobacco. Since these commodities were not in the nature of inputs therefore they were not modvatable.

The standard rate of excise duty (CENVAT) was brought down to 8 percent after two successive reductions in December 2008 and February 2009. It was increased to 10 percent in the Budget for 2010-11. It was further increased to 12 percent in the Budget for 2012-13 and remained the same for the financial year 2013-14 and 2014-15.

Undoubtedly, the Government provided a stable excise system to create confidence among the entrepreneurs, particularly the prospective ones, so that they could plan their investment and production without the Damocles sword of excise changes hanging over their heads. The application of CENVAT at fewer rates and the new system of CENVAT credits resulted in fewer classification disputes, reduced tax cascading, and greater neutrality of the tax. It was also hoped that CENVAT would encourage the State Governments to implement their agreed programme for converting their sales tax into VAT by April 1, 2001.

However, CENVAT was levied on goods manufactured or produced in India. This gave rise to definitional issues as to what constituted manufacturing, and valuation issues for determining the value on which the tax was to be levied. While these concepts had evolved through judicial rulings, it was recognized that limiting the tax to the point of manufacturing was a severe impediment to an efficient and neutral application of tax. Manufacturing itself formed a narrow base.

Moreover, the effective burden of tax became dependent on the supply chain, i.e. the taxable value at the point of manufacturing relative to the value added beyond this point. It was for this reason that virtually all countries had abandoned this form of taxation and replaced it by multi-point taxation system extending to the retail level.

The starting base for the CENVAT was narrow, and was further eroded by a variety of area-specific, and conditional and unconditional exemptions.

Under the Constitution, the Central Government was empowered to impose excise duty on goods produced or manufactured. It had no power to carry forward the tax up to the retail stage. Thus, CENVAT was a kind of VAT at the manufacturing stage. In any case, it paved the way for a national VAT.

17.10 Exemptions and Concessions

17.10.1 Rationale: As in other countries, exemptions and concessions were an integral part of the excise system. Excise preferences and reliefs were given to promote a wide spectrum of socio-economic objectives. Exemptions/concessions were justified on following grounds:

1. Exemptions/concessions ensured progressivity in the structure of commodity taxation.
2. They induced entrepreneurs to undertake activities which they would have otherwise shrunk, e.g. adopting labour-intensive techniques of production.
3. They were designed to promote enterprises deemed *vital* by society (though it is controversial as to which activities are *vital* and require governmental support).
4. Exemptions/concessions provided the desired flexibility to the tax system to deal with changing market situation. They were used as a corrective mechanism to stabilise demand, production, and profits of different industries.
5. Due to continuous diversification of the economy and inflation, markets for various commodities had not remained stable in India after Independence. Because of the changing market conditions, the levels of profit in different industries had also been fluctuating and on balance had shown a rising trend. Excise rates, it was argued, should be modified upward to mop up excess profits and downward to boost sluggish demand for idle-capacity industries.
6. Exemptions were sometimes granted on administrative considerations. The duty on unmanufactured tobacco was abolished in 1979 mainly on account of the administrative difficulty of assessing and collecting duty from a large number of growers, and curers. Similarly, exemption of smaller of the small industries was also due to administrative problems. Agricultural products were also exempt owing to the same reason.

17.10.2 General Exemptions: There were various general exemptions which purported to serve a wide variety of socio-economic objectives. Thus, goods of the following description were exempt from the whole of the duty of excise leviable thereon.

1. All excisable goods, produced in a technical, educational and research institute during the course of imparting technical training of an academic or vocational nature.
2. All excisable goods donated for the welfare of defence personnel.
3. All excisable goods donated to the National Defence Fund or to the Ministry of Defence.
4. Excisable goods, supplied as stores for consumption on board a vessel of the Indian navy.
5. All excisable goods sent abroad as exhibits in any international trade fair or exhibition.

Apart from these general exemptions, excise tariff was extensively used to serve a host of other objectives including export promotion, industrial development, and mopping up a part of high profits earned by certain industries.

17.10.3 Labour-intensive Technology: Excise exemptions and concessions were particularly important in promoting labour-intensive technology and small-scale industries. Central excise law contained provisions the sole objective of which was employment generation. Products of a number of industries were exempt from excise duty if they were manufactured without the aid of power. Duty differentials were used to discourage mechanisation in certain industries.

Similarly, concessions were available to the handloom sector of the textile industry. Processed *khadi* cloth woven on handloom wholly from hand spun cotton yarn or in admixture with similar silk and/or woollen yarn enjoyed full exemption since 1969. Cotton fabrics manufactured on handlooms and processed by a factory owned by a registered handloom co-operative society enjoyed full exemption from duty.

17.10.4 Concessions to Small Industries: In line with Government's policy of encouraging small-scale industries, a wide range of concessions and exemptions from excise duty was available to small producers to enable them to stand in competition with large-scale manufacturers. Also, relatively simple and concessional procedures were followed for the assessment and collection of excises from the small-scale sector. As a part of the Comprehensive Policy Package on SSI and Tiny Sector announced by the Prime Minister on August 30, 2000, the excise exemption limit for SSI was raised from ₹ 50 lakh to ₹ 1 crore with effect from September 1, 2000.

As regards duty exemption for the small-scale sector, the Task Force on Indirect Taxes (Chairman: Vijay Kelkar), 2002 recommended as under:

- Duty exemption should be extended to only small units with a turnover of ₹ 50 lakh.
- Duty exemption limit for the larger SSI units should be gradually brought down to ₹ 50 lakh as per the following time frame: from ₹ 100 lakh to ₹ 75 lakh by the year 2004-05 and from ₹ 75 lakh to ₹ 50 lakh by the year 2005-06.

17.10.5 Problems Created by Exemptions/Concessions: These were as follows:

1. Excise concessions narrowed the tax base and therefore adversely affected government revenues.
2. Excise concessions interfered with the designing of the excise system and led to complexities in the excise law which, in turn, led to tax evasion and litigation.
3. They also obscured the evaluation of excise system, particularly from equity angle.
4. Excise concession to a particular industry led to a chain reaction (i.e. similar demands by other industries), causing unsettling effects on producers, consumers, and the administration.
5. Exemptions/concessions were often the result of persistent representations and pressure tactics by industry and trade than any economic justification.
6. It was not always possible to segregate the effects of duty reduction on production, costs, prices, and consumption because duty concessions operated in conjunction with other non-tax policy measures to affect the production process.

17.10.6 Misuse of Concessions: Though preferential treatment to small units and labour-intensive methods of production was desirable, the misuse of these concessions created doubts as regards the ultimate beneficiaries of such facilities. Concerned about the misuse of excise concessions, the Finance Minister in his 2001-02 budget speech announced the withdrawal of exemption on certain items and observed, "Products of SSI are exempt from excise duty up to ₹ 1 crore. This exemption is intended to provide fiscal support to the genuinely small producers. I propose to withdraw this exemption in respect of the following items, in which misuse of the exemption is more than likely: (a) cotton yarn, (b) ball or roller bearings, and (c) arms and ammunition for private use". [12]

It was well-established that certain products—particularly footwear, domestic electrical appliances, electronic goods, and wires and cables—were purchased on a fairly large scale by established concerns from the exempted sector and marketed in the brand names of such concerns. However, under a scheme introduced in 1986, a small-scale manufacturer of excisable goods was allowed to clear his goods with the brand name of another manufacturer and was eligible for exemption for such clearances. Clearly, the small producers depended heavily on private marketing organisations to sell their products and this dependence needed to be reduced by strengthening and building up co-operatives and other officially sponsored marketing organisations to market the products of small sector.

See also chapters 5 and 12 of this book.

Endnotes

1. Excise duties on liquor and other narcotics are imposed by the State Governments under provisions of Entry 51 of List II (State List) in the Seventh Schedule.
2. Duties of excise on medicinal and toilet preparations containing alcohol were levied by the Centre under Article 268 but they were collected and appropriated by the States within which they were leviable. These were levied by the Centre to ensure uniformity in their rate throughout the country. Section 6 of the Constitution (One Hundred and First Amendment) Act, 2016 abolished the duties of excise on medicinal and toilet preparations.
3. Government of India, Ministry of Finance, *Long Term Fiscal Policy*, 1985, p. 25.
4. **Specific versus *Ad Valorem* Taxes:** This classification is relevant in the case of taxes/duties on commodities. Thus, excise levies, customs duties and sales taxes on commodities may take specific or *ad valorem* form.

   A specific or volumetric duty represents a fixed amount of tax on a unit of the physical quantity of the product. Specific duty is generally preferred for commodities the classifications and sub-classifications of which are not numerous, i.e. the commodity is a standardised one, e.g. sugar. A specific duty is easy to apply besides having the political and psychological advantages of obscuring the actual ratio of the tax to the selling price. It is, however, price-neutral in the sense that price changes, if any, in the commodity do not affect the revenue yield. Specific duty is quality-neutral also unless differential rates are prescribed with reference to the quality of the product. There can be many variants of the specific form of duty. If a flat amount per unit of a commodity is levied irrespective of the price range, it is a simple specific duty. It may be simple specific with initial exemption. However, if the flat amount per unit changes with the price range of the commodity, it becomes a graduated specific duty.

   An *ad valorem* (according to value) duty is imposed as a fixed percentage of the price of the product taxed. This form of duty is preferred when a commodity has many classifications and sub-classifications, e.g. textiles. An *ad valorem* duty is responsive to price changes and thus ensures an undiminished proportion of taxes in national income. The main problem in applying *ad valorem* rate is the determination of the tax base, i.e. valuation of production. An *ad valorem* duty may be a simple one, a duty collected as a fixed proportion of the price irrespective of the price range. As a variant of this, the commodity in question may be completely exempted till the price reaches a pre-determined maximum level. When different duty rates apply to different price brackets of a commodity, it becomes a graduated or bracketed *ad valorem* duty. So long as the price remains within a single bracket, the rate of the duty remains the same. Generally, commodities in higher price brackets bear a higher duty rate and vice versa.

Sometimes, both specific and *ad valorem* duties are levied on a single item. This pattern is called specific-cum-ad valorem duty or compound duty.

5. Government of India, Ministry of Finance, *Speeches of Union Finance Ministers, 1947-48 to 1984-85*, p. 313.
6. Government of India, Ministry of Finance, *Interim Report of the Tax Reforms Committee,* (Chairman: Raja Chelliah), 1991, p. 113.
7. Ibid., p. 114.
8. Government of India, Ministry of Finance, *Budget Speech of the Finance Minister*, 1999-2000, Part B, p. 21.
9. Excises on inputs enhance costs and profits and therefore increase the prices of goods much more than the amount of excise collected. The cost of production increases because producers and middlemen require larger amounts of working capital to maintain the necessary stocks of inputs. Prices of finished products tend to reflect taxes imposed on inputs used. If the middlemen apply fixed percentage mark ups to purchase prices as their profit and if the purchase prices include taxes, the mark ups will be applicable to the tax component of the purchase price as well. In other words, increase in the price of the manufactures is in excess of the excise revenue accruing from input taxes.

   Further still, excises on inputs may promote vertical integration in an industry, a trend which is harmful to the growth of small-scale sector. Lastly, input excises impose an inequitable burden on different economic classes by not discriminating between essential and non-essential uses of a product. For example, an excise on aluminium hits indiscriminately the use of the product for decoration purpose as well as for making utensils (generally used by the poor).

   Notwithstanding the various disadvantages of input excises, governments in many countries impose duties on inputs due to administrative convenience. Many items of inputs are the end-product of one manufacturer but merely a component for another (e.g. tyres and tubes) and are also used as replacement items. Exemption of such items will be discrimination in favour of replacement consumption and certain commodities (say motor cars) may be sold with avoidable components and accessories stripped off. Moreover, provisions can be made in tax laws to minimise the cascading effects of input excises.
10. Countervailing duty is an element of import duty equivalent to excise duty on domestically produced goods.
11. Government of India, Ministry of Finance, *Final Report of the Tax Reforms Committee,* (Chairman: Raja Chelliah), Part I, 1992, p. 36.
12. Government of India, Ministry of Finance, *Budget Speech of the Finance Minister, 2001-2002, Part B*, p. 27.

18

Service Tax

Service tax was abolished by Section 17 of Constitution (One Hundred and First Amendment) Act, 2016 to pave way for the introduction of GST from July 1, 2017. Main features of the service tax at the time of its abolition are presented below.

18.1 Need for Service Tax

From equity point of view, services should be taxed in the same way as goods. Taxation of goods and exclusion of services distorts the relative prices of goods vis-à-vis services, encouraging artificially the demand for services. In the process, the allocation of resources is also distorted. If tax is imposed on goods and not on services, a relatively high rate of tax would be required on goods to generate a given amount of revenue. If tax is imposed both on goods and services, a moderate tax rate can yield the given revenue. Administratively, taxation of both goods and services is desirable because it would reduce disputes pertaining to distinction between goods and services.

Service sector is very wide in its range. It includes, *inter alia*, healthcare, education, social security, leasing, entertainment, credit rating agencies, telecommunications, transport, publicity and advertising, insurance, banking, legal and financial services.

Till 1994, Indian tax system traditionally relied on commodity taxation for generating revenue for the Central and State Governments. The two major commodity taxes of the Central Government were excise duties and customs duties while at the level of the States, sales tax/VAT was the main commodity tax. Tax revenue from the agricultural sector being negligible, the industrial sector continued to constitute the only principal tax base till the mid-1990s. The extension of excise duties to more and more commodities of the industrial/manufacturing sector reached a saturation point in due course of time.

The composition of national income in India had changed steadily over the years. While the share of agriculture and allied activities in the gross domestic product (GDP) had declined, that of the tertiary sector had increased. The expansion of services sector was conducive for employment generation and improved quality of life. The compositional shift of GDP in favour of the services sector, was in line with the development experience of a number of countries. It is well-known that as an economy develops, the shares of industrial and service sectors in GDP increase at the cost of the agricultural sector.

Despite the fact that the services sector had shown substantial buoyancy , it remained outside the tax net till 1994. This pattern of tax structure development in India was contrary to the experience of most other countries where taxation of commodities and services grew hand in hand. In this connection, the Finance Minister, in his 1994-95 Budget

Speech to Parliament, observed, "There is no sound reason for exempting services from taxation when goods are taxed and many countries treat goods and services alike for tax purpose". [1]

The Tax Reforms Committee (TRC) [Chairman: Raja Chelliah], 1991 also recommended imposition of tax on certain select services, viz. advertising, non-life insurance and telephone services and services of stock brokers.

Thus, in order to impart buoyancy to government revenues and to provide consistency and equity in the tax structure via-a-via the composition of income, a modest effort was made in the 1994-95 budget when a 5 percent tax was imposed on telephone and non-life insurance services and services of stock brokers with effect from July 1, 1994.

The introduction of service tax ushered in a major structural change in the system of indirect taxes in the form of a wider tax base and facilitated the process of rationalization of excise duties, resulting in lower tax burden on productive sectors. Over the years, the number of services subject to service tax increased and so also the rate leviable on them.

18.2 Constitutional Provisions

The Central Government had no specific powers to tax services when it introduced service tax on select services from July 1, 1994. It was done under its residual powers of taxation vide Entry 97 of List I (Union List) in the Seventh Schedule of the constitution. The tax extended to the whole of India except the State of Jammu and Kashmir. The service tax being an indirect tax, its administrative control was vested with the Central Board of Excise and Customs (CBEC). The sharing of the revenue from service tax was on the basis of the recommendations of the Finance Commission, as applicable to other central taxes.

However, the Constitution (Eighty-eighth Amendment) Act, 2003 put service tax in List I (Union List) of the Seventh Schedule by inserting Entry 92C in that List. Furthermore, this amendment inserted a new Article 268A which provided for service tax to be levied by the Union and collected and appropriated by the Union and the States. The new Article was as follows:

268A. "(1) Taxes on services shall be levied by the Government of India and such tax shall be collected and appropriated by the Government of India and the States in the manner provided in clause (2).

(2) The proceeds in any financial year of any such tax levied in accordance with the provisions of clause (1) shall be:

(a) collected by the Government of India and the States;

(b) appropriated by the Government of India and the States;

in accordance with such principles of collection and appropriation as may be formulated by Parliament by law".

Thus, Article 268A specified that the principles of collection and appropriation of taxes on services will be determined by Parliament. In other words, the revenue from taxation of services was excluded from the purview of the Finance Commission.

In this connection, the Twelfth Finance Commission remarked, "With service taxes having been excluded from the ambit of the recommendations of the finance commission, the idea of an overall shareable pool of central taxes appears to be in the process of being reversed. While service taxes are likely to prove highly buoyant in the near future, these will not be subjected to sharing with the states under the Constitution, although other statutory arrangements can be made, which can include sharing as well as assignment. It may be noted that hitherto items under Articles 268 and 269 were subjects that were generally of inter-state nature with limited revenue importance. These were wholly assigned to the states. In this context, it needs to be stressed that any legislation passed by Parliament with respect to appropriation of service tax proceeds must take care to ensure that the revenue accruing to the states through any proposed changes should not be less than the share that would accrue to them, had the entire service tax proceeds been part of the shareable pool". [2]

It is noteworthy that the above mentioned provisions (Entry 92C and Article 268A) of Constitution (Eighty-eighth Amendment) Act, 2003 were never brought into force. In other words, these provisions were never notified. Hence, tax on services continued to be levied under the residuary entry, i.e. Entry 97 of List I (Union List) in the Seventh Schedule of the constitution These two items (Entry 92C and Article 268A) were omitted by the Constitution (One Hundred and First Amendment) Act, 2016 to pave way for the introduction of Goods and Services Tax (GST) which was finally rolled out on July 1, 2017.

Apart from the Centre, the States also had powers to tax certain services specified in clause (29A) of Article 366 of the Constitution. This sort of division of taxing powers created a grey zone which led to confusion and legal disputes. This problem was solved with the implementation of GST.

18.3 Introduction and Widening of Service Tax

In view of the need for additional resources, rising contribution of service sector to GDP and the recommendations of Tax Reforms Committee, 1991, a modest effort was made in the 1994-95 budget when a 5 percent tax was imposed on telephone and non-life insurance services and services of stock brokers with effect from July 1, 1994. The coverage of service tax was extended to advertising, courier and radio paging services from November 1, 1996.

In his 1997-98 budget speech, the Finance Minister maintained that services are products as much as manufactured goods and hence both must bear taxes. With these considerations in view he extended the service tax to the services provided by the following: transporters of goods by road, consulting engineers, custom houses, steamer and clearing and forwarding agents, air travel agents, tour operators and car rental agencies, outdoor caterers, *pandal* contractors and *mandap* keepers, and manpower recruitment agencies.

In the 1998-99 budget, service tax on the transportation of goods by road, outdoor caterers, and *pandal* contractors was abolished. However, its net was extended to services provided by architects, interior decorators, management consultants, chartered accountants, cost accountants, company secretaries, private security services, real estate agents and real estate consultants, market research agencies, credit rating agencies, underwriting agencies, and slaughter houses using mechanised means for large animals.

Acknowledging the potential of service tax, the Finance Minister in his 2000-2001 budget speech announced the setting up of an Expert Group to go into all its aspects and make suitable recommendations. The net of service tax was greatly expanded when the following 15 services were added to the list of taxable services in the 2001-02 budget.

1. Specified banking and financial services.
2. Authorised service stations for servicing of vehicles including two wheelers.
3. Port services.
4. Broadcasting services.
5. Photographic services.
6. Convention services.
7. Sound recording services.
8. Scientific and technical consulting services.
9. Telex services.
10. Telegraph services.
11. Facsimile services.
12. Online information and data base retrieval services.
13. Video tape production services.
14. Services auxiliary to insurance.
15. Services provided to lease circuit line holders.

In his 2004-05 budget speech, the Finance Minister announced the inclusion of some more services under the service tax ambit. These were the following.

1. Business exhibition services.
2. Airport services.
3. Services provided by transport booking agents.
4. Transport of goods by air.
5. Survey and exploration services.
6. Opinion poll services.
7. Intellectual property services other than copyright.
8. Brokers of forward contracts.
9. *Pandal* and *shamiana* contractors.
10. Outdoor caterers.
11. Independent TV/radio programme producers.
12. Construction services in respect of commercial or industrial constructions.
13. Life insurance services to the extent of the risk premium.

In the 2005-06 budget, the following 9 items were added to the list of taxable services.

1. Transport of goods through pipeline or other conduit.
2. Site preparation and clearance, excavation, earth moving and demolition services, other than those provided to agriculture, irrigation and watershed development.
3. Dredging services of rivers, ports, harbours, backwaters and estuaries.
4. Survey and map making other than by Government Departments.

5. Cleaning services other than in relation to agriculture, horticulture, animal husbandry or dairying.
6. Membership of clubs or associations.
7. Packaging services.
8. Mailing list compilation and mailing.
9. Construction of residential complexes having more than twelve residential units of apartments together with common areas and other appurtenances.

The 2005-06 budget also expanded the scope of certain existing services in the following manner.

1. Commercial or industrial construction services to include renovation of such building or civil structure, post-construction completion and finishing services for such building or civil structure, construction, repair, alteration, renovation or restoration of pipeline or conduits.
2. Erection, commissioning or installation services to include specified installation services.
3. Maintenance or repair services to include maintenance or management of immovable properties, maintenance or repair including reconditioning or restoration undertaken as part of any contract or agreement.
4. Broadcasting services to include charges recovered by broadcasting agencies from multi-system operator and provision of direct to home signals to the customers.
5. Sound recording to include recording of sound on any media and includes post-production services such as sound mixing or re-mixing.
6. Videotape production to include recording of any programme, event or function on any media and includes post-production services.
7. Taxable services provided by authorised service station to include reconditioning or restoration of motor cars, two wheeled and light motor vehicles.
8. Beauty parlour services to include all services provided by beauty parlours.
9. Manpower recruitment services to include supply of manpower, temporary or otherwise.
10. Franchisee services to cover all agreements by which the franchisor grants representational rights to franchise to sell or manufacture goods or provide services identified with the franchisor.
11. Business auxiliary services to include production or processing of goods for or on behalf of the client.
12. Outdoor catering services to include catering from a place or premises provided by way of tenancy or otherwise by the person receiving such services.

The budget for 2006-07 added the following new services under the service tax net.

1. Services provided by registrars to capital issues.
2. Services provided by share transfer agents.
3. Automated teller machine operations, maintenance or management.
4. Services provided by recovery agents.
5. Sale of space or time for advertisements, other than in print media.

6. Sponsorship services provided to anybody, corporate or firm, other than sponsorship of sports events.
7. Transport of passengers, other than economy class passengers, embarking on international journey by air.
8. Transport of goods in containers by rail by any person.
9. Business support services.
10. Auctioneers' services, other than auction of property under directions or orders of a court of law or auction by the Central Government.
11. Public relation services.
12. Ship management services.
13. Internet telephony services.
14. Transport of persons by cruise ship.
15. Credit card, debit card, charge card or other payment card related services.

In the 2007-08 budget, service tax net was extended to the following services.

1. Services outsourced for mining of minerals, oil or gas.
2. Renting of immovable property for use in commerce or business.
3. Development and supply of content for use in telecom and advertising purposes.
4. Asset management services provided by individuals.
5. Design services.

The budget for 2011-12 retained the service tax rate at 10 percent (increased to 12 percent in the budget for 2012-13) and focused on achieving a closer fit between the existing service tax regime and the proposed GST. This was sought to be done by: (a) adding a few new services on the ability-to-pay principle, (b) expanding or rationalizing the scope of existing services, (c) rationalizing certain provisions relating to important services and valuation, and (d) modifying provisions of the CENVAT credit scheme seeking to effect the right balance between input credits and output tax, and harmonizing the provisions of the scheme across goods and services, incentivizing honesty and penalizing dishonesty in compliance, and adoption of point of taxation rules to facilitate accrual basis of the collection.

Besides, the budget for 2011-12 imposed service tax on the following services:

1. Services provided by air-conditioned restaurants having a licence to serve alcoholic beverages in relation to serving of food and/or beverages.
2. Short-term accommodation provided by a hotel, inn, guesthouse, club or campsite, or any other similar establishment for a continuous period of less than three months.

Scope of certain existing services was expanded or altered as under:

1. Scope of *life insurance services* was widened to cover all services provided to a policy holder or any person, by an insurer, including re-insurer carrying on life insurance business. Tax to be charged on the portion of the premium other than what is allocated for investment, when the break-up of premium is shown separately in any document given to the policy holder. Rate of composition increased from 1 percent to 1.5 percent.
2. Scope of *club or association services* expanded to include services provided to non-members within its ambit.

3. Scope of the service of *authorized service stations* expanded to: (a) include services provided by any person; (b) cover all motor vehicles other than those meant for goods carriage and three-wheeler scooter (auto-rickshaws); and (c) cover decoration and other similar services in respect of vehicles along with the services already covered.
4. Definition of *business support services* amended so as to include services provided by way of operational or administrative assistance in any manner.
5. Scope of legal consultancy services expanded by bringing within their ambit: (a) services provided by a business entity to individuals in relation to advice, consultancy, or assistance in any branch of law, in any manner; (b) representational services provided by any person to any business entity (representational services provided to individuals to continue to be exempt); and (c) arbitration services provided by an arbitral tribunal to any business entity.
6. In commercial training or coaching services, the definition of *commercial training or coaching centre* amended so as to bring all unrecognized courses within the tax net, irrespective of the fact that such courses were conducted by an institute which also conducted courses that might lead to grant of a degree or diploma.

Certain exemptions were extended as follows:

1. Exemption provided to services rendered in relation to business exhibitions held abroad.
2. An abatement of 25 percent from the taxable value provided for the purpose of levy of service tax under *transport of goods through coastal and inland shipping*.
3. Exemption provided to *works contract* services rendered for construction or finishing of new residential complexes under the Jawaharlal Nehru National Urban Renewal Mission and Rajiv Awaas Yojana.
4. Exemption provided to services rendered within a port or other port or an airport under *works contract* services for specified areas.
5. Exemption provided to the Rashtriya Swasthya Bima Yojana under general insurance service.
6. Value of air freight included in the assessable value of goods for charging customs duties excluded from taxable value for the purpose of levy of service tax under *transport of goods by air* services.
7. Services related to transportation of goods by road, rail, or air when origin and destination are located outside India exempted from service tax.
8. A modified scheme introduced to refund service tax to SEZ units and developers.
9. Some existing exemptions on domestic and international travel and club or association services were withdrawn.

Keeping in view the social objectives of state policy, the Government of India refrained from taxing services in the field of health and education. [3]

18.4 Revenue Significance of Service Tax

Table 18.1 records the growth in revenue from service tax during its operation.

For the financial year 2016-17, the standard rate of service tax was 14 percent. In addition, Swachh Bharat Cess @ 0.5 percent was also leviable. From June 1, 2016, Krishi Kalyan

Cess @ 0.5 percent was also leviable.

Table 18.1: Trends in the Relative Significance of Service Tax in Gross Tax Revenues* of the Central Government: 1994-95 to 2016-17

(₹ crore)

Year	Gross Central Taxes	Revenue from Service Tax	Col. 3 as % of Col. 2
1	2	3	4
1994-95	92,297	407	0.4
1995-96	1,11,224	862	0.8
1996-97	1,29,762	1,059	0.8
1997-98	1,39,220	1,586	1.1
1998-99	1,43,797	1,957	1.4
1999-00	1,71,752	2,128	1.2
2000-01	1,88,603	2,613	1.4
2001-02	1,87,060	3,302	1.8
2002-03	2,15,905	4,122	1.9
2003-04	2,54,348	7,891	3.1
2004-05	3,04,957	14,200	4.7
2005-06	3,66,151	23,055	6.3
2006-07	4,73,513	37,598	7.9
2007-08	5,93,147	51,301	8.6
2008-09	6,05,298	60,941	10.1
2009-10	6,24,527	58,422	9.4
2010-11	7,93,072	71,016	9.0
2011-12	8,89,176	97,509	11.0
2012-13	10,36,235	1,32,601	12.8
2013-14	11,38,734	1,54,778	13.6
2014-15	12,44,885	1,67,969	13.5
2015-16	14,59,611	2,10,000	14.4
2016-17	16,30,888	2,31,000	14.2

* Before transferring States' share in Central taxes.

Sources: Government of India, Ministry of Finance, *Explanatory Memorandum on the Budget of the Central Government* (various years); *Receipts Budget* (various years); and *Budget at a Glance*, 2016-17.

18.5 Service Tax: A Critique

The expanding base of service tax provided a promising source of revenue, but there were some caveats which had to be kept in mind. First, the scope for expanding the service tax net to more and more services got narrower as the net was widened. The contribution of the expanding net, therefore, reduced over time. Second, the preponderance of small service providers below the taxable limit of turnover constrained the scope of revenue mobilization beyond a certain level.

The introduction of the service tax was a mixed blessing. While it broadened the tax base, its structure was complex. The tax was levied on specified services, classified into one hundred odd different categories. This approach spawned many disputes about the scope of each category. Unlike goods, services are malleable, and can and are often packaged into composite bundles that include taxable as well as non-taxable elements. Also, there is no standardized nomenclature for services, such as the Harmonised System Nomenclature (HSN) for goods.

Furthermore, there was a complicated rate structure. Although there was one statutory rate, in practice there were 10 other rates because of the so-called *abatement* which amounted to fixing a rate different from the standard rate and not allowing further input tax credits. Abatement was necessitated, in some part, because of uncertainty in the base, and specifically being unable to distinguish *goods* from *services*. Further, there was incomplete provision of input tax crediting for goods, and incomplete cross-crediting between goods and services. Added to this was the Central sales tax (CST) which was levied on the sale or purchase of goods in the course of inter-State trade.

The key problem with the service tax was the basic approach of levying it on specified services, each of which generated an extensive debate as to what was included in the base. Ideally, the tax base should be defined to include all services, with a limited list of exclusions (the so-called negative list). The Government was reluctant to adopt this approach for the fear that it could bring into the tax net many services that are politically sensitive. [4]

Endnotes

1. Government of India, Ministry of Finance, *Budget Speech of the Finance Minister, 1994-95, Part B*, p. 24.
2. *Report of the Twelfth Finance Commission (2005-10)*, November 2004, pp. 15-16.
3. In the case of excise and sales tax also, commodities such as medicines and books were either exempt or taxed at very low rates.
4. From July 1, 2012, the concept of taxation on services was changed from a Positive List of services to a Negative List regime. This changed the taxation system of services from tax on the specified services to tax being levied on all services, other than those mentioned in the Negative List or which were exempted by a notification.

19

Customs Duties

Before the tax reforms initiated in 1991, import tariff had a variety of rates for different items, and even for the same item depending on its end use. Such a cumbersome system led to legal disputes pertaining to import classifications and encouraged corruption in the administration of customs tariff.

In mid-1991 when the new government assumed office at the Centre, it began the process of reducing import duties. The Finance Act (No. 2), 1991, reduced the *ad valorem* rate of basic plus auxiliary duties of customs to a maximum of 150 percent where it was more than that. Thus, tariff peaks above 150 percent were eliminated with the exceptions of duty on imported alcoholic beverages and passenger baggage. The then prevailing rates of import duty on capital goods for general projects and machinery were reduced from 85 percent to 80 percent. The rate of duty on their components was also reduced by 5 percentage points from the existing level of 65 percent.

19.1 Tax Reforms Committee (TRC), 1991

Reform of the customs tariff was high on the agenda of the Tax Reforms Committee (Chairman: Raja Chelliah) constituted by the government in August 1991. Its terms of reference enjoined it to examine and make recommendations, *inter alia*, on "simplification and rationalisation of customs tariffs with a view to reducing the multiplicity and dispersion of rates and to eliminate exemptions which have become unnecessary; (and) reducing the level of tariff rates, keeping in view the need for mobilising resources to facilitate fiscal adjustment and the objective of promoting international competitiveness". [1]

In its Interim Report submitted to the government in December 1991, the Committee suggested the following as elements of the programme of import tariff reform: "(a) reduction of the general level of tariff, (b) reduction of the spread or dispersion of tariff rates, (c) simplification of the tariff system, (d) rationalisation of tariff rates, along with the abolition of numerous exemptions and concessions, and (e) abolition of the practice of making changes in effective rates through notifications". [2] Stressing the need for time-bound action, the Committee observed, "By 1995-96, the average tariff rate should be brought down to about 50 percent and the peak rate to about 80 percent. In the years 1996-97 to 1998-99, tariff rates should be reduced further to bring down the average rate to around 25 percent and the maximum rate to 50 percent by 1998-99". [3]

Following the recommendations of the Tax Reforms Committee, 1991, the Finance Act, 1992, lowered the peak level of import duties to 110 percent with the exception of passenger baggage and alcoholic beverages. With a view to reduce the cost of new investment, the duty on project imports was lowered from 80 percent to 55 percent and in the case of electronic industry to 50 percent. A deeper reduction to 30 percent was granted for capital goods for projects of coal mining and crude petroleum refining. For power projects, a uniform duty of 30 percent was fixed.

The underlying philosophy of reduction in tariffs was to promote competitiveness in the Indian industry. There was a feeling in Government circles that high tariff rates had the effect of creating a high cost industrial structure.

The Finance Act, 1993, made a significant simplification in the import tariff by merging auxiliary duty with basic duty, and also by reducing the maximum rate of import duty from 110 percent to 85 percent. The peak rate of import duty was further reduced from 85 percent to 65 percent by the Finance Act, 1994.

Continuing the process of reducing the high level of protection to domestic industry is continuing so as to foster competition and promote efficiency. The peak rate of import duty was reduced from 65 percent to 50 percent in 1995, and further down to 40 percent in the 1997-98 budget.

A special customs duty of 2 percent was imposed in the 1996-97 budget and a further special customs duty of 3 percent was imposed on certain items in 1997-98. In other words, special customs duty of 5 percent was in force for a period valid till 31.3.1999. However, the Finance Minister announced in his 1999-2000 budget speech the discontinuance of the 5 percent special customs duty with effect from 28.2.1999.

In another significant move, the Finance Minister reduced the then existing 7 major ad valorem rates of customs duty to the following 5 basic rates.

1. 5 percent (the existing one).
2. 15 percent (by substituting the existing 10 percent rate).
3. 25 percent (by merging the 20 percent and 25 percent rates).
4. 35 percent (by merging the 30 percent and 35 percent rates).
5. 40 percent (the existing one).

However, in another move the Finance Minister imposed a uniform surcharge of 10 percent on all commodities excluding the following categories: (a) crude oil and petroleum products, (b) items attracting 40 percent rate of basic duty, (c) certain GATT-bound items, and (d) gold and silver.

In other words, the imposition of surcharge raised the basic rate by 10 percent. For example, basic rate of 5 percent became 5.5 percent and 15 percent became 16.5 percent.

Still further, the Finance Minister reduced the peak rate of basic customs duty from 40 percent to 35 percent in his 2000-01 budget, thereby reducing the total number of customs duty rates from 5 to 4, i.e. 35 percent, 25 percent, 15 percent and 5 percent. The surcharge of 10 percent imposed in the 1999-2000 budget became applicable to new peak rate of 35 percent. However, in the 2001-02 budget, the surcharge of 10 percent was discontinued, making the peak level of customs duty decline from 38.5 percent to 35 percent. As regards further reduction in the peak rate of duty, the Finance Minister observed, "I have already promised that our customs tariff would be brought down to East Asian levels. I will like to move progressively within three years to reduce the number of rates to the minimum with a peak rate of 20 percent". [4] Government reduced the peak customs duty from 30 percent to 25 percent in the 2003-04 budget.

19.2 Customs Tariff Report, 2002

Customs Tariff Report (Chairman: Arvind Virmani) was submitted to the government by the Inter-ministerial Group in January 2002.

The Report made the following main recommendations to the government.

1. Introduction of a single customs duty (20 percent) on all products by 2004-05. Tariff rates below 20 percent on some products be brought to 20 percent while peak tariff rate be brought down to 20 percent. According to the Report, a single uniform import tariff implies that the effective protection for all producers is also equal to this single uniform tariff.
2. Phasing out all exemptions, barring those on security considerations, by 2004-05.
3. Removal of all anomalies in the levy of customs duty by reclassifying all goods and services into two broad categories, viz. producer goods and consumer goods instead of raw materials, components and parts, and final goods.

The Report made out a case for reducing import duties to a near-uniform basic rate of 10 percent by the end of 2005-06 and 5 percent by the end of 2011-12. The ASEAN free trade agreement proposes to bring down ASEAN rates to the 0-5 percent range by 2010 even for highly sensitive agricultural goods.

It is noteworthy that producers seek a low import tariff on raw materials and intermediate goods, and high tariff on finished goods.

19.3 Import Duty Structure Recommended by Task Force on Indirect Taxes, 2002

Government of India had appointed two task forces on direct and indirect taxes in September 2002 under the chairmanship of Vijay Kelkar. These Task Forces made important recommendations on toning up tax administration to put in place a system that is simple, effective and at par with international standards (see section 15.2 of chapter 15 of this book).

The Task Force on Indirect Taxes laid down a broad approach to customs tariff reforms in India. It envisaged a zero duty for essential items, 10 percent duty for raw materials, inputs and intermediate goods and 20 percent for final goods by 2004-05. Following introduction of value added tax (VAT) by the states, these duties were proposed to be further reduced to 5 percent for basic raw materials, 8 percent for intermediate goods, 10 percent for finished goods and 20 percent for consumer durables by 2006-07. In order to reap efficiency gains from further opening up of the economy, the Task Force emphasized the need for systemic changes in customs procedures and trade facilitation based on modern best practices, which rely on self compliance,

As regards customs exemptions, the Task Force recommended removal of all exemptions except in case of: (a) life-saving goods, (b) goods of security and strategic interest, (c) goods for relief and charitable purposes, and (d) international obligations including contracts. The Task Force recommended the following pattern of import duty (Table 19.1).

19.4 Off-budget Package of Tax Concessions, January 2004

Finance Minister Jaswant Singh announced on January 8, 2004 an off-budget package of tax concessions which mainly pertained to indirect taxes (excise and customs). The most notable of these was the reduction in the peak rate of import duty across the board (except for agricultural goods) from 25 percent to 20 percent. Simultaneously, he abolished the 4 percent special additional customs duty (SACD). Both these changes became effective from January 9, 2004. These measures considerably lowered the protection levels for the domestic industry. However, the two measures are expected to bring down input costs of the manufacturing sector, enabling it to make Indian products globally competitive.

Table 19.1: Import Duty Structure Recommended by the Task Force on Indirect Taxes

0 percent	For items like life-saving drugs and equipments, sovereign imports (defence and security related goods) and imports by RBI.
For other goods by 2004-05	10 percent for raw materials, inputs and intermediate goods. 20 percent for consumer durables.
By 2006-07	5 percent for basic raw materials like coal, ores and concentrates, xylenes etc. 8 percent for intermediate goods which will be used for future manufacture (capital goods, basic chemicals, metals etc.) 10 percent for finished goods other than consumer durables. 20 percent for consumer durables.

Source: Government of India, Ministry of Finance and Company Affairs, *Report of the Task Force on Indirect Taxes*, December 2002, p. 169.

It may be recalled that former Finance Minister Yashwant Sinha announced an 8 percent SACD in 1998-99 and rolled it back to 4 percent in the official amendments. SACD was meant to offset the burden of local taxes borne by the domestic industry.

In the 2005-06 Union budget, the peak rate of import duty on non-agricultural products was reduced from 20 percent to 15 percent. It was further reduced to 12.5 percent and 10 percent in the 2006-07 and 2007-08 budgets respectively. Table 19.2 records the progressive reductions in the peak rate of import duty. In this context, *Economic Survey*, 2009-10 observed, "India has been progressively lowering peak customs duty. Contrary to popular belief, the fall in peak duty has neither led to a fall in revenue collections, nor a wiping out of the domestic manufacturing sector. In fact, peak duty falls have been accompanied by rise in customs duty collections. The trend follows the Laffer Curve Effect which indicates that lowering of taxes produces higher economic activity and higher revenue realization". [5]

To recapitulate, radical reforms have been introduced in the import tariff since 1991. These reforms were necessary because the customs tariff had become, over the years, very complicated in terms of multiple rates, innumerable exemptions, excessive controls, and elaborate procedures. These infirmities of the customs tariff often led to delays, harassment, corruption, and litigation. Moreover, rationalisation and simplification of the customs duties was needed to move towards a market economy, freedom of trade, and opening up the Indian economy to the outside world. The country has moved towards moderate rates of taxation with a view to improve compliance and reduce litigation.

After successive downward revisions, the peak rate of import duty on non-agricultural products at present stands at 10 percent.

Table 19.2: Progressive Reductions in Peak Rate of Import Duty

(percent)

Year	Rate of Peak Duty
1999-00	40
2000-01	38.5
2001-02	35
2002-03	30
2003-04	25
2004-05	20
2005-06	15
2006-07	12.5
2007-08 to 2022-23	10

Source: Government of India, *Budget Papers* (various years).

19.5 Revenue Significance

The relative contribution of customs revenue in the total tax yield of the Central Government has shown fluctuations due to changes in the foreign exchange situation, domestic production levels, and trends in international trade. For example, in the late 1950s, several restrictions and bans were imposed on imports in view of the difficult foreign exchange position, resulting in fall in revenue from import duties.

During pre-Independence days and even during early post-Independence period, customs duties formed the mainstay of Central tax revenues. However, the relative share of customs duties started declining from early 1950s in view of protective trade policy and dwindling foreign exchange reserves. The share of customs revenue in Centre's total tax collections dropped from 38.9 percent in 1950-51, to 19.1 percent in 1960-61 and to as low as 16.3 percent in 1970-71. After that, customs revenue maintained an upward swing, accounting for 25.8 percent in 1980-81, and 35.8 percent in 1990-91 (Table 19.3). This upward trend was attributable to the changed emphasis from physical to fiscal controls to regulate imports. As the Long Term Fiscal Policy, 1985, maintained, "The basic thrust of customs tariff reforms will be to place increasing reliance on tariffs to regulate imports and progressively reduce the role of quantitative restrictions in this regard. The move in this direction should increase revenues, encourage less import-intensive forms of production, moderate the unjustifiably high protection granted by quantitative restrictions to certain industries and reduce the delays and uncertainties associated with the administration of import licensing". [6]

During the post-liberalization period (i.e. 1991 onwards), a sharp fall is noticeable in the relative share of customs duties in gross tax revenues of the Central Government. The relative share fell to 25.2 percent in 2000-01 and further down to 17.1 percent in 2010-11. This was due to drastic reductions in the tariff rates across the rate categories, including the peak rate, in the wake of WTO commitments and the policy to become globally competitive. In the budget estimates for 2022-23, revenue from customs duties was shown at ₹ 2,13,000 crore, forming 7.7 percent of gross tax revenue (₹ 27,57,820) of the Centre (Table 19.3).

Table 19.3: Trends in the Relative Significance of Customs Duties in Gross Tax Revenues* of the Central Government: Selected Years

(₹ crore)

Central taxes	1950-51	1960-61	1970-71	1980-81	1990-91	2000-01	2010-11	2022-23
A+B Gross tax revenues	404 (100.0)	888 (100.0)	3,206 (100.0)	13,179 (100.0)	57,576 (100.0)	1,88,603 (100.0)	7,93,072 (100.0)	27,57,820 (100.0)
A. Direct taxes	174 (43.1)	290 (32.6)	870 (27.1)	3,004 (22.8)	11,025 (19.1)	68,306 (36.2)	4,45,962 (56.2)	14,20,000 (51.5)
B. Indirect taxes of which	229 (56.7)	599 (67.5)	2,337 (72.9)	10,175 (77.2)	46,552 (80.9)	1,20,297 (63.8)	3,47,110 (43.8)	13,37,820 (48.5)
Customs duties	157 (38.9)	170 (19.1)	524 (16.3)	3,409 (25.8)	20,644 (35.8)	47,542 (25.2)	1,35,813 (17.1)	2,13,000 (7.7)

* Before transferring States' share in Central taxes.
Figures in parentheses are corresponding percentages of gross tax revenues.
Figures for 2022-23 are budget estimates.
Sources: Government of India, Ministry of Finance, *Explanatory Memorandum on the Budget of the Central Government* (various years); *Receipts Budget* (various years); and *Budget at a Glance*, 2022-23.

Presently, customs revenue is mainly composed of import duties levied on a wide range of commodities. In the budget estimates for 2022-23, import duties accounted for ₹ 2,11,450 crore (99.3 percent) of total customs revenue of ₹ 2,13,000 crore (Table 19.4).

Although at present the share of export duties in customs revenue is very low (0.7 percent in the 2022-23 budget), it was not always so. In the early 1950s, export duties formed a significant proportion of customs revenue, though this situation could not be maintained for long. The yield from export duties reached a peak figure when it formed 29.9 percent of total customs revenue in 1950-51. By 1960-61, export duty revenue had been reduced to 8.2 percent of total customs revenue.

Another upsurge in the relative share of export duties is observed in 1970-71 when they formed 12.0 percent of customs revenue. Since then, the revenue importance of export duties has decreased (Table 19.4).

Like excise levies, the revenue from import duties is also concentrated in a select few commodities including petroleum oils and crude, electrical machinery, organic chemicals, project imports, plastics etc. These are the items which form the bulk of

India's imports and hence customs revenue.

Table 19.4: Trends in the Relative Shares of Import and Export Duties in Total Customs Duties: Selected Years

(₹ crore)

Year	Customs Duties	Import Duties	Export Duties	As Percent	
				Col.3 of Col. 2	Col. 4 of Col. 2
1	2	3	4	5	6
1950-51	157	110	47	70.1	29.9
1955-56	166	128	38	77.1	22.9
1960-61	170	156	14	91.8	8.2
1965-66	539	537	2	99.6	0.4
1970-71	524	461	63	88.0	12.0
1975-76	1,419	1,336	83	94.1	5.9
1980-81	3,409	3,292	117	96.6	3.4
1985-86	9,526	9,443	83	99.1	0.9
1990-91	20,644	20,532	36	99.5	0.5
1995-96	35,757	35,647	110	99.7	0.3
2000-01	47,542	47,400	142	99.7	0.3
2005-06	81,800	81,015	795	99.1	0.9
2010-11	1,35,813	1,32,541	3,272	97.6	2.4
2015-16	2,08,336	2,01,397	6,939	96.7	3.3
2020-21	1,34,750	1,20,911	13,839	89.7	10.3
2022-23*	2,13,000	2,11,450	1,550	99.3	0.7

.*Budget estimates

Sources: Government of India, Ministry of Finance, *Explanatory Memorandum on the Budget of the Central Government* (various years); *Receipts Budget* (various years).

19.6 Legislative Framework

The Constitution of India grants exclusive powers to the Central Government to impose duties of customs. By virtue of Entry 83 of List I (Union List) in the Seventh Schedule of the Constitution of India, the Central Government is empowered to impose 'duties of customs including export duties'.

During the British rule, various customs and tariff enactments were passed from time to time, the following two being the main: (a) The Sea Customs Act, 1878, and (b) The Tariff Act, 1934.

After Independence, the Sea Customs Act, 1878 and other allied enactments (Inland Bounded Warehousing Act, 1896 and the Land Customs Act, 1924) were repealed by a consolidating and amending legislation entitled the Customs Act, 1962. Similarly, the Tariff Act of 1934 was repealed by the Customs Tariff Act, 1975.

19.6.1 Customs Act, 1962: This is the main Act which provides, vide Section 12, for the levy and collection of customs duty. This power is derived by virtue of Entry 83 of List I (Union List) in the Seventh Schedule of the Constitution of India. Besides, the Act provides import/export procedures, prohibition on importation and exportation of goods, offences penalties etc. It stands as a complete code in itself as to the levy and collection of duties on import and export of goods.

A. Rules under Customs Act, 1962: Section 156 of Customs Act empowers the Central Government to make rules, consistent with provisions of the Act, to carry out the purposes of the Act. Thus, the Government has framed various rules some of which are as under:

- Customs Valuation (Determination of Value of Imported Goods) Rules, 2007.
- Customs Valuation (Determination of Value of Export Goods) Rules, 2007.
- Baggage Rules, 1998.

B. Regulations under Customs Act, 1962: Under Section 157 of the Customs Act, the Central Board of Indirect Taxes and Customs (CBIC) [Earlier Central Board of Excise and Customs (CBEC)] is empowered to make regulations, consistent with the provisions of the Act, to carry out the purposes of the Act. Different regulations have been framed within the parameters of these powers as, for example, Project Import Regulations, 1986.

Similarly, CBIC can issue circulars, instructions, directions for the purpose of uniformity in classification of goods and with respect to the levy of duty thereon.

19.6.2 Customs Tariff Act, 1975: It contains two schedules. Schedule 1 includes various import items in systematic categories—in accordance with the international scheme of classification of internationally-traded goods known as Harmonized System of Commodity Classification—and specifies the rate of import duties thereon, as prescribed by the legislature. Schedule 2 incorporates items that are subject to export duties and the rate of duties thereon. Further, it makes provisions for additional duty, preferential duty, anti-dumping duty, protective duties etc.

Customs duties are generally levied either on specific or *ad valorem* basis, but in some cases specific-cum-ad valorem duties are also levied.

19.7 Various Types of Customs Duties

In accordance with the provisions of the Constitution, various types of customs duties are imposed by the Government under different Acts of Parliament.

Goods become liable to import duty when there is *import into* India. Import is completed only when goods cross the customs barrier. This crossing of customs barrier is the taxable event in the case of imports.

Goods become liable for export duty when there is *export from* India. Export is completed when goods cross territorial waters of India. [7] Although export duty is collected before the ship leaves the port, it does not mean that taxable event has taken place. One can say that export duty is collected in advance.

Following are the important customs duties levied on goods imported into or exported from India.

19.7.1 Basic Customs Duty (BCD): Under Section 12 of the Customs Act, 1962 (the main enactment), duty of customs is levied at such rates as may be specified under Customs Tariff Act, 1975 on goods imported into, or exported from India. This is known as basic customs duty (BCD). It is levied under Section 12 of the Customs Act and specified under Section 2 of the Customs Tariff Act.

As per Section 2 of the Customs Tariff Act, the rates at which duties of customs shall be levied are indicated in the First Schedule and the Second Schedule of this Act. First Schedule deals with import tariff and Second Schedule with export tariff.

.The duty may be a percentage of the value of the goods or at a specific rate. The Central Government has the power to reduce or exempt any goods from these duties.

19.7.2 Integrated Goods and Services Tax (IGST): It is noteworthy that Goods and Services Tax (GST) was introduced in India with effect from July 1, 2017. IGST—as a part of GST regime—is levied on inter-State supply of goods and services. IGST also applies on imports.

All exports (whether of goods or services) as well as supplies to SEZs have been categorized as zero-rated supplies in the IGST Act.

A. Applicability of IGST: IGST is applicable by virtue of Section 3(7) of the Customs Tariff Act, 1975 which was amended with effect from July 1, 2017. The amended version provides that any article which is imported into India shall be liable to IGST at such rate which is leviable under Section 5 of IGST Act, 2017 on a like article on its supply in India.

Section 3(7) of Customs Tariff Act, 1975 reads as follows, "any article which is imported into India shall, in addition, be liable to integrated tax at such rate, not exceeding forty percent, as is leviable under Section 5 of the Integrated Goods and Services Tax Act, 2017 on a like article on its supply in India, on the value of the imported article…".

Input tax credit pertaining to IGST paid is available on import of goods and services. BCD paid on import is not eligible for set-off.

IGST rate is broadly equal to Central Goods and Services Tax (CGST) rate plus State Goods and Services Tax (SGST) rate. SGST component of IGST accrues to the consumer state. In other words, the incidence of tax follows the destination principle and the SGST component of tax revenue accrues to the state where the imported goods and services are consumed. Unlike in the past, the states where imported goods are consumed now gain their share from the IGST paid on imported goods.

B. Rationale for IGST on Imports: BCD on imports indicates the *level of protection* which the Government wants to provide to domestic industries, subject to WTO rules, regulations and norms.

IGST on imports ensures *level playing field* between imported goods and domestically produced goods.

In the pre-GST era, *level playing field* was ensured through Additional Duty of Customs [commonly known as Countervailing Duty (CVD)] under Section 3(1) of the Customs Tariff Act, 1975, on goods imported into the country. The rate of this duty was equal to the excise duty on like articles if produced or manufactured in India. [8]

Similarly, Special Additional Duty of Customs (SAD), also known as Special CVD, was levied under Section 3(5) of the Customs Tariff Act, 1975. This duty was equal to sales tax/VAT, local taxes or any other charge on a like article on its sale, purchase or transportation in India. Again, the purpose of SAD was to counter balance various state level taxes and provide *level playing field* to indigenous goods which had to bear these taxes/charges.

With effect from July 1, 2017, these duties (CVD and Special CVD) were replaced by IGST. As already stated, the underlying philosophy of IGST is to endure *level playing field* between imported goods and domestically produced goods. In other words, IGST ensures that that the *level of protection* provided by the basic import duty (under Section 2 of the Customs Tariff Act, 1975) to domestic industry is not reduced.

C. Calculation of IGST: IGST is calculated on the aggregate of the following:

1. Assessable value.
2. Basic customs duty.
3. Social welfare surcharge (10 percent of basic customs duty).

(a) Compensation Cess: It is a cess levied under Section 8 of the Goods and Services Tax (Compensation to States) Act, 2017. It is applicable—in addition to the regular GST taxes (CGST + SGST/UT - GST on intra-state supplies and IGST on inter-state supplies—on the supply of certain notified goods/services. The following goods—which mostly belong to the luxury and demerit categories—have been notified for the purpose so far.

1. *Pan masala.*
2. Tobacco and tobacco products.
3. Coal.
4. Aerated waters.
5. Motor vehicles.

The rate of compensation cess varies for different notified goods. It is imposed to compensate states for any revenue loss on account of implementation of GST.

In case compensation cess is applicable on goods imported into India, then it is levied and collected in accordance with the provisions of section 3 of the Customs Tariff Act, 1975, at the point when duties of customs are levied on the said goods under Section 12 of the Customs Act, 1962, on a value determined under the Customs Tariff Act, 1975.

The cess is levied and collected along with customs duty and IGST.

D. Other Notable Points: These are as under:

1. IGST is applicable in case of import of goods/services.
2. IGST is not applicable on baggage.
3. Input tax credit pertaining to IGST paid is available.
4. If an exemption is given on inter-state supply under IGST Act, 2017, it is taken into consideration while calculating IGST for the purpose of import.

E. Exemptions from IGST on Certain Imports: At its Twenty-third Meeting held in Guwahati (Assam) on November 10, 2017, the GST Council took major decisions relating to GST rates, ITC eligibility criteria, and exemptions and clarifications on levy of GST on services. In the context of imports it approved the following exemptions:

1. Exemption from IGST on imports of lifesaving medicine supplied free of cost by overseas supplier for patients, subject to certification by DGHS of Centre or State and certain other conditions.
2. Exemption from IGST on imports of goods (other than motor vehicles) under a lease agreement if IGST is paid on the lease amount.
3. Exemption from IGST on imports of specified goods by a sports person of outstanding eminence, subject to specified conditions.
4. Exemption from GST on specified goods, such as scientific or technical instruments, software, and prototype supplied to public funded research institution or a university or IISc, or IITs or NIT.
5. Coverage of more items, such as temporary import of professional equipment by accredited press persons visiting India to cover certain events, broadcasting equipments, sports items, testing equipment, under ATA carnet system. These goods are to be re-exported after the specified use is over.

19.7.3 Anti-dumping Duty: Dumping occurs when one country (say China) exports an article to another country (say India) at a price lower than its normal value. Since this is an unfair trade practice having a disruptive effect on international trade, anti-dumping duty comes in handy as a measure to rectify the situation.

Thus, if an article is exported from outside India to India at less than its normal value, the Central Government can impose anti-dumping duty on such transaction. It can be imposed by issue of a notification under Section 9A of the Customs Tariff Act, 1975. However, anti-dumping duty cannot exceed *margin of dumping* in relation to such article. Margin of dumping means the difference between *normal value* and *export price*. Normal value means comparable price in ordinary course in trade, for like article, when destined for consumption in the exporting country. Export price means the price at which goods are exported.

Anti-dumping duty is generally imposed in cases where Indian production units are manufacturing similar articles.

It is noteworthy that Section 9B(1)(b) of Customs Tariff Act, 1975 provides restrictions on the power of the Government to impose anti-dumping duty in the case of imports from a WTO member country. In such cases, anti-dumping duty can be imposed only if the Central Government declares that import of such articles in India causes material injury to Industry established in India or materially retards the establishment of any industry in India.

19.7.4 Safeguard Duty: Central Government can impose safeguard duty under Section 8B of the Customs Tariff Act, 1975. This duty can be imposed on specified imported goods if the Government is satisfied that the goods are being imported in such increased quantity and under such conditions that they are causing serious injury to the domestic industry. Safeguard duty is valid for 4 years. The period of 4 years can be extended but the aggregate period cannot be more than 10 years.

19.7.5 Protective Duty: It is a duty imposed on imported goods for protection of interests of any industry in India on the recommendation of Tariff Commission. As per Sections 6 and 7, protective duty is effective from the date specified in the First Schedule of the Customs Tariff Act, 1975.

19.7.6 Social Welfare Surcharge: It is levied at the rate of 10 percent of the aggregate duties of Customs, on imported goods, to help provide for social welfare schemes of the Government.

19.8 Exemptions from Customs Duty

Customs duty exemptions are provided through provisions of Customs Act, 1962 and Customs Tariff Act, 1975. Central Government can also grant exemptions by issuing a notification under Section 25 of the Customs Act. Exemptions given by notifications may be unconditional or subject to conditions given in the notification. Different exemption notifications have been issues for duty free imports by Ministry of Defence, Indian Navy, Coast Guards and other Central/State organizations.

General exemptions have been granted for imports by privileged organizations like United Nations agencies.

19.9 Export Tariff Policy

In India, about 99 percent of customs revenue is derived from import duties which are levied on a wide range of commodities. Apart from revenue function, import duties act as policy instrument to provide protection to domestic industry, conserve and ration scarce foreign exchange, and frame external trade policy of the Government. Export duties, accounting for the rest of 1 percent revenue, are imposed on a few commodities, namely coffee, mica, black pepper, hides and skins, and leather. Government has generally refrained from levying export duties in order to ensure competitiveness of India's exports in the world market.

Export duties can become an important source of revenue when a country enjoys monopoly or near-monopoly in certain products in the international market. In the early 1950s, India had foreign market dominance in commodities such as jute, tea, and textiles. Hence, export duties fetched sizeable revenues. As this dominance grew weaker over the years, the rates of export duty had to be reduced.

The devaluation of rupee, along with the sterling, against the dollar in September 1949, and the Korean boom considerably increased the demand for India's exports. The comparatively strong position in respect of certain commodities in the world market led to wide profit margins, encouraging the Government to impose or enhance export duty on a number of items including jute manufactures, cotton textiles, and black pepper. Apart from raising revenue, export duties also served to stabilise domestic prices. However, the need to promote India's exports led to a gradual scaling down of export duties. Following the devaluation of the rupee in 1966, export duties were re-imposed on a number of goods including jute manufactures, tea, raw cotton, groundnuts, hides and skins, and mineral ores. The objective was to mop up a part of the windfall gain accruing to the exporters as a result of devaluation. However, they had to be withdrawn in course of time to ensure competitiveness of our exports in the world market. Exports are encouraged, in certain cases through subsidies, to narrow the ever-widening deficit in the balance of payments.

Despite the fact that export duties have lost their importance from revenue angle, they have not been completely dispensed with. Occasions do arise when there is considerable disparity between the domestic and international prices of certain goods enjoying a comparatively stronger position in the export market, and levying of export duties may be justified to mop up a part of the profits of the exporters. At present, export duties are levied on a few commodities such as coffee, mica, black pepper, hides and skins and leather. Export duty on an item is levied after considering such factors as domestic production and likely exportable surpluses, demand for the item in the foreign markets, changes in exchange rates, and the prices prevailing in the international market. It is noteworthy that the Government can impose/enhance export duties without prior approval of the Parliament because such duties do not fall on the Indian consumers.

See also chapters 6 and 13 of this book.

Endnotes

1. Government of India, Ministry of Finance, *Interim Report of the Tax Reforms Committee,* (Chairman: Raja Chelliah), December 1991, p. l.
2. Ibid., p. 97.
3. Ibid., pp. 143-144.
4. Government of India, Ministry of Finance, *Budget Speech of the Finance Minister, 2001-02, Part B*, p. 31.
5. Government of India, Ministry of Finance, *Economic Survey*, 2009-10, p. 172.
6. Government of India, Ministry of Finance, *Long Term Fiscal Policy,* 1985, p. 40.
7. Territorial sea, as defined by the 1982 United Nations Convention on the Law of the Sea, is a belt of coastal waters extending at most 12 nautical miles (22.2 km) from the baseline (usually the mean low-water mark) of a coastal state.
8. The rate of additional duty of customs, popularly known as countervailing duty, was equal to the excise duty on like articles if produced or manufactured in India. If the rate of this duty was on *ad valorem* basis, the value for this purpose was the total of the value of the imported article and the customs duty on it (both basic and auxiliary). The underlying philosophy of a countervailing duty is to ensure that the protection provided by the import duty to domestic industry is not reduced. Till the early 1960s, countervailing duty was levied on a select basis on products which were considered to erode the margin of protection to the domestic industry on account of the excise duty. In course of time when the number of excisable goods increased, the selective use of countervailing duty was found to be inadequate and complicated. Therefore, the Indian Tariff Act, 1934, was amended in 1963 to insert a new Section 2A to provide for the levy of countervailing duty in all cases where excise duty was leviable on a similar indigenous commodity.

20

Sales Tax/Value Added Tax (VAT)

Under Entry 54 of List II (State List) in the Seventh Schedule of the Constitution, the States were given the power to levy "a tax on sales or purchases of goods other than newspapers". Each State was, therefore, empowered to collect tax on the sale of goods within its territory according to the rules framed by it. Prior to tax reforms initiated in early 1990s, sales tax was characterized by a multiplicity of tax rate and exemptions, lack of uniformity across States, large number of exemptions and concessions, and differing procedures for tax collection. It was a nightmare for a business entity doing business in more than one State.

In mid-1990s, most states had agreed to phase out the incentive related exemptions and implement floor rates of sales tax. As part of the nation wide efforts to redesign commodity taxation and the implementation of CENVAT at the level of the Centre, many States modified their sales tax regimes to launch a state level VAT under the scheme prepared by the Empowered Committee for this purpose.

At a meeting of the State Finance Ministers with the Union Finance Minister on June 18, 2004, it was decided that all States would introduce a uniform VAT from April 1, 2005 to replace sales tax. After missing many deadlines, VAT was finally introduced in all the States. Broadly speaking, the experience of implementing VAT was quite encouraging. The new system was received well by all the stakeholders, and the transition was quite smooth.

To pave way for the introduction of GST, sales tax/VAT was abolished by Section 17 of Constitution (One Hundred and First Amendment) Act, 2016.

20.1 Present Constitutional Provisions Regarding Sales Tax/VAT

Prior to the introduction of goods and services tax (GST) on July 1, 2017, taxation of goods by the States was characterized by a base (sales) that extended all the way to the retail stage. Lists of exemptions, rates of taxation, compounding schemes and rules and regulations varied across States. It was a nightmare for a business entity doing business in more than one State.

By virtue of powers vested in them under Entry 54 of List II (State List) in the Seventh Schedule of the Constitution, the states were authorised to impose, "taxes on the sale or purchase of goods other than newspapers, subject to the provisions of Entry 92A of List I".

To pave the way for GST, Section 17 of the Constitution (One Hundred and First Amendment) Act, 2016 substituted the following entry for the old Entry 54:

"54. Taxes on the sale of petroleum crude, high speed diesel, motor spirit (commonly known as petrol), natural gas, aviation turbine fuel and alcoholic liquor for human consumption, but not including sale in the course of inter-State trade or commerce or sale in the course of international trade or commerce of such goods" (Table 20.1).

Table 20.1: Entry 54 of List II (State List) in the Seventh Schedule of the Constitution

Before Constitution (One Hundred and First Amendment) Act, 2016	After Constitution (One Hundred and First Amendment) Act, 2016
Taxes on the sale or purchase of goods other than newspapers, subject to the provisions of Entry 92A of List I.	Taxes on the sale of petroleum crude, high speed diesel, motor spirit (commonly known as petrol), natural gas, aviation turbine fuel and alcoholic liquor for human consumption, but not including sale in the course of inter-State trade or commerce or sale in the course of international trade or commerce of such goods.

Petroleum and petroleum products have been constitutionally included as *goods* under GST. However, it has also been provided that petroleum and petroleum products shall not be subject to the levy of GST till notified at a future date on the recommendation of the GST Council. The present taxes levied by the Centre and the States on petroleum and petroleum products—excise duty/CENVAT by the Centre and sales tax/VAT by the States—will continue to be levied in the interim period. The five petroleum products which have been kept in abeyance for the purpose of GST are the following: (a) petroleum crude, (b) motor spirit [petrol], (c) high speed diesel, (d) natural gas, and (e) aviation turbine fuel.

It is noteworthy that GST Council is entrusted to make recommendations to the Union and the States on taxes, cesses and surcharges levied by the Union, the States and the local bodies which may be subsumed in the goods and services tax [(Article 279A(4)(a)].

Pre-GST system of sales tax/VAT is explained in the rest of this chapter.

20.2 Revenue Significance of Sales Tax

An outstanding development in the sphere of State finances after Independence in 1947 was the precipitous growth in the relative revenue significance of sales tax levied under Entry 54 of List II (State List) in the Seventh Schedule of the Constitution. It grew considerably in depth and coverage, and formed the mainstay of States' tax revenue. It was levied not only on consumer goods but also on raw materials and capital goods. In 1950-51, the relative share of sales tax was 26.1 percent: ₹ 58 crore out of a total collection of ₹ 222 crore from States' taxes. Recording a precipitous growth in relative revenue significance, sales tax was estimated to contribute 62.0 percent to States' own tax revenues in the 2015-16 budgets of the state governments (Table 20.2). As already noted, sales tax/VAT was subsumed under GST effective July 1, 2017.

20.3 White Paper on State-Level Value Added Tax, 2005

A White Paper on State-Level Value Added Tax was prepared by the Empowered

Committee of State Finance Ministers (Convenor: Asim Kumar Dasgupta), constituted by the Ministry of Finance, Government of India. The White Paper was prepared on the basis of a Resolution adopted in the Conference of the Chief Ministers on November 16, 1999. It was the result of collective efforts of all the States in formulating the basic design of the State-level Value Added Tax (VAT) through repeated and candid discussions in the Empowered Committee of State Finance Ministers.

Table 20.2: Trends in the Relative Revenue Significance of Sales Tax in Total Revenue from States' Own Taxes: Selected Years

(₹ crore)

State taxes	1950-51	1960-61	1970-71	1980-81	1990-91	2000-01	2010-11	2015-16
A+B Revenue from States' own taxes	222 (100.0)	455 (100.0)	1,546 (100.0)	6,665 (100.0)	30,145 (100.0)	1,16,717 (100.0)	4,78,594 (100.0)	9,69,594 (100.0)
A. Direct taxes	55 (24.7)	110 (24.2)	140 (9.1)	271 (4.1)	1,230 (4.1)	3,457 (2.9)	12,307 (2.6)	21,774 (2.2)
B. Indirect taxes of which	167 (75.3)	345 (75.8)	1,406 (90.9)	6,394 (95.9)	28,915 (95.9)	1,13,260 (97.1)	4,66,287 (97.4)	9,47,820 (97.8)
1. Sales tax	**58 (26.1)**	**158 (34.7)**	**755 (48.8)**	**3,887 (58.3)**	**16,476 (54.6)**	**68,386 (58.6)**	**2,90,682 (60.7)**	**6,00,851 (62.0)**

Figures in parentheses indicate corresponding percentages of the total revenue from States' own taxes.

Sources: Reserve Bank of India, *Report on Currency and Finance,* Volume II, (various years); and Government of India, Ministry of Finance, *Indian Public Finance Statistics, 2015-2016*, Tables 1.7 and 3.2 (excerpted).

According to the White Paper, in the existing sales tax structure, there were problems of double taxation of commodities and multiplicity of taxes, resulting in a cascading tax burden. For instance, in the existing structure, before a commodity was produced, inputs were first taxed, and then after the commodity was produced with input tax load, output was taxed again. This caused an unfair double taxation with cascading effects.

The State-level VAT, as elaborated in the White Paper, had certain distinct advantages over the existing sales tax structure. The VAT would not only provide full set-off for input tax as well as tax on previous purchases, but it would also abolish the burden of several of the existing taxes, such as turnover tax, surcharge on sales tax, additional surcharge, special additional tax etc. In addition, Central Sales Tax (CST) would also be phased out. As a result, the overall tax burden would be rationalised, and prices, in general, would fall. Moreover, VAT would replace the existing system of inspection by a system of built-in self-assessment by traders and manufacturers. The tax structure would become simple and more transparent. This would significantly improve tax compliance and would also help increase revenue growth.

The White Paper listed the following benefits from VAT adoption:

1. A set-off would be given for input tax as well as tax paid on previous purchases.
2. Other taxes, such as turnover tax, surcharge, additional surcharge etc. would be abolished.

3. Overall tax burden would be rationalized.
4. Prices would in general fall.
5. There would be self-assessment by dealers.
6. Transparency would increase.
7. There would be higher revenue growth.

The VAT would therefore help common people, traders, industrialists and also the Government. It is indeed a move towards more efficiency, equal competition and fairness in the taxation system.

The White Paper also struck a balance between what was possible in the VAT design to begin with and what could be improved upon in subsequent years as more experience is gathered. It further mentioned how after working out a consensus on this VAT design, nearly all the States had finalized their VAT Bills and were in the process of obtaining Presidential assent.

It is noteworthy that sales tax was replaced by State-VAT (i.e. sales tax with set-off provisions). Haryana was the first state to replace its sales tax by VAT on April 1, 2003. Other States followed suit. State-VAT, in turn, was subsumed under GST.

20.4 Replacement of Sales Tax by Value Added Tax (VAT)

The replacement of the state sales taxes by VAT in 2005 marked a significant step forward in the reform of domestic trade taxes in India. Implemented by the Empowered Committee of State Finance Ministers (Chairman: Asim Dasgupta) [1], it addressed the distortions and complexities associated with the levy of tax at the first point of sale under the erstwhile system and resulted in a major simplification of the rate structure and broadening of the tax base. The consensus reached among the States for uniformity in the VAT rates brought an end to the harmful tax competition among them. It also lessened the cascading of tax.

In mid-1990s, most states had agreed to phase out the incentive-related exemptions and implement floor rates of sales tax. As part of the nation wide efforts to redesign commodity taxation and the implementation of CENVAT at the level of the Centre, many States modified their sales tax regimes to launch a state level VAT under the scheme prepared by the Empowered Committee of State Finance Ministers for this purpose.

20.4.1 Minimum Rate Agreement among States, 1989: As already noted, some States had been indulging in a sort of *rate-war* to attract trade and industry to their respective regions. To avoid this unhealthy competition, the Chief Ministers agreed, at their conference in New Delhi on February 9-10, 1989, that all the States would adopt the minimum floor level rates as recommended by the Committee of Sales Tax Commissioners in its report of 1984 in respect of 29 identified items. The Chief Secretaries of northern States (Punjab, Haryana, Himachal Pradesh, Rajasthan, Delhi, and Uttar Pradesh) had recommended in May 1994 that there should not only be a uniform rate of sales tax but the slabs of this tax be reduced in these States.

In this connection the Tax Reforms Committee, 1991, observed, "As regards sales tax, the Committee is of the view that this tax could be converted into a form of State VAT within the manufacturing sector. There may be no need for levying sales tax at more than two rates since the distributional and other non-revenue objectives could be left to be performed by the Central taxes which apply uniformly throughout the country". [2]

20.4.2 State Finance Ministers' Conference, 1994: The State Finance Ministers' Conference held in New Delhi on May 27, 1994, failed to arrive at a consensus on the replacement of indirect taxes at the State level by a value added tax. The matter was deferred indefinitely by appointing a ten-member Committee of State Finance Ministers to go into this and related questions.

20.4.3 Preliminary Discussion on State-level VAT, 1995: The first preliminary discussion on State-level VAT took place in a meeting of Chief Ministers convened by Dr. Manmohan Singh, the then Union Finance Minister in 1995. In this meeting, the basic issues on VAT were discussed in general terms and this was followed up by periodic interactions of State Finance Ministers.

20.4.4 Chief Ministers Conference, 1999: In a significant meeting of all the Chief Ministers, convened on November 16, 1999 by Yashwant Sinha, the then Union Finance Minister, two important decisions, among others, were taken. First, before the introduction of State-level VAT, the unhealthy sales tax *rate war* among the States must end, and sales tax rates would need to be harmonised by implementing uniform floor rates of sales tax for different categories of commodities with effect from January 1, 2000. Secondly, on the basis of achievement of the first objective, steps would be taken by the States for introduction of State-level VAT after adequate preparation. For implementing these decisions, a Standing Committee of State Finance Ministers was formed which was then made an Empowered Committee of State Finance Ministers.

20.5 Report of Empowered Committee, 2001

The Empowered Committee met regularly. All the decisions were taken on the basis of consensus. On the strength of these repeated discussions and collective efforts, involving the Ministers and the concerned officials, it was possible within a period of about a year and a half to achieve nearly 98 percent success in the first objective, namely harmonisation of sales tax structure through implementation of uniform floor rates of sales tax.

After reaching this stage, steps were initiated for systematic preparation for introduction of State level VAT. Again, in order to avoid any unhealthy competition among the States which might lead to distortions in manufacturing and trade, attempts were made from the very beginning to harmonise the VAT design in the States, keeping also in view the distinctive features of each State and the need for federal flexibility. This was done by the States collectively agreeing, through discussions in the Empowered Committee, to certain common points of convergence regarding VAT, and allowing at the same time certain flexibility to accommodate the local characteristics of the States.

Along with these measures, steps were taken for necessary training, computerization and interaction with trade and industry. While these preparatory steps were taken, the Empowered Committee got a significant support from P. Chidambaram, the then Union Finance Minister, when he responded positively in providing Central financial support to the States in the event of loss of revenue in transitional years of implementation of VAT.

The Empowered Committee, through its deliberations over the years, finalised a design of VAT to be adopted by the States. The model design sought to retain the essential features of VAT, while at the same time, providing a measure of flexibility to the States, to enable them to meet their local requirements. The main features of the VAT design finalised by the Empowered Committee were the following:

1. Rates of VAT on various commodities were to be uniform for all the States/UTs. There were 2 basic rates of 4 percent and 12.5 percent, besides an exempt category and a special rate of 1 percent for a few selected items. The items of basic necessities were put in the zero-rate bracket or the exempted schedule. Gold, silver and precious stones were put in the 1 percent schedule. There was also a category with 20 percent floor rate of tax, but the commodities listed in this schedule were not eligible for input tax rebate/set off. This category covered items like motor spirit (petrol), diesel, aviation turbine fuel, and liquor.
2. Model VAT design made provision for eliminating the multiplicity of taxes. In fact, all the State taxes on purchase or sale of goods (excluding entry tax in lieu of octroi) were required to be subsumed in VAT.
3. Provision was made for allowing input tax credit, which was the basic feature of VAT. However, since the VAT being implemented was intra-State VAT only and did not cover inter-State sale transactions, input tax credit was not made available on inter-State purchases.
4. There were provisions to make the system more business-friendly. For instance, there was provision for self-assessment by the dealers. Similarly, there was provision of a threshold limit for registration of dealers in terms of annual turnover of ₹ 5 lakh. Dealers with turnover lower than this threshold limit were not required to obtain registration under VAT and were exempt from payment of VAT. There was also provision for composition of tax liability up to annual turnover limit of ₹ 50 lakh.
5. Regarding the industrial incentives, the States were allowed to continue with the existing incentives, without breaking the VAT chain. However, no fresh sales tax/VAT-based incentives were permitted.
6. Exports were zero-rated, with credit given for all taxes on inputs/purchases related to such exports.

It was emphasised that the States must think in terms of economic development of the country as a whole and encourage the free flow of trade and commerce in the economy.

At a Conference of Chief Ministers and Finance Ministers of various States held on July 5, 2001 in New Delhi, the Report of the Empowered Committee of State Finance Ministers on VAT (Chairman: Asim Kumar Dasgupta), was accepted and adopted for the introduction of VAT with effect from April 1, 2002. The VAT design recommended by the Empowered Committee was geared to achieve the following objectives:

1. Eliminate the cascading burden of taxation by setting off the tax paid on inputs against that on output.
2. Reduce distortions in the economy caused by double taxation.

3. End market fragmentation with a uniform regime of taxation followed in all the States.
4. Ensure one category of tax-exempted commodities for all the States.
5. Ensure two VAT rates: a uniform 4 percent for all States on goods of basic necessities and a uniform floor rate of 10 percent for other commodities (except a few items such as bullion and liquor).
6. Ensure uniform set of procedures for VAT assessment to be followed by all the States, including the use of permanent account number (PAN) as a common business identifier.
7. Ensure that States implemented uniform floor rates of sales tax by July-end 2001, failing which faulting States could be penalised by discontinuing Central Government assistance.

In view of the apprehensions expressed by a large number of States about possible revenue losses in the initial years of introduction of VAT, an assurance was given to the States that the Government of India would compensate the States to the extent of 100 percent of revenue loss in the first year (2002-03), 75 percent of the loss in the second year (2003-04) and 50 percent of the loss in the third year (2005-06). A Committee of State Finance Secretaries was appointed to evolve clear and measurable criteria for judging revenue loss, if any, due to the introduction of VAT.

20.6 Agreement of January 23, 2002

At the Conference of State Finance Ministers held on January 23, 2002 a final decision was taken that all States and Union Territories would introduce VAT from April 2003. This position was reiterated by all States at the Conference of State Chief Ministers held on October 18, 2002. Empowered Committee of State Finance Ministers endorsed the suggestion that every State Legislation on VAT should have a minimum set of common features. Accordingly, a model VAT Bill was circulated to all the States.

20.7 Meeting of State Finance Ministers, 2003

Again, at a meeting of the Finance Ministers of all States/Union Territories on January 17, 2003, States and Union Territories again reiterated their firm commitment to introduce VAT from April 1, 2003. It was decided that the VAT legislations of all States and UTs would have common provisions in respect of all important matters and that a simple VAT legislation with maximum convergence would be implemented. It was also agreed that along with the introduction of VAT, the origin-based Central sales tax (CST) would be phased out. It was also agreed that the Additional Duties of Excise (Goods of Special Importance) Act would be suitably amended to empower States to levy sales tax/VAT on sugar, textiles and tobacco with a ceiling rate of 4 percent. This would be done without affecting the existing levy of Additional Duties of Excise on these items by the Union Government.

The Empowered Committee of State Finance Ministers agreed upon the following sequence of steps to ensure introduction of VAT in place of retail sales tax system in States.

1. Passing of VAT legislation and framing of rules and regulations.
2. Computerisation of dealers who would fall within the ambit of VAT.
3. Training of tax officials, traders and consumer associations.
4. Publicity for consumers.
5. Implementation of VAT, assigning VAT identification numbers to tax payers.
6. Implementing transitional measures for introduction of VAT.

20.8 Agreement of June 2004

At a meeting of the State Finance Ministers with the Union Finance Minister on June 18, 2004, it was decided that all States would introduce a uniform VAT from April 1, 2005. The proposed VAT would replace the taxes levied by different States like sales tax and octroi. Coinciding with the introduction of VAT, the Central Government would bring down the Central sales tax (CST) rate from 4 percent to 2 percent. The CST would be phased out in 2006-07. It was also decided that traders with an annual turnover up to ₹ 5 lakh would be exempt from VAT. This decision was aimed at ending traders' opposition to VAT. It may be recalled that States had missed at least five deadlines for the introduction of VAT, mainly due to resistance from trading community.

As a consequence of all these steps, the States started implementing VAT beginning April 1, 2005. After overcoming the initial difficulties, all the States and Union Territories were able to implement VAT. The Empowered Committee monitored closely the process of implementation of State-level VAT.

20.9 Role of the Central Government

Introduction of State VAT was an important reform measure at the State level. The State VAT replaced the earlier sales tax systems of the States. VAT, being a 'tax on sale or purchase of goods within a State' was a State Subject by virtue of Entry 54 of List II (State List) of the Seventh Schedule of the Constitution of India. Since sales tax/VAT was a State subject, the Central Government played the role of a facilitator for successful implementation of VAT. Some of the steps taken by the Central Government in this regard were as follows:

1. A package for payment of compensation to States for any revenue loss on account of introduction of VAT was implemented.
2. Financial support under Mission Mode Project (MMP) was provided to States/UTs in order to enable them to take up computerization of their tax departments.
3. A separate project for computerization of tax administration of Himachal Pradesh and Jammu and Kashmir was sanctioned.
4. 50 percent funding was provided to the Empowered Committee of State Finance Ministers for implementation of the TINXSYS Project for tracking of inter-State transactions.

20.10 Shortcomings of State VAT

Complexities under the State VAT related primarily to classification of goods to different tax rate schedules. Theoretically, one might expect that the lower tax rates would be applied to basic necessities that are consumed largely by the poor. This was not the case under the State VAT. The lowest rate of 1 percent applied to precious metals and jewellery, and related products—was unacceptable from the distributional perspective. The middle rate of 4 percent applied to selected basic necessities and also a range of industrial inputs and IT products. In fact, basic necessities fell into three categories—exempted from tax, taxable at 4 percent, and taxable at the standard rate of 12.5 percent. The classification was arbitrary, with no well-accepted theoretical underpinning. Whatever the political merits of this approach, it was not conducive to lower compliance costs. Most retailers found it difficult to determine the tax rate applicable to a given item without referring to the legislative schedules. Consumers were even less aware of the tax applicable to various items. This gave rise to leakages and rent-seeking.

Another source of complexity under the State VAT was determining whether a particular transaction constituted a sale of goods or not. This problem was most acute in the case of software products and intangibles such as the right to distribute/exhibit movies or time slots for broadcasting advertisements.

The issue of cascading taxation was partly addressed when all the states adopted the concept of VAT for state sales tax. Several central and state taxes were excluded from VAT. Sectors such as real estate, oil and gas production etc. were exempt from VAT. Further, goods and services were taxed differently, thereby making the taxation of products complex.

Broadly speaking, the experience of implementing VAT was quite encouraging. The new system was received well by all the stakeholders, and the transition was quite smooth with the Empowered Committee (EC) constantly reviewing the progress of implementation. The EC advised the States to constantly interact with trade and industry to remove their apprehensions, if any, and to ensure that the benefits of VAT due to input tax credit and reduction in tax rates (wherever applicable) were passed on to the consumers.

Introduction of VAT in the States was a more challenging exercise in a federal country like India, where each State, in terms of constitutional provision, is sovereign in levying and collecting State taxes. In the sales tax regime (before the introduction of VAT), apart from the problem of multiple taxation and burden of adverse cascading effect of taxes, there was also no harmony in the rates of sales tax on different commodities among the States. Not only were the rates of sales tax numerous (often more than ten in several States), and different from one another for the same commodity in different States, but there was also an unhealthy competition among the States in terms of sales tax rates—so-called *rate war*—often resulting in revenue loss.

It is in this background that attempts were made by the States to introduce a harmonious VAT in the States, keeping at the same time in mind the issue of sovereignty of the States regarding the State tax matters.

See also chapters 7 and 14 of this book.

Endnotes

1. Empowered Committee of State Finance Ministers (EC) was originally set up on July 17, 2000 by the Government of India with the State Finance Ministers of West Bengal, Karnataka, Madhya Pradesh, Maharashtra, Punjab, Uttar Pradesh, Gujarat, Delhi and Meghalaya as members with an objective to monitor the implementation of uniform floor rates of sales tax by States and Union territories, to monitor the phasing out of the sales-tax based incentive schemes, to decide milestones and methods of States to switch over to VAT and to monitor reforms in the Central Sales Tax system existing in the country. Subsequently, State Finance Ministers of Assam, Tamil Nadu, Jammu and Kashmir, Jharkhand and Rajasthan were also notified as the members of the Empowered Committee. On August 12, 2004, the Government of India decided to reconstitute the Empowered committee with State Finance/Taxation Ministers of all States as its members.
   The body was later registered as a Society under the Societies Registration Act (XXI of 1860). The registration certificate was issued on August 17, 2004. Presently, all the Ministers in-charge of Finance/Taxation of all State Governments and Union Territories with legislatures, Additional Secretary (Revenue), Government of India and Member Secretary, Empowered Committee are the members of the Empowered Committee. The Empowered Committee has its office in Delhi Sachivalaya, I.P. Estate, New Delhi where Government of NCT of Delhi has provided accommodation and other facilities. The Society has been receiving contribution from the State Government and Government of India to meet its administrative expenditure and undertake various other activities.
   Recently, in order to strengthen the EC, Thirteenth Finance Commission recommended that a grant of ₹ 30 crore be made to EC, so that they can pursue GST related research work and enhance capacities. Amount of ₹ 30 crore has accordingly been released to EC for creating a corpus of for this purpose.
2. Government of India, Ministry of Finance, *Tax Reforms Committee-Final Report*, Part I, (Chairman: Raja Chelliah), August 1992, p. 174.

21

Goods and Services Tax (GST)

The pre-GST system of indirect taxes in India was marked by multiplicity of taxes and rates at the central and state levels which resulted in a complex tax structure ridden with hidden costs for trade and industry. GST subsumed a profusion of central and state indirect taxes to create a single unified market. In all, 8 central and 9 state taxes/duties were abolished to pave way for the introduction of GST. In sharp contrast to the earlier system, GST is an all-India unified, uniform and harmonized indirect tax system. The old system was mainly manual and opaque while the new system is technology-based and hence transparent.

21.1 Commodity Taxation in India Prior to the Introduction of GST

Prior to the introduction of GST on July 1, 2017, the indirect tax system of India suffered from various disabilities. There was a burden of *tax-on-tax* in the pre-GST system of central excise duty and the sales tax system of the states. State level sales tax (later VAT) was a levy on commodities which, in most cases, were also subject to excise duties imposed by the centre. As excise duty and sales tax were levied by different layers of government, it became difficult to determine judiciously the impact of these levies on production, investment, and the consumers. Since the centre and states acted independently without co-ordination among themselves, there was hardly any possibility to rationalize commodity tax system successfully.

21.1.1 Multiplicity of Taxes and Rates: The multiplicity of taxes at the central and state levels resulted in a complex indirect tax structure in the country that was ridden with hidden costs for the trade and industry. There was no uniformity of tax rates and structure across states. Differential rates of sales tax on the same set of commodities in different states often led to uneconomic diversion of trade as well as production centres. It was not uncommon for people of one state making purchases in other states to avoid or reduce sales tax liability. In order to attract trade and industry to their respective areas, some states indulged in a kind of *rate war* (competitive reductions in sales tax rates). Rate differentials caused flight of capital and enterprise from high to low tax rate states thereby distorting natural selection of production centres based on geographical advantages, leading to unnecessary transportation of raw materials and finished goods and hence cost escalations. In contrast, GST is a single tax on the supply of goods or services or both, right from the manufacturer to the consumer. Credits of input taxes paid at each stage are available in the subsequent stage of value addition, which makes GST essentially a tax only on value addition at each stage.

21.1.2 Complexity of Administration and Compliance: In spite of the improvements made in the tax design and administration, the systems at both the central and state levels remained complex. Their administration left a lot to be desired. There were often disputes and court challenges, and the process for resolution of disputes was slow and expensive. At the same time, the systems suffered from substantial compliance gaps, except in the highly organized sectors of the economy. There were several factors contributing to this unsatisfactory state of affairs. The most significant cause of complexity was the existence of exemptions and multiple rates, and the irrational structure of the levies.

Compounding the structural or design deficiencies of each of the taxes was the poor or archaic infrastructure for their administration. Taxpayer services were virtually non-existent or grossly inadequate under both central and state administrations. Many of the administrative processes were still manual, not benefiting from the efficiencies of automation. All this not only increased the costs of compliance, but also undermined revenue collection.

21.1.3 Tax Cascading: Tax cascading [1] was the most serious flaw of the pre-GST indirect tax system. There was a burden of *tax-on-tax* in the erstwhile system of central excise duties and states' sales taxes. It increased the cost of production and put Indian suppliers at a competitive disadvantage in the international markets. It created a bias in favour of imports, which did not bear the hidden burden of taxes on production inputs. It also detracted from a neutral application of tax to competing products. Although the statutory rate was uniform, the effective tax rate (i.e. statutory rate on finished products and the implicit or hidden tax on production inputs) varied from product to product depending on the magnitude of the hidden tax on inputs used in their production and distribution. The intended impact of government policy towards sectors or households was negated by the indirect or hidden taxation in a cascading system of taxes.

21.2 Introduction of GST: A Historic Tax Reform

After an arduous journey of 12 years—beginning with the mention of Goods and Services Tax (GST) by the then Finance Minister P. Chidambaram in his Budget Speech for 2005-06 on February 28, 2005—GST finally became operative on July 1, 2017. The historic tax reform saw various ups and downs during this period.

21.2.1 What is GST? GST is a tax on goods and services with comprehensive and continuous chain of set-off benefits up to the retailer level. It is essentially a tax only on value addition at each stage, and a supplier at each stage is permitted to set-off, through a tax credit mechanism, the GST paid on the purchase of goods and services. Ultimately, the burden of GST is borne by the end-user (i.e. final consumer) of the commodity/service.

According to clause 12A of Article 366 of the Constitution, *goods and services tax* means any tax on supply of goods, or services or both except taxes on the supply of the alcoholic liquor for human consumption. According to the same Article, *goods* includes all materials, commodities, and articles (clause 12), *services* means anything other than goods (clause 26A) and *State* with reference to Articles 246A, 268, 269, 269A and Article 279A includes a Union Territory with legislature (clause 26B).

The power to levy GST is derived from Article 246A of the Constitution which confers concurrent powers to both Parliament and State Legislatures to make laws with respect to GST. However, clause 2 of Article 246A read with Article 269A provides exclusive power to the Parliament to legislate with respect to inter-state trade or commerce. The taxable event under GST is the supply of goods and/or services. CGST and SGST are levied on intra-state supplies while IGST is levied on inter-state supplies.

GST is a comprehensive indirect tax levy on manufacture, sale and consumption of goods as well as services at the national level. GST is an indirect tax for the whole of India to make it one unified common market. GST is designed to give India a world class tax system and improve tax collections. It has ended the long-standing distortions of differential treatment of manufacturing sector and services sector. GST has facilitated seamless credit across the entire supply chain and across all States under a common tax base.

21.2.2 Objectives of GST: The basic objective of tax reforms in any country should be to establish a tax system that is economically efficient, distributionally acceptable, and simple to administer. GST is India's most ambitious and remarkable indirect tax reform. Its objective is to levy a single uniform tax across India on all goods and services. Implementing a new tax, encompassing both goods and services, by the centre and the states in a large and complex federal system, is perhaps unprecedented in modern global tax history.

Since major central and state indirect taxes have got subsumed under GST, the multiplicity of taxes has been substantially reduced which, in turn, has decreased the administrative costs [2] of the indirect tax system. The uniformity in tax rates and procedures across the country have also reduced the compliance costs. [3]

Signifying the spirit of co-operative federalism, GST is a historic and game-changing tax reform. Domestically, it will help improve governance, strengthen tax institutions, facilitate *Make-in-India by making-one-India*, and impart buoyancy to the tax base. The Indian GST is 21st century's global standard for VAT in large federal systems.

Implementation of GST left behind an inefficient, complicated and fragmented indirect tax system. GST requires a very high level of compliance. The age of hand-written ledgers, account books, balance sheets and manual record-keeping is gone. Everything is now online and needs to be updated regularly.

21.3 Salient Features of GST

GST has subsumed a profusion of Central and State indirect taxes to create a single unified market. GST has made India a seamless national market, boosting trade and industry and hence growth rate. As against the erstwhile system of tax on the manufacture of goods or on sale of goods or on provision of services, GST is applicable on *supply* of goods or services or both.

21.3.1 GST is Levied on Supply: Taxable event in law is the event the happening of which results in imposition of a tax. In other words, tax liability is activated when tax event takes place.

What is taxable event in GST? Taxable event in GST is the *supply* of goods or services or both. GST becomes applicable only if there is supply of goods/services. Therefore, the word *supply* holds the greatest significance in determining the taxability of various types of transactions. In fact, the concept of supply is the pivot around which GST revolves.

The concept of supply under GST includes all sorts of activities like manufacture, sale, barter, exchange, transfer etc. It also includes supplies made without consideration when such supplies are made in certain specified situations.

It is noteworthy that in the pre-GST system of indirect taxes, excise duties were imposed on manufacture/production of goods, sales tax (later VAT) on sale of goods and service tax on provision of services,

21.3.2 Destination-based Consumption Tax: GST is a destination-based consumption tax as against the erstwhile origin-based tax system. This implies that the tax would accrue to the taxing authority which has jurisdiction over the place of consumption which is also termed as place of supply.

21.3.3 Input Tax Credit (ITC): According to Section 16(1) of the Central Goods and Services Tax Act, 2017, "Every registered person shall, subject to such conditions and restrictions as may be prescribed and in the manner specified in Section 49, be entitled to take credit of input tax charged on any supply of goods or services or both to him which are used or intended to be used in the course or furtherance of his business and the said amount shall be credited to the electronic credit ledger of such person".

ITC is an important feature of GST. There are well-defined rules for availing ITC.

21.3.4 GST and Foreign Trade: Exports are zero-rated supplies under GST law. Supplies made to special economic zones (SEZs) are zero-rated and considered as physical exports. As per explanation to clause (1) of Article 269A of the Constitution, IGST (CGST plus SGST) will be levied on all imports into the territory of India. Thus, import of goods is treated as inter-state supplies and hence subject to IGST in addition to the applicable customs duties. Import of services is treated as inter-state supplies and hence subject to IGST.

21.3.5 Goods and Services Tax Network (GSTN): GSTN is the information technology (IT) infrastructure of GST. In fact, it is GSTN the backbone of GST. GSTN provides shared IT infrastructure and services to Central and State Governments, tax payers and other stakeholders. GSTN is a special purpose vehicle (SPV) which aims to provide a standard and uniform interface to the taxpayers, and shared infrastructure and services to Central and State/UT Governments. It is the interface between the government and the taxpayers.

21.3.6 GST Council: GST Council is a joint forum of the Centre and the States created under Article 279A of the Constitution. The recommendations made by the Council act as benchmark or guidance to Union as well as State Governments. The guiding principle of GST Council is to ensure harmonization on different aspects of GST between the Centre and the States as well as among States. It has been provided in Article 279A that the GST Council, in its discharge of various functions, shall be guided by the need for a harmonized structure of GST and for the development of a harmonized national market for goods and services.

21.4 Components of GST

The introduction of GST on July 1, 2017 was a significant reform in the field of indirect taxes in India. Multiple taxes levied on goods and services by the centre and the states were replaced by GST.

A dual GST model is in place in view of the federal structure of India. Centre and the states now simultaneously levy GST on every supply of goods or services or both which takes place within a state or union territory (i.e. intra-state trade). Hence, there are three components of GST so far as intra-state trade is concerned.

1. Central Goods and Services Tax (CGST).
2. State Goods and Services Tax (SGST).
3. Union Territory Goods and Services Tax (UT-GST).

Another important component of GST is Integrated Goods and Service Tax (IGST) which is levied by the centre on inter-state supply of goods or services or both. IGST rate is broadly equal to CGST rate plus SGST rate. SGST component of IGST accrues to the consumer state.

Similarly, a compensation cess on certain specified goods is imposed to compensate states for any revenue loss on account of implementation of GST.

21.4.1 Central Goods and Services Tax (CGST): GST levied by the Centre on intra-State supply of goods or services or both is called CGST. It is levied under Central Goods and Services Tax (CGST) Act, 2017 which makes provisions for the levy and collection of tax on intra-state supply of goods or services or both by the Central Government. The Act is divided into 21 chapters which deal with matters connected with the levy, collection and administration of GST.

21.4.2 State Goods and Services Tax (SGST): GST levied by the States on intra-state supply of goods or services or both under their respective SGST Acts is called SGST. Union territories with legislature (Delhi, Puducherry and Jammu and Kashmir) are covered under the definition of *state*. However, Union territories without legislature are governed by Union Territory Goods and Services Tax (UT-GST), Act, 2017.

21.4.3 Union Territory Goods and Services Tax (UT-GST): Union Territories without legislature are governed by a separate Act, namely the Union Territory Goods and Services Tax (UT-GST), Act, 2017 which makes provisions for the levy and collection of tax on intra-UT supply of goods or services or both in the Union Territories without legislature. Thus, it extends to the following five Union Territories:

1. Andaman and Nicobar Islands.
2. Lakshadweep.
3. Dadra and Nagar Haveli and Daman and Diu.
4. Chandigarh.
5. Ladakh.

21.4.4 Integrated Goods and Service Tax (IGST): IGST is levied by the Centre on inter-state supply of goods or services or both. IGST is a mechanism to monitor the inter-state supply of goods or services or both. It is levied by the Central Government on all inter-state transactions of taxable goods and services. IGST rate is broadly equal to CGST rate plus SGST rate. SGST component of IGST accrues to the consumer state. IGST maintains the integrity of input tax credit (ITC) chain in inter-state supplies.

GST makes distinction between intra-state and inter-state supply of goods and services. Hence, IGST—as a part of GST regime—is levied on inter-State supply (including stock transfers) of goods and services. It is levied and collected by the Centre so that the credit chain is not disrupted. IGST also applies on imports.

21.4.5 Compensation Cess: It is a cess levied under Section 8 of the Goods and Services Tax (Compensation to States) Act, 2017. It is applicable—in addition to the regular GST taxes (CGST + SGST/UT-GST on intra-state supplies and IGST on inter-state supplies—on the supply of certain notified goods/services. The following goods—which mostly belong to the luxury and demerit categories—have been notified for the purpose so far.

1. *Pan masala.*
2. Tobacco and tobacco products.
3. Coal.
4. Aerated waters.
5. Motor vehicles.

21.5 Rate Structure of GST

Implementation of GST involved several issues which were debated in policy circles. Primary among them was the issue of the revenue neutral rate—the rate which would ensure that the migration to the proposed GST would not entail any revenue shortfall for the centre and states from the current level. In order to achieve this goal, rates had to be appropriately set, exemplifying the true spirit of fiscal federalism, in which revenues are equitably shared by the centre and states. To get the design of the GST right, it was necessary to aim at tax rates that would protect revenue, simplify administration, encourage compliance, avoid adding to inflationary pressures, and keep India in the range of countries with reasonable levels of indirect taxes.

21.5.1 Rate Structure of GST on Goods: First of all there is a notified list of goods exempted from GST. Most of the essential goods of mass consumption are exempt from GST through notifications. There is a long list of such goods as, for example, bread, all fresh fruits and vegetables, fresh milk and curd and hearing aids. The exemption list also includes items which have symbolic value in terms of tax relief as, for example *rakhis,* bangles and *puja samagri.* The purpose of exemptions is to ensure tax equity, i.e. not to put tax burden on low income earners.

Essential food items and necessities of life are subject to 5 percent rate of GST as, for example, sugar, tea roasted coffee beans, edible oils, skimmed milk powder, milk food for babies, domestic LPG, low-priced footwear (i.e. costing below ₹ 1,000). Again, the purpose is not to put heavy tax burden on low income earners.

12 percent rate is applicable to semi-comfort goods such as butter, *ghee,* almonds mobiles, telephones, LED lights, umbrellas and cutlery.

18 percent rate is applicable on comfort goods as, for example TVs, computers, digital cameras, hair oil, soap, toothpaste, toiletry, footwear costing ₹ 1,000 and above.

The highest 28 percent rate is applicable on luxury goods as, for example, air conditioners and dish washing machines.

Ultra luxury goods like aerated waters and motor cars are also subject to GST compensation cess in addition to the 28 percent rate. Similarly, certain demerit or sinful goods like *pan masala* and tobacco products are subject to compensation cess in addition to 28 percent rate.

It is apparent that the rate structure on goods is designed to ensure progressivity in the indirect tax system of the country. In simple words, the burden of tax should fall on economically well-off sections of society and not on economically disadvantaged.

21.5.2 Rate Structure of GST on Services: First of all there is a notified list of services exempted from GST. In the long list of exempt services, health and educational services stand out prominently.

5 percent rate is applicable on essential services like transport of goods by rail, transport of goods in a vessel, renting of motor cab, tour operators services, food parcels (or takeaways).

12 percent rate is applicable, among others, on cinema tickets up to ₹ 100 and third-party insurance premium of goods-carrying vehicles.

18 percent rate is applicable on cinema tickets above ₹ 100.

Highest rate of 28 percent is applicable on luxury services like services by way of admission to entertainment events or access to amusement facilities, services provided by a race club, gambling, accommodation in hotels including 5 star and above rated hotels where room rent is ₹ 7,500 and above per night per room.

21.6 Impact of GST on Indian Economy

The pre-GST system of indirect taxes was marked by multiplicity of taxes and rates at the central and state levels. This resulted in a complex tax structure which was ridden with hidden costs for trade and industry. There was no uniformity of tax rates and collection procedures across States.

In sharp contrast to the earlier system, GST has ensured uniform exemption list, uniform rates and uniform collection procedures throughout the country. It has paved the way for a common national market. The country has moved from an inefficient and fragmented indirect tax system to an efficient and unified tax regime in the form of GST. The old system was mainly manual and opaque while the new system is technology-based and hence transparent.

21.6.1 From Fragmented to Unified Indirect Tax System: Prior to the introduction of GST, the indirect tax system of India was fragmented and complicated. Tax powers were clearly demarcated between the centre and the states. There was no joint occupancy of tax fields. As a result, tax bases were fragmented in the sense that duties of excise were imposed on goods manufactured or produced in India by the centre and taxes on the sale or purchase of goods were levied by the states.

The central government imposed excise duty on the manufacture/production of commodities. These duties were imposed on almost all industrial products at varying rates. Apart from the basic excise duty, there were additional excise duties, surcharges and cesses. Exemptions and concessions were an integral part of the excise system. Excise preferences and reliefs were given to promote a wide spectrum of socio-economic objectives. Excise taxation in India was an interesting example of multitude of rates which were subject to frequent revisions. Numerous considerations contributed to the complexity of excise rates. The labyrinthine intricacies of the tariff often led to confusion and litigation amongst the taxpayers and revenue authorities. Moreover, there were different procedures to assess and collect excise duties, viz. physical control system, self-removal procedure (SRP) and compounded levy scheme. All Union duties of excise were abolished—except those on petroleum products and tobacco—to pave way for the introduction of GST.

In all, 8 Central taxes, including the above-mentioned, were abolished to pave way for the roll out of GST from July 1, 2017.

States governments, on their part, imposed sales tax (later VAT) on almost the same commodities as were subject to excise duties. All the States had their own Sales Tax Acts. Lists of exemptions, rates of taxation, compounding schemes and rules and regulations varied across states. It was a nightmare for a business entity doing business in more than one State.

Differential rates of sales tax on the same set of commodities in different states often led to uneconomic diversion of trade as well as production centres. It was not uncommon for people of one state making purchases in other States to avoid or reduce sales tax liability. Apart from sales tax, states also imposed various types of cesses and taxes of local nature like entry tax, octroi, terminal tax etc.

Then there was the central sales tax (CST). When goods were sold within the state, sales tax was levied, collected and appropriated by the concerned state. In case goods were sold in the course of inter-state trade, then CST was levied by the centre but collected and appropriated by the exporting state.

In all, 9 state taxes/duties were abolished, including the above-mentioned, to prepare ground for the introduction of GST.

Thus, GST subsumed under it 17 taxes/duties (8 belonging to centre and the rest 9 belonging to states). Now, GST is a single tax on the supply of goods or services or both, right from the manufacturer to the consumer. Credits of input taxes paid at each stage are available in the subsequent stage of value addition, which makes GST essentially a tax only on value addition at each stage.

In GST, the country has moved from a fragmented indirect tax system to a unified tax regime. Now there is joint occupancy of tax fields by the centre and the states. In other words, there is a common tax base (i.e. supply of goods and services) for the centre and the states. This exercise at consolidation and unification of taxation of goods and services was historic and unprecedented.

21.6.2 From Differing to Uniform Tax Practices: In the pre-GST era, multiple taxes were imposed at the level of central and state governments. In the case of excise duty and service tax imposed by the central government, there was all-India uniformity in terms of rates, exemptions and compliance procedures. However, in the case of state taxes (mainly sales tax/VAT), every state had its own rate structure, exemption list and collection procedures. Many of the administrative processes were manual, not benefiting from the efficiencies of automation. All this not only increased the costs of compliance, but also undermined revenue collection. Businesses had to maintain multiple-record-keeping for a variety of taxes.

In fact, there was no national policy as regards the burden of taxes on different goods and services. The scenario has changed with the introduction of GST. Instead of multiple taxes at different levels of the government, there is one tax with common base, exemption list, rate structure and administrative procedures. This has reduced investment of resources and manpower in maintaining records. GST has improved the ease-of-doing-business and transportation of goods across the country.

Apart from reducing compliance costs, common tax rates and procedures across the country have made business tax neutral, irrespective of the choice of place of doing business. GST rate structure, with some exceptions, is based on the following four rates (know as *four-tax slabs-rule*): 5 percent, 12 percent, 18 percent and 28 percent.

21.6.3 From Tax Rivalry to Tax Harmony: In the pre-GST system of indirect taxes, the centre had a commanding position over the states in the sense that the former had the first right to levy tax (excise duties) on a wide range of industrial products. State levied sales tax (later VAT) on almost the same set of commodities, but with whatever little scope left after the imposition of excise duties. In other words, states played second fiddle to the centre in terms of revenue from commodity taxation. Since the centre and states acted independently without co-ordination among themselves, there was hardly any possibility to harmonize commodity tax system successfully. Similarly, as excise duty and sales tax were levied by different layers of government, it became difficult to determine judiciously the impact of these levies on production, investment, and the consumers.

Another point of rivalry was the taxation of services. In the pre-GST regime, services per se remained outside the scope of state taxation powers. In other words, centre had the exclusive power to tax services. Exclusion of services from the state taxation powers had negative impact on the buoyancy of state tax revenues. With the growth in per capita incomes, services were accounting for a growing fraction of the total consumer basket, which the states could not tax. With no powers to levy tax on fastest growing components of consumer expenditure, the states had to rely almost exclusively on compliance improvements or rate increases for any buoyancy in their *own-source revenues*.

Centre-State revenue antagonism has subsided with the imposition of GST on goods and services. Article 246A of the Constitution confers concurrent powers to both Parliament and State Legislatures to make laws with respect to GST. The dual GST imposes tax on the same taxable event—supply of goods and services—simultaneously by both the centre and the states. Both the centre and the states are empowered to levy GST across the value chain from the stage of manufacture to consumption.

The assignment of concurrent jurisdiction to the centre and the states for the levy of GST requires a unique institutional mechanism that would ensure that decisions about the structure, design and operation of GST are taken jointly by the two. GST Council is the institutional mechanism for this purpose with constitutional force.

GST has charted out a new course for co-operative federalism in India, focusing on mutual understanding and accommodation between the centre and states as regards the structure of taxation of goods and services.

21.6.4 End to Inter-State Tax Rivalry: In the pre-GST era, state governments levied sales tax/VAT on a wide range of commodities at different rates with diverse procedures and rules for its collection. The rate structure of sales tax/VAT was further complicated in view of different lists of exemptions/concessions in each of the States. In order to attract trade and industry to their respective areas, some states indulged in a kind of *rate war* (competitive reductions in sales tax/VAT rates). It is true that some States lacked infrastructural facilities and to compensate for that, sales tax concessions came handy to attract industries, but this shortcut eroded the resource-base of the states, so vital for the development of infrastructure which alone could guarantee their speedy development on permanent footing.

GST has ensured uniform exemption list, uniform rates and uniform collection procedures throughout the country. GST represents fiscal integration of the country on the same pattern as political integration of India after attaining Independence in 1947.

21.6.5 From Manually-operated Opaque to an IT-based Transparent Tax System: The use of technology for tax administration, particularly at the level of states, was limited in the pre-GST era. Taxpayers, in most cases, were following traditional practices of hand-written ledgers, account books, balance sheets and manual record-keeping. Manually-operated administrative and compliance procedures lacked transparency, leading to delays and corruption. GST is an IT-based tax system. Everything is now online—from tax payment to filing of returns and to claiming of refunds. Moreover, IT-based tax information has to be updated regularly.

Goods and Services Tax Network (GSTN) provides shared IT infrastructure and services to central and state governments, tax payers and other stakeholders. GSTN is a state-of-the-art comprehensive IT infrastructure including the common GST portal which provides front-end services of registration, payments and returns to taxpayers. It also assists some States with back-end IT modules that include processing of returns, registrations, audits, assessments, appeals etc.

21.6.6 E-way Bill and Hassles-free Movement of Goods: In the pre-GST era, different states had different requirements of documentation to allow goods pass through their check-posts. However, such check posts, by the very nature of their operations, generated enormous delays in road traffic. The arrangement also encouraged rent-seeking behaviour. Introduction of e-way bill system is a fundamental shift from the earlier departmental policing model to self-declaration model. The new system envisages one EWB for movement of goods throughout the country, thereby ensuring a hassle-free movement for transporters throughout the country.

Soon after the introduction of GST from July 1, 2017, most of the states dismantled border check posts for commercial taxes. Many state governments, through advisories to their field staff, are ensuring that truckers are not harassed. This has significantly reduced travel time, minimized delays and reduced transaction costs.

The objective of dismantling internal trade barriers to create a common economic space within the country, which is an essential element of nationhood, depends critically upon the recognition of commonality of interests by the states. This need has gained urgency as external barriers to trade and commerce have been brought down in the wake of establishment of World Trade Organization (WTO) with effect from January 1, 1995. Barriers to internal trade are specifically barred by the Constitution of India, and it is the responsibility of the Central Government to ensure that no policy, which has the effect of abridgement of inter-State trade and commerce, is permitted as envisaged in Article 301 of the Constitution. In short, GST has improved the logistics environment of India.

21.6.7 Reduced Interface between Taxpayer and Tax Collector: All interactions under GST are through the common GSTN portal and hence there will be less public interface between the taxpayer and the tax administration. Timelines have been provided for important activities like obtaining registration, refunds etc.

In short, GST is a comprehensive indirect tax levy on manufacture, sale and consumption of goods as well as services at the national level. GST is an indirect tax for the whole of India to make it one unified common market. GST is designed to give India a world class tax system and improve tax collections. It would end the long-standing distortions of differential treatment of manufacturing sector and services sector. GST will facilitate seamless credit across the entire supply chain and across all States under a common tax base.

Endnotes

1. The concept of tax cascading is associated with a traditional turnover tax which is levied on transaction of goods and services at all levels of production and distribution. For example, excise duty may be levied on raw materials, components, semi-finished and finished goods. This system of taxation increases the price of a commodity much more than the tax collected, resulting in *cascading*.
2. Administrative costs are costs incurred by public authorities in administering a tax. These costs (also called expense ratio) include wages of tax officials and expenditures on stores and supplies for running tax administration. They are interpreted in terms of cost-yield ratio which means cost of collection expressed as a proportion of tax revenue. A lower cost-yield ratio is considered indicative of the efficiency of tax administration. Unusually high cost-yield ratio is a drag on the public exchequer. Thus, cost-yield ratios may be used to evaluate administration of competing taxes.
3. Compliance costs refer to costs incurred by taxpayers or third parties in complying with a tax, over and above the tax payment made to public authorities. The third party compliance costs are those incurred by firms in discharging their legal responsibility as tax collectors, e.g. deducting income tax from salaries and passing it on to the tax authorities. The following three types of compliance costs may be distinguished:

- Money Costs: These include payment for legal advice, fees to accountants or to valuers for valuation of property (for purposes of death duties, wealth tax etc.), cost of postage, telephone calls, travelling, books, and in some cases litigation.
- Time Costs: These include time taken to consult tax advisers, complete tax returns, and to travel to tax offices.
- Psychic Costs: These refer to the worries and anxieties associated with tax payment.

22

Changed Landscape of Fiscal Federalism Due to Implementation of GST

Enactment of the Constitution (One Hundred and First Amendment) Act, 2016 and the subsequent introduction of Goods and Services Tax (GST) from July 1, 2017 marked a clear departure from the initial scheme of distribution of taxation powers between the Centre and the States envisaged in the Constitution.

22.1 From Mutually Exclusive to Concurrent Powers of Taxation

Prior to enactment of the Constitution (One Hundred and First Amendment) Act, 2016, taxation powers between the Centre and the States were clearly demarcated in the Constitution of India with no overlaps between their respective domains. In other words, there were no concurrent powers of taxation (or joint occupancy of tax fields) by the two levels of government. The absence of joint occupancy of tax fields successfully minimised double taxation, tax rivalry between the Centre and the States, and duplicate tax administration.

Broadly speaking, the important sources of indirect tax revenue for the Centre were customs duty, excise duty (except on alcoholic liquors) and service tax. States collected the major part of their indirect tax revenue from tax on sales and purchases, excise duty on alcoholic liquors, octroi or entry tax, electricity duty and taxes on luxuries, entertainments and amusements.

In the case of inter-State sales, the Centre had the power to levy Central Sales Tax (CST), though the tax was collected and retained entirely by the originating States.

In fact, taxes with inter-State base and those in the case of which all-India uniformity in rates was desirable—to facilitate industry and trade—were vested in the Central Government. Taxes which were location-specific and related to subjects of local consumption were with the States.

In the pre-GST arrangements, the indirect tax system of India suffered from various disabilities like multiplicity of taxes and rates, complexity of administration and compliance and tax cascading (*tax-on-tax*).

The Constitution (One Hundred and First Amendment) Act, 2016 inserted Article 246A in the constitution which now confers concurrent powers to both Parliament and State Legislatures to make laws with respect to goods and services tax (GST). The dual GST imposes tax on the same taxable event—supply of goods and services—simultaneously by the Centre and the States. Both the Centre and the States are empowered to levy GST across the value chain from the stage of manufacturing to consumption. The credit of GST paid on inputs at every stage of value addition is available for the discharge of GST liability on the output, thereby ensuring that GST is charged only on the value addition component at each stage. This mechanism has ensured that there is no *tax-on-tax* on goods and services.

By amalgamating a large number of Central and State taxes into a single tax and allowing set-off of prior-stage taxes, GST has mitigated the ill effects of *cascading* or *pyramiding* and paved the way for a common national market. Introduction of GST would make India's products competitive in the domestic and international markets. GST is not merely a tax reform. It is also a reform that would revolutionize the way business is conducted in India.

Since major Central and State indirect taxes have got subsumed under GST, the multiplicity of taxes has been substantially reduced which, in turn, is expected to decrease the operating costs of the indirect tax system. With GST in place, the burden of Central sales tax (CST) has also been removed. The uniformity in tax rates and procedures across the country will go a long way in reducing compliance costs.

As already stated, introduction of GST has concurrently empowered the Centre and the States to levy and collect it. The assignment of concurrent jurisdiction to the Centre and the States for the levy of GST requires a unique institutional mechanism that would ensure that decisions about the structure, design and operation of GST are taken jointly by the two levels of government. Goods and Services Tax Council (GST Council) is the institutional mechanism for this purpose with constitutional force.

22.2 Compensation to States for the Loss of Revenue Due to GST Implementation

22.2.1 Need for Compensation: In the pre-GST era, when goods were sold within the state, then sales tax (later VAT) was levied, collected and appropriated by the concerned state. In case goods were sold in the course of inter-state trade, then central sales tax (CST) was levied by the Central Government but the revenue was collected and appropriated by the exporting state (state of origin) where production or sale took place rather than the state where consumption happened (importing state).

Switchover from origin-based sales tax/VAT to destination-based GST was a thorny issue in the designing of the new tax. Many manufacturing states expressed concerns over the loss of revenue on account of such a shift. To allay their fears, it was decided to compensate states which may suffer revenue loss consequent upon the introduction of GST.

22.2.2 Constitutional Provisions and the Law for Compensation to States: Despite the sincere attempts made by the Empowered Committee (EC) of State Finance Ministers [1] on the determination of revenue neutral GST rates, it was difficult to estimate accurately as to how much the States would gain from service taxes and how much they would lose on account of removal of cascading effect, payment of input tax credit and phasing out of CST. In view of this, it was essential to provide adequately for compensation for loss that might emerge during the process of implementation of GST. The payment of this compensation was ensured in terms of special grants to be released to the States on the basis of neutrally-monitored mechanism. Section 18 of the Constitutional (One Hundred First Amendment) Act, 2016—reproduced below—incorporated provisions for such compensation.

"Compensation to States for Loss of Revenue on Account of Introduction of Goods and Services Tax: Parliament shall, by law, on the recommendation of the Goods and Services Tax Council, provide for compensation to the States for loss of revenue arising on account of implementation of the goods and services tax for a period of five years".

Goods and Services Tax (Compensation to States) Act, 2017 was enacted to levy compensation cess for providing compensation to the States for the loss of revenue arising on account of implementation of the goods and services tax with effect from July 1, 2017, for a period of 5 years or for such period as may be prescribed on the recommendations of the GST Council.

Compensation to the affected states is provided through GST compensation cess which is levied—on top of the peak rate of GST (28 percent)—on a few specified goods (which are mainly luxury and demerit items), viz. *pan masala*, tobacco, coal, aerated waters, and motor cars to create a fund for compensating states.

In the very First Meeting of GST Council held on September 22-23, 2016, it was decided, *inter alia*, that Financial year 2015-16 would be the base year for compensating the States in case of any revenue loss to States following the implementation of GST.

Growth rate of revenue for a state during the 5 year period is assumed to be 14 percent.

The base year tax revenue consists of revenue from: (a) state VAT, (b) central sales tax, (c) entry tax, octroi, local body tax, (d) taxes on luxuries and (e) taxes on advertisements etc. In other words, revenue from all taxes of a state—subsumed under GST—in 2015-16 is the base year revenue. However, any revenue among these taxes related to supply of alcohol for human consumption, and five specified petroleum products, is not accounted as part of the base year revenue.

22.3 Earlier Instances of Compensation

Compensation to States under GST is not the first instance of its kind in the post-Independence tax history of India. It can be recalled that following a voluntary agreement between the Centre and the States in December, 1956, it was decided to replace sales tax on textiles, tobacco, and sugar by additional duties of excise and to distribute revenues derived therefrom among the States. The agreement provided also that the share accruing to each State *shall not in any case be less than the revenue realised from the levy of sales tax on these goods for the financial year 1956-57 in that State.* The decision was implemented through the Additional Duties of Excise (Goods of Special Importance) Act, 1957.

The Act did not debar States from the levy of sales tax on the specified commodities, but it did provide that if in any year any State levied and collected a tax on the sale or purchase of such commodities, no sum shall be paid to that State in that year by way of share out of the net proceeds of the additional duties of excise. The commodities covered under the scheme (textiles, tobacco, and sugar) were declared goods of special importance in inter-State trade so that no state could find it worthwhile to opt out of the voluntary agreement not to impose sales tax on these goods. [2]

Further, the scheme of additional excise duties was proposed to be extended to some more commodities in 1983. An expert committee (Chairman: Kamlapati Tripathi) in its Report [3] submitted in January 1983, recommended the replacement of sales tax by additional excise duty on *vanaspati*, drugs and medicines, cement, paper and paper board, and petroleum products. The recommendations were considered in a conference of Chief Ministers held on November 2, 1983. However, the six Chief Ministers of the non-Congress(I) States, viz. Andhra Pradesh, Jammu and Kashmir, Karnataka, Tamil Nadu, Tripura, and West Bengal opposed the centre's initiative to implement the recommendations.

The opposition of non-Congress(I) States was based on the belief that implementation of the scheme would erode their revenue position. However, a close perusal of the recommendations of the Tripathi Committee suggests that it evolved elaborate formulae for *protecting the financial interests of the States*. In the case of three commodities, namely paper and paper board, *vanaspati*, and drugs and medicines, it suggested that the annual growth rate of the amount to be collected by way of additional excise duty in lieu of sales tax should be related to the future annual growth rate of sales tax revenue of all the States. For petroleum products and cement, which were substantially subject to administered prices, the Committee recommended and worked out linkages between the amount to be collected by way of additional excise duty from year-to-year and value of consumption on which normal sales tax would be leviable.

In spite of these safeguards, the apprehension of some States that their resource position would be adversely affected reflected their lack of confidence in the Centre in implementing the scheme sincerely. Thus, an important tax reform became a casualty of distrust between the central and the state governments.

In the case of switch over from sales tax to VAT, compensation was provided to the states for three years, at 100 percent in the first year, 75 percent in the second year and 50 percent in the third year.

22.4 GST Compensation Cess

22.4.1 What is a Cess? A cess is a levy to raise funds for a particular purpose and not for the general revenues of the government. A cess is different from a tax in that the proceeds of the former are earmarked for a defined purpose. For example, under the Income Tax Act, 1961, education and health cess @ 4 percent is leviable on the amount of income tax and surcharge, if any. The money collected through it is used only for education and health facilities in India. Out of the total 4 percent, 3 percent is spent on education and 1 percent for giving health insurance.

In the pre-GST era, 26 cesses were in existence at the level of Central Government. In its very first meeting held on September 22-23, 2016, GST Council decided to subsume all Central cesses under the GST.

22.4.2 What is GST Compensation Cess: It is a cess levied under Section 8 of the Goods and Services Tax (Compensation to States) Act, 2017. It is applicable—in addition to the regular GST taxes (CGST + SGST/UT-GST on intra-state supplies and

IGST on inter-state supplies—on the supply of certain notified goods/services. The following goods—which mostly belong to the luxury and demerit categories—have been notified for the purpose so far.

1. *Pan masala.*
2. Tobacco and tobacco products.
3. Coal.
4. Aerated waters.
5. Motor vehicles.

22.4.3 Purpose of Compensation Cess: GST cess is levied to compensate states which may suffer any loss of revenue due to the implementation of GST from July 1, 2017. The revenue collected from compensation cess is credited to a non-lapsable fund known as Goods and Services Tax Compensation Fund. The Fund is used for compensating tax revenue loss to states on account of GST implementation.

The Act specifies that compensation payable to states has to be released at the end of every two months. The cess will be levied for a period of 5 years (transition period) from the date of implementation of GST.

If any funds remain unutilized at the end of the transition period, the same would be shared in half by the Central Government and all the State Governments. The share of State Governments would be distributed in the ratio of their total revenues from State/UT GST, in the last year of the transition period.

Goods and Services Tax (Compensation to States) Act, 2017 was amended by Goods and Services Tax (Compensation to States) Amendment Act, 2018 by inserting sub-Section 3A in Section 10 of the principal Act. As per the amended Act, fifty percent of such amount, as may be recommended by the GST Council, which remains unutilized in the compensation fund, at any point of time in any financial year during the transition period shall be transferred to the Consolidated Fund of India as the share of the Centre, and the balance fifty percent shall be distributed amongst the States in the ratio of their base year revenue.

In case of shortfall in the amount collected in the fund against the requirement of compensation to be released for any two months' period, fifty percent of the same, but not exceeding the total amount transferred to the Centre and the States, as recommended by the Council, shall be recovered from the Centre and the balance fifty percent from the States in the ratio of their base year revenue.

The new arrangement would partly address the GST revenue deficit for the Centre and come in aid of states worried over stagnant growth in their own (non-GST) revenue. However, it also indicates an excess collection of cess beyond the losses contemplated by the states. This calls for justification because the only purpose of cess is to compensate the states for any revenue loss arising out of GST implementation.

22.4.4 Collection and Calculation of Cess: All taxable persons supplying the notified goods, except taxpayers registered under composition scheme, are liable to collect and remit the cess to the government. The cess is calculated on the basis of the taxable value of the supply and as per the rate schedule for compensation cess. It is levied in addition to the regular GST taxes, i.e. CGST + SGST/UT-GST in the case of intra-state supplies and IGST in the case of inter-state supplies.

A. On Exports: Compensation cess is not charged on goods exported by an exporter under bond and the exporter is eligible for refund of input tax credit of cess relating to goods exported. In case goods are exported on the payment of cess, the exporter is eligible for refund of cess paid on goods exported by him, along with refund of input tax credit of cess relating to goods exported.

B. On Imports: In case compensation cess is applicable on goods imported into India, then it is levied and collected in accordance with the provisions of Section 3 of the Customs Tariff Act, 1975, at the point when duties of customs are levied on the said goods under section 12 of the Customs Act, 1962, on a value determined under the Customs Tariff Act, 1975.

The cess is levied and collected along with customs duty and IGST.

22.4.5 Input Tax Credit (ITC): ITC can be availed on compensation cess paid on inward supplies of the notified goods. However, the credit of the cess paid can be utilized only towards payment of cess liability.

22.4.6 Valuation if Cess to be Levied on Value: GST cess can be specific, ad valorem or even specific-cum-ad valorem. Thus, cess on coal is specific (or volumetric), representing a fixed amount of tax on a unit of the physical quantity of the product. In other words, there is no need for valuation of the commodity. It is ad valorem (according to value) in the case of pan masala, aerated waters and motor vehicles. Still further, it is specific-cum-ad valorem in the case of tobacco and tobacco products.

In case the compensation cess is chargeable on any supply of goods with reference to their value, then for each such supply, the value has to be determined under Section 15 of the CGST Act, 2017.

22.4.7 Laws and Rules Applicable: The provisions of the CGST Act, 2017 and the rules made thereunder—including those relating to assessment, input tax credit, appeals, offences and penalties—apply in relation to the levy and collection of the cess on the intra-state supply of goods and services.

Similarly, in the case of inter-state supplies the provisions of the IGST Act, 2017 and the rules made thereunder shall apply.

In short, compensation cess has the following characteristics:

1. Compensation cess is collected on the supply of notified goods or services or both.
2. Beginning July 1, 2017, it will be levied for a period of 5 years or for such period as may be prescribed on the recommendations of the GST Council.
3. The cess is meant to compensate the states for any revenue loss on account of implementation of GST.
4. It is not be payable by exporters.
5. It is not payable by composition scheme dealers.
6. Input tax credit of the cess can be used only to pay compensation cess and not the other taxes like CGST, SGST/UT-GST or IGST.

Endnotes

1. While declaring its intention to introduce GST from April 1, 2010, the Central Government had indicated that the Empowered Committee (EC) of State Finance Ministers would work with the Central Government to prepare a road map for the introduction of GST. Hence, EC—which had formulated the design of State level VAT—prepared a report on a Model and Road Map for GST.
2. Internal as well as inter-State sales tax on goods of special importance was governed by the Central Sales Tax Act, 1956. The existing rate of CST was 4 percent.
3. Government of India, Ministry of Finance, *Report of the Expert Committee on Replacement of Sales Tax by Additional Excise Duty,* (Chairman: Kamlapati Tripathi), January 1983.

Appendix

Appendix

Current Constitutional Provisions Pertaining to Distribution of Taxation Powers between the Centre and the States

This chapter explains the constitutional provisions pertaining to taxation powers of different tiers of government in India. The Constitution makes elaborate, albeit complex, arrangements relating to the distribution, between the Union and the States, of taxes, the power of borrowing, and provision for grants-in-aid by the Union to the States. The underlying philosophy of these arrangements is to place at the disposal of the two tiers of government adequate financial resources to enable them to discharge their respective responsibilities under the Constitution.

A.1 Distribution of Taxation Powers

Article 265 of the Constitution specifically states that no taxes shall be levied or collected except by the authority of law.

Article 246 (read with Seventh Schedule of the Constitution) mentions the matters on which the Centre and the States can legislate. Thus, the Centre has exclusive powers to legislate in respect of matters contained in List I (Union List) of the Seventh Schedule. Entries 82 to 92C of this list refer to taxation powers of the Union Government (Table A.1). Similarly, the States have exclusive powers to legislate in respect of matters contained in List II (State List) of the Seventh Schedule. Entries 45 to 63 of this list refer to taxation powers of the States (Table A.2). Furthermore, the Centre and the States have concurrent powers to make laws on any matter contained in List III (Concurrent List) of the Seventh Schedule. However, this list does not contain any head of taxation.

The residual powers of taxation, as in general legislation, belong to the Union vide Article 248 read with Entry 97 of List I (Union List) in the Seventh Schedule. The Article reads, "(1) Subject to Article 246A, Parliament has exclusive power to make any law with respect to any matter not enumerated in the Concurrent List or State List.

(2) Such power shall include the power of making any law imposing a tax not mentioned in either of those Lists".

For example, gift tax was imposed by the Union Government in 1958 under these residual powers (gift tax was abolished in 1998). Similarly, prior to the Constitution (Eighty-eighth Amendment) Act, 2003, service tax was imposed under these residual powers.

As regards Union Territories, the Parliament has the power to impose any tax included in the State List.

A scrutiny of the taxation powers contained in List I Union List) and List II (State List) of the Seventh Schedule of the Constitution reveals that major and elastic sources of tax revenue belong to the Centre while relatively inelastic sources of revenue come under the purview of State Governments.

Table A.1: Taxes within Union Jurisdiction as Enumerated in List I (Union List) in the Seventh Schedule (Read with Article 246) of the Constitution of India

Entry No. in List I	Description of the Tax/Duty	
	Before Constitution (One Hundred and First Amendment) Act, 2016	**After Constitution (One Hundred and First Amendment) Act, 2016**
82	Taxes on income other than agricultural income.	Same
83	Duties of customs including export duties.	Same
84	Duties of excise on tobacco and other goods manufactured or produced in India except: (a) alcoholic liquors for human consumption; (b) opium, Indian hemp and other narcotic drugs and narcotics, but including medicinal and toilet preparations containing alcohol or any substance, included in sub-paragraph (b) of this entry.	Duties of excise on the following goods manufactured or produced in India, namely: (a) petroleum crude; (b) high speed diesel; (c) motor spirit (commonly known as petrol); (d) natural gas; (e) aviation turbine fuel; and (f) tobacco and tobacco products.
85	Corporation tax.	Same
86	Taxes on the capital value of assets, exclusive of agricultural land, of individuals and companies, taxes on the capital of companies.	Same
87	Estate duty in respect of property other than agricultural land.	Same
88	Duties in respect of succession to property other than agricultural land.	Same
89	Terminal taxes on goods or passengers carried by railway, sea or air; taxes on railway fares and freights.	Same
90	Taxes other than stamp duties on transactions in stock exchanges and future markets.	Same
91[1]	Rates of stamp duty in respect of bills of exchange, cheques, promissory notes, bills of lading, letters of credit, policies of insurance, transfer of shares, debentures, proxies, and receipts.	Same
92	Taxes on the sale or purchase of newspapers and on advertisements published therein.	Omitted

contd...

92A[2]	Taxes on the sale or purchase of goods other than newspapers, where such sale or purchase takes place in the course of inter-State trade or commerce.	Same
92B[3]	Taxes on the consignment of goods (whether the consignment is to the person making it or to any other person), where such consignment takes place in the course of inter-State trade or commerce.	Same
92C[4]	Taxes on services.	Omitted
97[5]	Any other matter not enumerated in List II or List III including any tax not enumerated in either of these lists.	Same

1. To be read with Article 268.
2. Inserted by the Constitution (Sixth Amendment) Act, 1956; to be read with Article 269.
3. Inserted by the Constitution (Forty-sixth Amendment) Act, 1982; to be read with Article 269.
4. Inserted by the Constitution (Eighty-eighth Amendment) Act, 2003.
5. To be read with Article 248.

Source: Government of India, Ministry of Law, Justice and Company Affairs, *The Constitution of India,* Seventh Schedule, List I (Union List).

A.2 Special Provisions with Respect to Goods and Services Tax

Article 246A of the Constitution [1] makes special provision with respect to goods and services tax by the Centre and the States. It reads, "246A. (1) Notwithstanding anything contained in Articles 246 and 254, Parliament, and, subject to clause (2), the Legislature of every State, have power to make laws with respect to goods and services tax imposed by the Union or by such State. (2) Parliament has exclusive power to make laws with respect to goods and services tax where the supply of goods, or of services, or both takes place in the course of inter-State trade or commerce.

Explanation—The provisions of this article, shall, in respect of goods and services tax referred to in clause (5) of Article 279A, take effect from the date recommended by the Goods and Services Tax Council".

A.3 Restrictions on the Taxation Powers of the States

Constitution also imposes certain restrictions on the taxation powers of the States. Although a State legislature enjoys the power to levy Goods and Services Tax (GST) under Article 246A and any of the taxes mentioned in List II (State List) of the Seventh Schedule, in the case of certain taxes, this power is subject to restrictions imposed by substantive provisions of the Constitution. Some examples of these restrictions are as follows.

A.3.1 Restriction on States to Impose Tax on the Supply of Goods or Services or Both: Article 286 ensures that taxes imposed by the States do not interfere with imports and exports or inter-State trade and commerce which are matters of national importance. The Article reads as under:

Table A.2: Taxes within State Jurisdiction as Enumerated in List II (State List) in the Seventh Schedule (Read with Article 246) of the Constitution of India

Entry No. in List II	Description of the Tax/Duty	
	Before Constitution (One Hundred and First Amendment) Act, 2016	**After Constitution (One Hundred and First Amendment) Act, 2016**
45	Land revenue, including the assessment and collection of revenue, the maintenance of land records, survey for revenue purposes and records of rights, and alienation of revenues.	Same
46	Taxes on agricultural income.	Same
47	Duties in respect of succession to agricultural land.	Same
48	Estate duty in respect of agricultural land.	Same
49	Taxes on lands and buildings.	Same
50	Taxes on mineral rights subject to any limitations imposed by Parliament by law relating to mineral development.	Same
51	Duties of excise on the following goods manufactured or produced in the State and countervailing duties at the same or lower rates on similar goods manufactured or produced elsewhere in India: (a) alcoholic liquors for human consumption; (b) opium, Indian hemp and other narcotic drugs and narcotics but not including medicinal and toilet preparations containing alcohol or any substance included in sub-paragraph (b) of this entry.	Same
52	Taxes on the entry of goods into a local area for consumption, use or sale therein.	Omitted
53	Taxes on the consumption or sale of electricity.	Same
54*	Taxes on the sale or purchase of goods other than newspapers, subject to the provisions of Entry 92A of List I.	Taxes on the sale of petroleum crude, high speed diesel, motor spirit (commonly known as petrol), natural gas, aviation turbine fuel and alcoholic liquor for human consumption, but not including sale in the course of inter-State trade or commerce or sale in the course of international trade or commerce of such goods.

contd...

55**	Taxes on advertisements other than advertisements published in the newspapers (and advertisements broadcast by radio or television).	Omitted
56	Taxes on goods and passengers carried by road or on inland waterways.	Same
57	Taxes on vehicles, whether mechanically propelled or not, suitable for use on roads, including tramcars subject to the provisions of Entry 35 of List III.	Same
58	Taxes on animals and boats.	Same
59	Tolls.	Same
60***	Taxes on professions, trades, callings and employment.	Same
61	Capitation taxes.	Same
62	Taxes on luxuries, including taxes on entertainment, amusements, betting and gambling.	Taxes on entertainments and amusements to the extent levied and collected by a panchayat or a municipality or a regional council or a district council.
63	Rates of stamp duty in respect of documents other than those specified in the provisions of List I with regard to rates of stamp duty.	Same

*Substituted by the Constitution (Sixth Amendment) Act, 1956: ** The words 'and advertisements broadcast by radio or television' inserted by the Constitution (Forty-second Amendment), Act, 1976: *** The scope of these taxes is spelt out in Article 276, clause (2) of which fixes the amount payable by a person on account of these taxes.

Source: Government of India, Ministry of Law, Justice and Company Affairs, *The Constitution of India,* Seventh Schedule, List II (State List).

"286. (1) No law of a State shall impose, or authorise the imposition of, a tax on the supply of goods or services or both, where such supply takes place: (a) outside the State; or (b) in the course of the import of the goods or services or both into, or export of the goods or services or both out of, the territory of India.

(2) Parliament may by law formulate principles for determining when a supply of goods or of services or both takes place in any of the ways mentioned in clause (1).

A.3.2 Exemption from State Taxes on Electricity Consumed by the Government of India (Article 287): The Article reads: "287. Save in so far as Parliament may by law otherwise provide, no law of a State shall impose, or authorise the imposition of, a tax on the consumption or sale of electricity (whether produced by a Government or other persons) which is:

(a) consumed by the Government of India, or sold to the Government of India for consumption by that Government; or (b) consumed in the construction, maintenance or operation of any railway by the Government of India or a railway company operating that railway, or sold to that Government or any such railway company for consumption in the construction, maintenance or operation of any railway, and any such law imposing, or authorising the imposition of, a tax on the sale of electricity shall secure that the price of electricity sold to the Government of India for consumption by that Government, or to any such railway company as aforesaid for consumption in the construction, maintenance or operation of any railway, shall be less by the amount of the tax than the price charged to other consumers of a substantial quantity of electricity".

A.3.3 Monetary Limit on Taxes on Professions etc.: A State legislature is empowered to levy a tax on professions, trade, calling or employment vide Entry 60 of List II. However, the total amount payable in respect of any one person to the State by way of such tax is not to exceed ₹ 2,500 per annum [Article 276(2)].

A.4 Exemption of Property of the Union from State Taxation

The property of the Centre is exempt from State taxation under Article 285(1) which reads as follows: "285. (1) The property of the Union shall, save in so far as Parliament may by law otherwise provide, be exempt from all taxes imposed by a State or by any authority within a State. (2) Nothing in clause (1) shall, until Parliament by law otherwise provides, prevent any authority within a State from levying any tax on any property of the Union to which such property was immediately before the commencement of this Constitution liable or treated as liable, so long as that tax continues to be levied in that State".

A.5 Exemption of Property and Income of a State from Union Taxation

Under Article 289 the property and incomes of the States are exempt from Union taxes, except that Parliament may by law provide for Central taxation of any trading activities of a State which are not incidental to the ordinary functions of Government. Article 289 reads as follows: "289. (1) The property and income of a State shall be exempt from Union taxation. (2) Nothing in clause (1) shall prevent the Union from imposing, or authorising the imposition of, any tax to such extent, if any, as Parliament may by law provide in respect of a trade or business of any kind carried on by, or on behalf of, the Government of a State, or any operations connected therewith, or any property used or occupied for the purposes of such trade or business, or any income accruing or arising in connection therewith. (3) Nothing in clause (2) shall apply to any trade or business, or to any class of trade or business, which Parliament may by law declare to be incidental to the ordinary functions of Government".

A.6 Sharing of Central Taxes

All the taxes and duties levied by the Union are not meant entirely for the purpose of the Union. In fact, revenues from certain taxes and duties leviable by the Union are totally assigned to States [2] or shared with them to supplement their revenues in accordance with their needs. It is a tribute to the foresight of the founding fathers that they realised that the sources of revenue allocated to the States may not prove sufficient in view of their growing welfare, maintenance, and developmental activities. Hence, specific provisions were made to set apart a portion of Central revenues for the benefit of States. These provisions indicate the flexibility of India's Constitution in terms of distribution of financial resources between different layers of the Government. They also make a distinction between the legislative power to *levy* a tax and the power to *appropriate* the proceeds of a tax so levied.

A.6.1 From Itemised Sharing to Global Sharing: Prior to the Constitution (Eightieth Amendment) Act, 2000, two main Central taxes were shared with the states, namely income tax (other than corporation tax) and the Union excise duties. The sharing of the income tax was mandatory under Article 270 while that of the Union excise duties was discretionary under Article 272. There were also two tax rental arrangements with the States, where the Union Government collected the tax on behalf of the States and then distributed the proceeds among the States on the basis of criteria recommended by the Finance Commission. These were: (i) additional duties of excise in lieu of sales tax on textiles, tobacco and sugar, and (ii) grant in lieu of tax on railway passenger fares.

The Constitution (Eightieth Amendment) Act, 2000, significantly changed the manner of distribution of Central tax collections between the Central and State Governments. It substituted a new Article for Article 270 and omitted the old Article 272. The new Article 270 provides for the sharing of the net proceeds of all Union taxes and duties with the States, subject to the provisions of Article 271 (explained below). In other words, all central taxes were brought into a shareable pool and it became mandatory to assign a share from each central tax to the States. Eleventh Finance Commission was the first to make recommendations in accordance with the new provisions of the Constitution.

It is noteworthy that only *net proceeds* are to be shared, and as such *cost of collection* has to be deducted to obtain the net proceeds as prescribed under Article 279. The proceeds are to be distributed among the States where the central taxes are *leviable* in *that year*.

Article 270 reads as follows: "270. (1) All taxes and duties referred to in the Union List, except the duties and taxes referred to in Articles 268, 269 and 269A, respectively, surcharge on taxes and duties referred to in Article 271 and any cess levied for specific purposes under any law made by Parliament shall be levied and collected by the Government of India and shall be distributed between the Union and the States in the manner provided in clause (2).

(1A) The tax collected by the Union under clause (1) of Article 246A shall also be distributed between the Union and the States in the manner provided in clause (2).

(1B) The tax levied and collected by the Union under clause (2) of Article 246A and Article 269A, which has been used for payment of the tax levied by the Union under clause (1) of Article 246A, and the amount apportioned to the Union under clause (1) of Article 269A, shall also be distributed between the Union and the States in the manner provided in clause (2).

(2) Such percentage, as may be prescribed, of the net proceeds of any such tax or duty in any financial year shall not form part of the Consolidated Fund of India, but shall be assigned to the States within which that tax or duty is leviable in that year, and shall

be distributed among those States in such manner and from such time as may be prescribed in the manner provided in clause (3).

(3) In this article, "prescribed" means—(i) until a Finance Commission has been constituted, prescribed by the President by order, and (ii) after a Finance Commission has been constituted, prescribed by the President by order after considering the recommendations of the Finance Commission".

The objective of the Constitution (Eightieth Amendment) Act, 2000 was to construct a pool of all central taxes for sharing so that a holistic view could be taken and both sides could share in the aggregate buoyancy of the central tax revenues.

A.7 Surcharges on Certain Duties and Taxes for the Purposes of the Union (Article 271)

The Article reads, "271. Notwithstanding anything in Articles 269 and 270, Parliament may at any time increase any of the duties or taxes referred to in those articles [except the goods and services tax under Article 246A [3] by a surcharge for purposes of the Union and the whole proceeds of any such surcharge shall form part of the Consolidated Fund of India".

A.8 Duties Levied by the Union but Collected and Appropriated by the States (Article 268)

These include such stamp duties as are mentioned in Entry 91 of List I (Union List) of the Seventh Schedule. The Article reads as follows: "268. (1) Such stamp duties as are mentioned in the Union List shall be levied by the Government of India but shall be collected: (a) in the case where such duties are leviable within any Union Territory by the Government of India, and (b) in other cases, by the States within which such duties are respectively leviable. (2) The proceeds in any financial year of any such duty leviable within any State shall not form part of the Consolidated Fund of India, but shall be assigned to that State".

Stamp duties are leviable on bills of exchange, cheques [4], promissory notes, bills of lading, letters of credit, policies of insurance, transfer of shares, debentures, proxies, and receipts. These documents are executed in the course of business and trade and they find place in the Union List to ensure uniformity of rates throughout the country for the smooth conduct of commercial and related transactions. Inter-State disparities in their rates and tax regulations can hinder, and even disrupt, the free flow of trade and commercial activities. The levy and collection of stamp duty is governed by the Indian Stamp Duty Act, 1899 which was last amended in 1976 when rates of stamp duty on certain instruments were revised. [5]

A.9 Taxes Levied and Collected by the Union but Assigned to the States (Article 269)

Article 269 reads as follows: "269. (1) Taxes on the sale or purchase of goods and taxes on the consignment of goods, except as provided in Article 269A, shall be levied and collected by the Government of India but shall be assigned and shall be deemed to have been assigned to the States on or after the 1st day of April, 1996 in the manner provided in clause (2).

Explanation—For the purposes of this clause: (a) the expression "taxes on the sale or purchase of goods" shall mean taxes on sale or purchase of goods other than newspapers, where such sale or purchase takes place in the course of inter-State trade or commerce and (b) the expression "taxes on the consignment of goods" shall mean taxes on the consignment of goods (whether the consignment is to the person making it or to any other person), where such consignment takes place in the course of inter-State trade or commerce.

(2) The net proceeds in any financial year of any such tax, except in so far as those proceeds represent proceeds attributable to Union territories, shall not form part of the Consolidated Fund of India, but shall be assigned to the States within which that tax is leviable in that year, and shall be distributed among those States in accordance with such principles of distribution as may be formulated by Parliament by law.

(3) Parliament may by law formulate principles for determining when a sale or purchase of, or consignment of, goods takes place in the course of inter-State trade or commerce".

The above two taxes correspond to Entries 92A and 92B in List I (Union List) of the Seventh Schedule. [6]

It is noteworthy that out of these two taxes only one was being levied till recently, viz. inter-State sales tax (Entry 92A). Central Sales Tax (CST) on inter-State sales was subsumed under GST.

A.9.1 Philosophy of Articles 268 and 269: Taxation arrangements under Articles 268 and 269 of the Constitution are of special importance. They place under the charge of the Union the taxes and duties which have inter-State character and require uniformity in rate structure for the smooth conduct of business and trade activities throughout the country. These two Articles mention taxes/duties which shall be levied by the Centre but assigned completely to the States within which they are leviable. [7]

A.10 Levy and Collection of Goods and Services Tax in the Course of Inter-State Trade or Commerce (Article 269A)

Inserted by Section 9 of the Constitution (One Hundred and First Amendment) Act, 2016 this new Article reads as follows: "269A. (1) Goods and services tax on supplies in the course of inter-State trade or commerce shall be levied and collected by the Government of India and such tax shall be apportioned between the Union and the States in the manner as may be provided by Parliament by law on the recommendations of the Goods and Services Tax Council.

Explanation—For the purposes of this clause, supply of goods, or of services, or both in the course of import into the territory of India shall be deemed to be supply of goods, or of services, or both in the course of inter-State trade or commerce.

(2) The amount apportioned to a State under clause (1) shall not form part of the Consolidated Fund of India.

(3) Where an amount collected as tax levied under clause (1) has been used for payment of the tax levied by a State under Article 246A, such amount shall not form part of the Consolidated Fund of India.

(4) Where an amount collected as tax levied by a State under Article 246A has been used for payment of the tax levied under clause (1), such amount shall not form part of the Consolidated Fund of the State.

(5) Parliament may, by law, formulate the principles for determining the place of supply, and when a supply of goods, or of services, or both takes place in the course of inter-State trade or commerce".

A.11 Goods and Services Tax Council (GST Council) (Article 279A)

Section 12 of the Constitution (One Hundred and First Amendment) Act, 2016 inserted a new Article 279A in the Constitution to provide for the constitution of Goods and Services Tax Council (GST Council) to make recommendations to the Union and the States on various aspects of the Goods and Services Tax (GST). The new Article reads as follows: "279A. (1) The President shall, within sixty days from the date of commencement of the Constitution (One Hundred and First Amendment) Act, 2016, by order, constitute a Council to be called the Goods and Services Tax Council.

(2) The Goods and Services Tax Council shall consist of the following members, namely: (a) the Union Finance Minister...Chairperson; (b) the Union Minister of State in charge of Revenue or Finance...Member; (c) the Minister in charge of Finance or Taxation or any other Minister nominated by each State Government...Members.

(3) The Members of the Goods and Services Tax Council referred to in sub-clause (c) of clause (2) shall, as soon as may be, choose one amongst themselves to be the Vice-Chairperson of the Council for such period as they may decide.

(4) The Goods and Services Tax Council shall make recommendations to the Union and the States on: (a) the taxes, cesses and surcharges levied by the Union, the States and the local bodies which may be subsumed in the goods and services tax; (b) the goods and services that may be subjected to, or exempted from the goods and services tax; (c) model Goods and Services Tax Laws, principles of levy, apportionment of Goods and Services Tax levied on supplies in the course of inter-State trade or commerce under Article 269A and the principles that govern the place of supply; (d) the threshold limit of turnover below which goods and services may be exempted from goods and services tax; (e) the rates including floor rates with bands of goods and services tax; (f) any special rate or rates for a specified period, to raise additional resources during any natural calamity or disaster; (g) special provision with respect to the States of Arunachal Pradesh, Assam, Jammu and Kashmir, Manipur, Meghalaya, Mizoram, Nagaland, Sikkim, Tripura, Himachal Pradesh and Uttarakhand; and (h) any other matter relating to the goods and services tax, as the Council may decide.

(5) The Goods and Services Tax Council shall recommend the date on which the goods and services tax be levied on petroleum crude, high speed diesel, motor spirit (commonly known as petrol), natural gas and aviation turbine fuel.

(6) While discharging the functions conferred by this article, the Goods and Services Tax Council shall be guided by the need for a harmonised structure of goods and services tax and for the development of a harmonised national market for goods and services.

(7) One-half of the total number of Members of the Goods and Services Tax Council shall constitute the quorum at its meetings.

(8) The Goods and Services Tax Council shall determine the procedure in the performance of its functions.

(9) Every decision of the Goods and Services Tax Council shall be taken at a meeting, by a majority of not less than three-fourths of the weighted votes of the members present and voting, in accordance with the following principles, namely: (a) the vote of the Central Government shall have a weightage of one-third of the total votes cast, and (b) the votes of all the State Governments taken together shall have a weightage of two-thirds of the total votes cast, in that meeting.

(10) No act or proceedings of the Goods and Services Tax Council shall be invalid merely by reason of: (a) any vacancy in, or any defect in, the constitution of the Council; or (b) any defect in the appointment of a person as a Member of the Council; or (c) any procedural irregularity of the Council not affecting the merits of the case.

(11) The Goods and Services Tax Council shall establish a mechanism to adjudicate any dispute: (a) between the Government of India and one or more States; or (b) between the Government of India and any State or States on one side and one or more other States on the other side; or (c) between two or more States, arising out of the recommendations of the Council or implementation thereof".

Section 15 of the Constitution (One Hundred and First Amendment) Act, 2016 also amended Article 368 of the Constitution which pertains to power of Parliament to amend the Constitution and procedure therefore. Thus, Article 279A (pertaining to GST Council) was included in the list of items amendments to which require ratification by the legislatures of not less than one-half of the States.

A.12 Taxes and Duties in List I (Union List) of the Seventh Schedule not being Levied at Present

These taxes/duties are discussed below individually along with the logic for retaining them with the Centre.

A.12.1 Entries 87 and 88: These two entries pertain to estate duty, and succession duty in respect of property other than agricultural land respectively. Since the incidence of both estate duty, and succession duty is on the same object, viz. property passing on the death of the owner to his successors, they are essentially similar in nature. However, while in the case of the estate duty, the value of the whole estate, even if situated in more than one State, is the base for taxation, the succession duty is relatable to the value of individual shares (i.e. parts of an estate) passing on to the successors.

The desirability of retaining both these duties with the Centre is self-evident. An individual may have properties located in more than one State and a total assessment of his estate can better be undertaken by the Union Government. Similarly, if succession duty is levied by the States, the persons inheriting properties in different States will have to deal with different tax rates and procedures. Moreover, if estate/succession duties are levied by the States, it may trigger unhealthy competition among the States, resulting into harassment of the assessees and hence litigation. On efficiency criterion (i.e. cost of collection) also it is desirable if these duties are levied and administered by the Union, thus avoiding duplication of tax administration. Moreover, the Union has better access to information and otherwise also it is in larger national interest to ensure uniformity with respect to these duties. It may be noted that estate duty was first imposed in India in 1953 when the Estate Duty Act of that year imposed a duty on the capital value of all property passing on the death of any person on or after October 15, 1953. It was abolished with effect from March 16, 1985.

A.**12.2 Entry 89:** It relates to terminal taxes on goods and passengers carried by railway, sea or air. However, under Entry 56 of List II, States are empowered to levy taxes on goods and passengers carried by road or on inland waterways. Thus, the taxation powers in regard to the services of the major means of transport rest with the Union.

In a developing and diversifying economy like India, the importance of transport sector is self-evident. The growth of this vital infrastructure enlarges the size of the market and determines, *inter alia*, the level of private enterprise. Lest the free flow of inter-State trade should be hampered by differential State levies, the taxation of transport services is, by and large, with the Union Government. The Fifth and the Eighth Finance Commissions examined the scope for levying these taxes but expressed themselves against their imposition on grounds of administrative difficulties and meagre revenue potential. It is noteworthy that there already exists a terminal tax on passengers carried by railway from or to certain places of pilgrimage or where fairs or exhibitions are held. The proceeds of the tax are credited to the Consolidated Fund of the concerned States. The tax is restrictive and limited in scope and not a general terminal tax on passengers carried by railways to all places.

Entry 89 also refers to taxes on railway fares and freights. The Eighth Finance Commission favoured levying tax on railway passenger fares but not until the present arrangement of giving grants in lieu of such a tax continues to exist.

A.**12.3 Entry 90:** It pertains to 'taxes other than stamp duties on transactions in stock exchanges and future markets'. Since stock exchanges and future markets [8] are at a formative stage and have an inter-State character therefore it is desirable to retain these taxes with the Union. The Eighth Finance Commission did not think it advisable to levy taxes on transactions in stock exchanges and future markets.

A.12.4 Entry 92: It refers to 'taxes on the sale or purchase of newspapers and on advertisements published therein'. This tax is retained with the Union to protect the freedom of the press, and avoid undue tax burden on newspaper industry, particularly the regional language newspapers. Since newspaper reading habit is not sufficiently developed and widespread in the country, it is not desirable to impose a tax on the sale or purchase of newspapers. Both the Fifth and the Eighth Finance Commissions did not recommend a tax on the sale or purchase of newspapers. However, both the Commissions opined that there was scope for tax on advertisements published in newspapers. The Eighth Commission cautioned that a tax on advertisement, if levied, should be borne by the advertisers themselves and not passed on to the newspapers and journals.

It is noteworthy that Entry 92 was omitted by Section 17 of the Constitution (One Hundred and First Amendment) Act, 2016.

A.13 Taxation Powers to Local Governments

The Constitution does not provide for any taxation powers to local governments. However, the implication of Article 276 is that the taxes on professions, trades, callings or employment are for the benefit of a State or of a municipality, district board, local board or any other local authority. The States on their own may assign any of the taxes in the State List to the local bodies. The taxes generally assigned to local governments are property taxes, and taxes on vehicles.

A.14 Powers of District Councils to Levy Taxes in Tribal Areas

Sixth Schedule of the Constitution [read with Articles 244(2) and 275(1)] pertains to provisions as to the administration of tribal areas in the States of Assam, Meghalaya, Tripura and Mizoram. Sub-paragraph (3) of paragraph 8 of the Sixth Schedule relates to powers of the District Council for an autonomous district to levy and collect all or any of the following taxes within such district: (a) taxes on professions, trades, callings and employments; (b) taxes on animals, vehicles and boats; (c) taxes on the entry of goods into a market for sale therein, and tolls on passengers and goods carried in ferries; (d) taxes for the maintenance of schools, dispensaries or roads; and (e) taxes on entertainment and amusements.

A.15 Freedom as to Payment of Taxes for Promotion of any Particular Religion

According to Article 27 of the Constitution of India, "No person shall be compelled to pay any taxes, the proceeds of which are specifically appropriated in payment of expenses for the promotion or maintenance of any particular religion or religious denomination".

A.16 Rationale for Constitutional Arrangements

The distribution of taxation powers between the Centre and the States is meant to minimise tax problems in a federal set up such as double taxation, tax rivalry among States, duplicate tax administration, and tax evasion. Constitutional division of taxation powers between the Union and the States in India rests on economic and administrative considerations. Taxes with an inter-State base, and those in the case of which uniformity in rates is desirable, are vested in the Central Government. Also, taxes which the taxpayer can evade by shifting his habitat, or where the place of residence is not a correct guide to the true incidence of the tax, belong to the Centre. Taxes which are location-specific and relate to subjects of local consumption are with the States.

Commenting upon the soundness of the constitutional arrangements regarding division of taxation powers, the Commission on Centre State Relations, 1988, observed, "A well balanced distribution of heads of taxation based on economic and administrative rationale between the Union and the States and adequate arrangements for sharing of resources is vital for the proper functioning of the two-tier polity. We are of the firm view that the basic scheme of the Constitution dividing the field of taxation between the Union and the States and incorporating adequate arrangements for sharing of resources between them, is sound and no major modifications in it are called for". [9]

Similarly, the Sixth Finance Commission made the following observations in this regard, "We must bear in mind that the country as a whole and every part thereof has gained significantly from the maintenance of a vast unified market within which there is free movement of goods and men. Having regard to the trends all over the world even for independent political entities to come together to forge closer economic links in the form of common markets and economic groupings, our best hopes of accelerated economic development lie in the further strengthening of our national market and in the promotion of fiscal arrangements that are most conducive to the effective functioning of this market. Given this basic fact, there can be no room for argument that the levy and administration of taxes with wide economic base such as income tax, corporation tax, Union excise duties and of course also import and export duties will have to remain with the Union Government. In fact the architects of our Constitution drew on the experience of some of the other federations in which the assignment of taxes with wide economic base to units had led to intractable problems of conflicting tax jurisdictions. They wisely averted the possibility of such conflicts by assigning such taxes right from the beginning to the Union Government. At the same time, the framers of our Constitution rightly allocated to the States' subjects such as agriculture, education, medical care, public health, irrigation and law and order that touch intimately the lives of the people. These can be efficiently administered in a vast country only by the State Governments which are closer to the people and are more keenly alive to their problems and needs. The heads of revenue and responsibilities were distributed on the basis of whether the Centre or the State was better equipped to deal with the particular head". [10]

A.17 Definitions

In relation to taxation, the Constitution provides the following definitions:

A.17.1 Goods: According to clause 12 of Article 366 of the Constitution, *goods* include all materials, commodities, and articles.

A.17.2 Goods and Services Tax: According to clause 12A [11] of Article 366 of the Constitution, *goods and services tax* means any tax on supply of goods, or services or both except taxes on the supply of the alcoholic liquor for human consumption.

A.17.3. Services: According to clause 26A [12] of Article 366 of the Constitution, *services* means anything other than goods.

A.17.4 State: According to clause 26B [13] of Article 366 of the Constitution, *State* with reference to Articles 246A, 268, 269, 269A and Article 279A includes a Union Territory with legislature.

A.18 Summary of Constitutional Provisions Pertaining to Taxes

Provisions regarding taxes in the Constitution of India are summarized in Table A.3.

Table A.3: Constitutional Provisions Pertaining to Taxes

Article	Brief Description
27	Freedom as to payment of taxes for promotion of any particular religion.
246 (read with Seventh Schedule of the Constitution)	Subject-matter (including taxes) of laws made by Parliament and by the Legislatures of States.
246A	Special provisions with respect to Goods and Services Tax (GST).
248 [read with Entry 97 of List I (Union List) of the Seventh Schedule]	Residuary powers of legislation, including taxes.
265	No tax shall be levied or collected except by authority of law.
268 [read with Entry 91 of List I (Union List) of the Seventh Schedule]	Duties levied by the Union but collected and appropriated by the States.
269 [read with Entries 92A and 92B of List I (Union List) of the Seventh Schedule]	Taxes levied and collected by the Union but assigned to the States.
269A	Levy and collection of Goods and Services Tax (GST) in the course of inter-State trade or commerce.
270	Taxes and duties levied and collected by the Union but distributed between the Union and the States.
271	Surcharges on certain duties and taxes for the purpose of the Union.
276 (2)	Monetary limit on taxes on professions, trade, calling or employment.
279A	Goods and Services Tax Council (GST Council).
285 (1)	Exemption of property of the Union from State taxation.
286	Restriction on States to impose tax on the supply of goods or services or both, where such supply takes place: (a) outside the State; or (b) in the course of the import of the goods or services or both into, or export of the goods or services or both out of, the territory of India.
287	Exemption from State taxes on electricity consumed by the Government of India.
289	Exemption of property and income of a State from Union taxation.
244 (2) and 275 (1) [read with sub-paragraph (3) of paragraph 8 of the Sixth Schedule	Powers of District Councils to levy taxes in tribal areas.
366 (12)	Definition of *goods.*
366 (12A)	Definition of *goods and services tax.*
366 (26A)	Definition of *services.*
366 (26B)	Definition of *state* with reference to Articles 246A, 268, 269, 269A and 279A.

Endnotes

1. Article 246A was inserted in the Constitution by Section 2 of the Constitution (One Hundred First Amendment) Act, 2016.
2. See sections A.8 and A.9 of this appendix.
3. Inserted by Section 11 of Constitution (One Hundred and First Amendment) Act, 2016.
4. Stamp duty was payable on cheques prior to 1927 but was withdrawn in that year.
5. **Indian Stamp Act:** The Indian Stamp Act, 1899 is a fiscal statute laying down the law relating to tax levied in the form of stamps on instruments recording transactions and stamp duties on instruments specified in Entry 91 of List I (Union List) of the Seventh Schedule of the Constitution. Because of large scale changes in the usage of the instruments since the Indian Stamp Act, 1899 was introduced, a need to amend a good number of provisions of this Act is being felt for quite some time. Law Commission in its 67th report submitted in 1976 made extensive recommendations in this regard. Serious efforts are now being made to bring in large scale amendments in Indian Stamp Act, 1899 to bring this law in tune with the times. Stamp duties on instruments other than those mentioned in Entry 91 of List I above are levied by the States as per Entry 63 of List II (State List). Thus, stamp duty and registration fees are levied on the registration of property or other conveyances. Provisions other than those relating to rates of duty fall within the legislative power of both the Union and the States by virtue of Entry 44 of List III (Concurrent List) of the Seventh Schedule. Stamp duties on all the instruments are collected and kept by the concerned States.

   Till recently, the stamp duty rates were quite high in most states and the procedures for evaluating the conveyances were also complicated. In this context, the Tenth Five Year Plan (2002-07) remarked, "Stamp duty needs to be paid on all documents which are registered and the rate varies from state to state. With stamp duty rates of 13 percent in Delhi, 14.5 percent in Uttar Pradesh and 12.5 percent in Haryana, India has perhaps one of the highest levels of stamp duty. Some states even have double stamp incidence, first on land and then on its development. In contrast the maximum rate levied in most developed markets whether in Singapore or Europe is in the range of 1-2 percent. Even the National Housing and Habitat Policy, 1998, recommended a stamp duty rate of 2-3 percent. Most of the methods to avoid registration are basically to avoid payment of high stamp duty.

   Another fall out of high stamp duty rates is the understatement of the proceeds of a sale. This is also linked to payment of income tax and capital gains tax. When registration has not been effected, a transfer is not deemed to have taken place and hence capital gains tax can be totally avoided. Thus, the present provisions in various laws and their poor implementation have led to a situation where there is considerable financial loss to the exchequer on account of understatement of sale proceeds, non-registration and consequent non-payment of stamp duty and avoidance of capital gains tax". [Government of India, Planning Commission, *Tenth Five Year Plan* (2002-07), Volume II, pp. 833-834.]

   Of late, states have undertaken reforms by reducing the duty rates and streamlining procedures for evaluation of property. After the reduction of rates, the general experience has been revenue-augmenting due to improved compliance of law.
6. Prior to the Eightieth Amendment of the Constitution, provisions of Article 269 were as follows.

   Taxes Levied and Collected by the Union but Assigned to the States (Article 269): These were: (a) duties in respect of succession to property other than agricultural land, (b) estate duty in respect of property other than agricultural land, (c) terminal taxes on goods or passengers carried by railway, sea or air, (d) taxes on railway fares and freights, (e) taxes other than stamp duties on transactions in stock exchanges and future markets, (f) taxes on the sale or purchase of newspapers and on advertisements published therein, (g) taxes on the sale or purchase of goods other than newspapers, where such sale or purchase takes place in the course of inter-State trade or commerce, and (h) taxes on the consignment of goods (whether the consignment is to the person making it or to any other person), where such consignment takes place in the course of inter-State trade or commerce. These taxes corresponded to Entries 87, 88, 89, 90, 92, 92A and 92B in the Union List.

7. **Assignment of Taxes:** Assignment of a tax means transfer of taxation power from a higher level to a lower level of government. Taxation power includes the following: the right to levy the tax, collect the tax, and appropriate the proceeds from the tax. Thus, there can be three interpretations of assignment of a tax. In the first case, the higher level government may levy and collect a tax but handover the entire proceeds to a lower level government. Taxes levied by the Government of India under Article 269 of the Constitution are a case in point. Secondly, the higher level government may levy a tax but allow the lower level government to collect it and retain fully the proceeds therefrom. Taxes levied by the Government of India under Article 268 of the Constitution fall under this category. Finally, the higher level government may transfer a tax to a lower level government lock, stock and barrel, a situation which defines assignment of a tax in its strictest sense.

   Assignment of taxes should not be unconditional. Along with the determination of tax domain for a state, the central government ought to prescribe conditions so that the underlying purpose of assignment is adequately served. Thus, it should be obligatory on the part of a state to levy the tax assigned to it. Not only this, the state should not have powers to alter the basic structure of the assigned tax. The state may enjoy flexibility in fixing the tax rates within a minimum and maximum range prescribed by the central government. Tax exemptions/concessions should be minimum because a state is not expected to serve national objectives through its tax policy. As at other levels, tax default through disputes should be discouraged by requiring full payments prior to disputing an assessment.

8. Future trading refers to contracts for sale and purchase of goods at a future date primarily with a view to avoid price fluctuations. Presently, future trading is allowed at specific centres in respect of four commodities, viz. jute products, paper, turmeric, and *gur*.
9. Government of India, *Report of the Commission on Centre State Relations* (Chairman: Justice R.S. Sarkaria) Part I, 1988, p. 271.
10. *Report of the Sixth Finance Commission*, 1973, p. 5.
11. Inserted by section 14 of the Constitution (One Hundred First Amendment) Act, 2016.
12. Ibid.
13. Ibid.

Bibliography

Bibliography

Ahmad, E. and N. Stern (1991), "Theory and Practice of Tax Reforms in Developing Countries", Cambridge University Press.

Ahmad, E. and N. Stern (1984), "The Theory of Tax Reform and Indian Indirect Taxes", *Journal of Public Economics*, Volume 25, pp. 259-298.

Bagchi, Amaresh et al. (1994), "Reform of Domestic Trade Taxes in India: Issues and Options", New Delhi: National Institute of Public Finance and Policy.

Bird, Richard and Oliver Oldman (eds.) (1967), "Readings on Taxation in Developing Countries", Baltimore: The Johns Hopkins Press.

Bird, Richard and P. Gendron (1998), "Dual VATs and Cross-border Trade, Two Problems and One Solution", *International Tax and Public Finance*, 5(3).

Chakraborty, Pinaki and Manish Gupta (2016), "Evolving Centre-State Financial Relations", *Economic and Political Weekly*, Volume L1, Number 16.

Cutt, James (1969), "Taxation and Economic Development in India", New Delhi: Vikas Publications.

Empowered Committee of State Finance Ministers (2008), "A Model and Roadmap for Goods and Services Tax in India", New Delhi.

—(2009), "First Discussion Paper on Goods and Services Tax in India", New Delhi, November 10.

—(2016), "Model GST Law".

Fazl, Abul (1873), "Ain-i-Akbari", translated from the original Persian by H. Blochmann, Asiatic Society of Bengal.

Ferdinand, H.M. Grapperhaus (1998), "Tax Tales from the Second Millennium", Amsterdam: International Bureau of Fiscal Documentation.

Fisher, Michael H. (ed.) (2007), "Beyond the Three Seas: Travellers' Tales of Mughal India", Random House India.

Gobin, Roy T. (1980), "An Analysis of the System of Sales Taxation in Caribbean Market", *Public Finance*, Volume XXXV, Number 2.

Government of India (1924-25), "Report of the Indian Taxation Enquiry Committee", (President: Charles Todhunter), Volume I.

— (1948), "Report of the Income Tax Investigation Commission", (Chairman: Srinivasa Varadachariar).

—(1953-54), "Report of the Taxation Enquiry Commission", (Chairman: John Matthai), Volumes I, II and III.

—(1963), "Report of the Central Excise Reorganisation Committee", (Chairman: A.K. Chanda).

—(1964), "Report of the Committee on Sales Tax", (Chairman: R.G. Saraiya).

—(1968), "Final Report on Rationalisation and Simplification of Tax Structure", (Chairman: S. Bhoothalingam).

——(1973), "Report of the Central Excise (Self-Removal Procedure) Review Committee", (Chairman: B. Venkatappiah).

——(1977), "Report of the Indirect Taxation Enquiry Committee", (Chairman: L.K. Jha). Part I.

——(1978), "Report of the Indirect Taxation Enquiry Committee", (Chairman: L.K. Jha), Part II, January.

——(1980), "Report of the Expert Committee on Tax Measures to Promote Employment", (Chairman: V.M. Dandekar).

——(1983), "Report of the Expert Committee on Replacement of Sales Tax by Additional Excise Duty", (Chairman: Kamlapati Tripathi).

——(1985), "Long Term Fiscal Policy".

——(1985), "Report of the Technical Study Group on Central Excise Tariff", (Chairman: J. Datta), Part I.

——(1988), "Report of the Commission on Centre-State Relations", (Chairman: R.S. Sarkaria), Part I.

——(1991), "Interim Report of the Tax Reforms Committee", (Chairman: Raja Chelliah), December.

——(1992), "Final Report of the Tax Reforms Committee", (Chairman: Raja Chelliah), Part I.

——(2002), "Report of the Task Force on Indirect Taxes", (Chairman: Vijay Kelkar), December.

——(2003), "Report on Implementation of the Fiscal Responsibility and Budget Management Act, 2003", (Chairman: Vijay Kelkar).

——(2005), "White Paper on State-Level Value Added Tax", (Chairman: Asim Kumar Dasgupta).

——(2012), "White Paper on Black Money", May.

——(2015), "Report on the Revenue Neutral Rate and Structure of Rates for the Goods and Services Tax (GST)", (Chairman: Arvind Subramanian).

——(2016), "The Constitution (One Hundred and First Amendment) Act", September.

——(2017), "GST: Concept and Status, Central Board of Excise and Customs (CBEC),

——Budget Papers", (various years).

——"Economic Survey", (various issues).

——"Reports of Finance Commissions".

——"Constitution of India (As on July 31, 2018)".

James, Simon and Christopher Nobes (1978), "The Economics of Taxation", Oxford: Philip Allen.

Keen, Michael (2015), "Targeting an Indirect Tax Design, Inequality and Fiscal Policy", International Monetary Fund.

Kuo, C.Y., Tom McGirr and Saya Poddar (1988), "Measuring the Non-neutralities of Sales and Excise Taxes in Canada", *Canadian Tax Journal*, Volume 38.

Leemput, E.V. and E.A. Wiencek (2017), "The Effect of the GST on Indian Growth", International Finance Discussion Paper, March.

Mahler, Walter (1970), "Sales and Excise Taxation in India", New Delhi: Orient Longman Ltd.

Makin, A.J. and R. Arora (2012), "Fiscal Sustainability in India at State Level", *Public Finance and Management*, Volume 12.

Musgrave, Richard and Peggy Musgrave (1989), "Public Finance in Theory and Practice", New York: McGraw-Hill Book Company.

National Council of Applied Economic Research (2009), "Moving to Goods and Services Tax in India: Impact on India's Growth and International Trade", Prepared for the Thirteenth Finance Commission Government of India, Working Paper Number 103, December.

Peacock, Alan and Francesco Forte (eds.) (1981), "The Political Economy of Taxation", Oxford: Basil Blackwell.

Poddar, S. and M. English (1997), "Taxation of Financial Services under a Value-added Tax: Applying the Cash-flow Method", *National Tax Journal*, pp. 89-111.

Poddar, Satya (1990), "Options for s VAT at the State Level", in M. Gillis, C.S. Shoup and G. Sicat (eds.), 'Value Added Taxation in Developing Countries', Washington D.C.: World Bank.

—(2003), "Consumption Taxes: The Role of the Value Added Tax", in Patrick Honohan (ed.), 'Taxation of Financial Intermediation: Theory and Practice in Emerging Economies', World Bank and Oxford University Press.

—(2007), "VAT on Financial Services: Searching for a Workable Compromise", in Richard Krever and David White (eds.), 'GST in Retrospect and Prospect', New Zealand: Brookers Ltd.

Poddar, Satya and Amaresh Bagchi (2007), "Revenue-neutral Rate for GST", *The Economic Times*, November 15.

Poddar, Satya and Nancy Harley (1989), "Problems in Moving from a Flawed to a Neutral and Broad-based Consumption Tax", *Australian Tax Forum*, Volume 6, Number 3.

Prest, A.R. (1970), "Public Finance in Theory and Practice", London: Weidenfeld and Nicolson.

Rangarajan, C. and D.K. Srivastava (2011), "Federalism and Fiscal Transfers in India", New Delhi: Oxford University Press.

Rao, Kavita (2014), "Revenue Implications of GST and Estimation of Revenue Neutral Rate: Estimates for 2011-12", New Delhi: National Institute of Public Finance and Policy.

Rao, M. Govinda (2001), "Report of the Expert Group on Taxation of Services", Government of India, March.

Rao, K. (2008), "Goods and Services Tax for India", NIPFP Working Paper Number 57, November.

Rao, M.G. and N. Singh (2005), "The Political Economy of Federalism in India", New Delhi: Oxford University Press.

Reserve Bank of India, "Report on Currency and Finance", (various years).

Sandford, C.T. et al. (1981), "Costs and Benefits of VAT", London: Heinemann Educational Books.

"Tuzuk-i-Jahangiri" (1909), translated by Alexander Rogers and edited by Henry Beveridge, London: Royal Asiatic Society.

World Bank (2015), "Fiscal Policy for Equitable Growth", India Development Report.

Zhou, L.Z., J. Tam and J. Heng-Contaxis (2013), "The Introduction of Goods and Services Tax in Malaysia: A Policy Analysis", CPSS Policy Paper Series, October 22.

Websites

Ministry of Finance
Central Board of Direct Taxes (CBDT)
Central Board of Indirect Taxes and Customs (CBIC)
Goods and Services Tax Council (GST Council)
Ministry of Law and Justice
Reserve Bank of India

Index

Index